AMC
Maine
Mountain
Guide

Appalachian Mountain Club
Trail Guides

AMC Maine Mountain Guide
6th Edition

**AMC Guide to Mount Desert Island
and Acadia National Park**
4th Edition

AMC White Mountain Guide
24th Edition

**AMC Guide to Mount Washington
and the Presidential Range**
4th Edition

**AMC Massachusetts and Rhode Island
Trail Guide**
6th Edition

North Carolina Hiking Trails
2nd Edition
Allen de Hart

**Hiking the Mountain State:
The Trails of West Virginia**
Allen de Hart

AMC Maine Mountain Guide

Sixth Edition

APPALACHIAN MOUNTAIN CLUB
Boston, Massachusetts

Maps by David Cooper
Cover design by Outside Designs
Cover photograph by Brian Sullivan

SIXTH EDITION

International Standard Serial Number: 0514-9738
Paperbound International Standard Book Number:
0-910146-68-3
Library of Congress Card Number: 68-7586

The paper used in this publication meets the minimum
requirements of the American National Standard for
Information Sciences—Permanence of Paper for Printed
Library Materials, ANSI Z39.48-1984.∞

**Due to changes in conditions,
use of the information in this book
is at the sole risk of the user.**

Printed in the United States of America

10 9 8 7 6 5 4 3 2   88 89 90 91 92

Contents

List of Maps

MAPS, FOLDED, IN BACK POCKET

Carter-Mahoosuc/Rangeley-Stratton
Katahdin/Camden Hills/Pleasant Mountain
Mount Desert/Weld

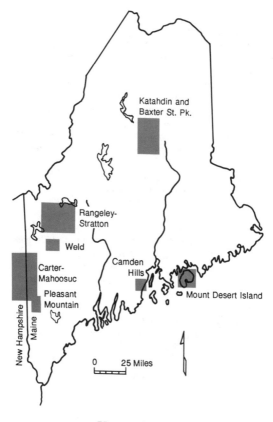

Katahdin and
Baxter St. Pk.

Rangeley-
Stratton

Weld

Camden
Hills

Mount Desert Island

New Hampshire

Maine

Carter-
Mahoosuc

Pleasant
Mountain

0   25 Miles

Key to Maps

To the Owner of This Book

With the object of keeping pace with the constant changes in mountain trails, the Appalachian Mountain Club publishes a revised edition of this guide at intervals of about four years.

Hiking and climbing in the Maine mountains should provide a combination of outdoor pleasure and healthful exercise. Plan your trip schedule with safety in mind. Determine the overall distance, the altitude to be reached, the steepness of the footway, and, if you are returning to the starting point the same day, allow ample time, as your morning quota of energy will have lost some of its get-up-and-go. Read the caution notes where they appear in this book. They are put there for your guidance and protection.

We request your help in preparing future editions. When you go over a trail, please check the description in the book. If you find errors or can suggest improvements, send a note to the Committee. Even if the description is satisfactory, "Description of such-and-such trail is o.k." will be appreciated. Do not be deterred by the lack of experience. The viewpoint of one unfamiliar with the trail is especially valuable.

Address: Maine Mountain Guidebook Committee, Appalachian Mountain Club, 5 Joy St., Boston, MA 02108.

Introduction

This, the sixth edition of the Appalachian Mountain Club's guide to the mountains and trails of Maine, describes nearly two hundred summits in all sections of Maine—from Mount Agamenticus in the southwestern corner of the state to DeBoulie Mountain in northern Aroostook County, and from Mount Aziscohos close to the New Hampshire line in northwestern Maine to Pocomoonshine Mountain, near the St. Croix River, which forms the New Brunswick border. Some examples are the trail-rich Mount Desert Island summits, the compact and scenic Camden Hills, the low but frequently climbed hills in southwestern Maine, and the isolated and interesting mountains close to the Quebec and New Brunswick boundaries.

This guide is intended for use as a pathfinder; therefore it does not include extended historical references or descriptions of views. In general, it describes trails for the ascent. Any difficulties going down a trail that would not be encountered going up are mentioned at the end of the description. Where a trail follows a range, the guide describes it for the direction usually traveled. Signs mark many paths, but hikers cannot rely on them, because they often fall down or disappear. Also, trails are constantly changing. Logging may destroy them; heavy storms may obscure them; and new trails are occasionally added.

The guide strives to remain current by adding or deleting trails or mountains depending on present conditions.

MAINE FOREST SERVICE FIRE TOWERS

For years, the Maine Forest Service maintained fire towers on many mountains. The trails built to the summit towers made excellent hiking paths. During the last two decades most of these towers have been abandoned as the state forest

service switched to aircraft for forest fire patrol. Several of
the towers have been removed or converted to other uses such
as microwave or cable television relay.

Some of the firewardens' cabins have been sold to private
owners; others are in disrepair or have been vandalized or
torn down. Do *not* expect to use them for camping or emergency shelter.

In many cases, continued use by hikers has kept trails to
fire towers open; in other, more remote regions, the trails are
becoming overgrown. No group has offered to maintain
them. Before heading for the more isolated areas with summit towers, hikers should check trail conditions with the
local Maine Forest Service office.

DISTANCES AND TIMES

The distances and times that appear in the tables at the end
of trail descriptions are cumulative from the starting point at
the head of each table. Estimated distances are preceded
by *est*.

Times are based on a speed of 2 mph, plus an additional
half-hour for every 1000 feet gained in elevation. Times are
included only to provide a consistent measure for compari-
son among trails and routes. When no time is given, the
route described may be considered a leisurely walk or stroll.
With experience, hikers will learn how to correct these standard times for their own normal paces. Bear in mind, however, that if your average pace is faster than the standard
time, it will not necessarily be so on trails with steep grades,
in wet weather, if you are carrying a heavy pack, or if you are
hiking with a group. And in winter, you should roughly double the time it would normally take for you to complete a
hike.

The final entry in the distance-time summaries at the end

of trail descriptions gives the metric equivalent of the total distance. The metric equivalent for the elevation of each summit is also listed.

GUIDELINES FOR WILDERNESS HIKERS AND CAMPERS

Below are some fundamentals of living in the outdoors without destroying it. Following these simple rules will help preserve the backcountry for all to enjoy.

Camp in Designated Areas

The backcountry can no longer withstand indiscriminate camping and hiking. Please cooperate.

Bring Your Own Tent or Shelter

Shelter buildings are often full, so each group should carry all needed equipment for shelter, including whatever poles, stakes, ground insulation, and cord are required. Do not cut boughs or branches for bedding.

Use a Portable Stove

In some camping areas, a "human browse line" is quite evident, because people have gathered firewood over the years: limbs are gone from trees, the ground is devoid of dead wood, and vegetation has been trampled by people scouring the area. A carefully operated stove puts the least pressure on the forest.

Help Preserve Nature's Ground Cover

If a shelter is full, or if you camp away from shelters, find a clear, level site on which to pitch your tent, away from trails and streams. Site clearing and ditching around tents are too damaging to soil and vegetation.

Hammock Camping

Some campers use hammocks rather than tents. Hanging between trees eliminates even that crushing of ground cover caused by tents. (Hammocks, however, have certain limitations during bug season!) We can all practice low-impact camping by making conscious efforts to preserve the natural forest.

Water for Drinking and Washing

Wash your dishes and yourself well away from streams, ponds, and springs. It's handy to carry a small screen or cloth to filter the dishwater, so you don't leave food remnants strewn about the woods.

Most hikers drink from the streams without ill effect, and indeed, the pleasure of quaffing a cup of water fresh from a (presumably) pure mountain spring is one of the traditional attractions of the mountains. Unfortunately, in many mountain regions the cysts of the intestinal parasite *giardia* are present in some of the water. A conservative practice is to boil water for 20 minutes or to use an *iodine*-based disinfectant. *Chlorine*-based products, such as Halazone, are ineffective in water that contains organic impurities and they deteriorate quickly in the pack. Remember to allow extra contact time (and use twice as many tablets) if the water is cold.

Think About Human Waste

Keep it at least 200 feet away from water sources. If there are no toilets nearby, dig a trench 6 to 8 inches deep for a latrine and cover it completely when you break camp. The bacteria in the organic layer of the soil will then decompose the waste naturally. (Don't dig the trench too deep, or you will be below the organic layer.)

Carry In–Carry Out

Trash receptacles are not available in trail areas (except at some trailheads), and visitors are asked to bring trash bags and carry out everything—food, paper, glass, cans—they carry in. Cooperation with the "carry in–carry out" program so far has been outstanding, and the concept has grown to "carry out more than you carried in." We hope you will join in the effort.

Use Special Care Above Timberline

Extreme weather and a short growing season make these areas especially fragile. Footsteps alone can destroy the toughest natural cover, so please try to stay on the trail or walk on rocks. And, of course, don't camp above timberline.

Limit the Size of Your Group

The larger the group, the greater the impact on the environment and on others. Please limit the size of your group to a dozen or less.

CAUTION

Hikers should always carry a map and compass, knife or small ax, waterproof matches, water, adequate food, a windbreaker, rain gear, a spare sweater or shirt, gloves or mittens, a hat, and extra socks. In addition, at least one member of the group should carry a lightweight survival kit that includes first aid supplies (bandaids, gauze pads, and adhesive tape; moleskin or a similar blister preventative; an antiseptic; and an analgesic), high-energy emergency food, a flashlight with extra batteries, a large plastic trash bag, some foil, a needle and thread, safety pins, cord, paper and a pencil, and perhaps a space blanket.

Before entering the woods, tell someone where you are going and when you plan to return, and get to know the area. Study a good map, and know how to use your compass. Pick out reference points along the trail after you start your hike, and check your compass from time to time. Dress for the terrain and weather. Don't depend on cotton clothing for warmth; once it is dampened by perspiration or precipitation it will pull warmth from your body. Wool and some of the newer synthetics such as polypropylene provide better insulation even when wet. Dress in layers: remember, you can always take off what you have on, but you can't put on what you don't have with you.

Compass directions given in this text are based on true north instead of magnetic north. This is important information, because in Maine the compass needle points up to 20 degrees west of true north.

Note: With reference to streams, the terms *right bank* and *left bank* mean right and left when facing downstream. Other abbreviations used frequently in the text are listed below.

HYPOTHERMIA

Hypothermia, the most serious danger to hikers, is the inability to stay warm because of injury, exhaustion, lack of sufficient food, or inadequate or wet clothing. Most cases occur in temperatures above freezing; the most dangerous conditions involve rain with wind. The symptoms are stumbling, poor coordination, garbled speech, amnesia, disorientation, and agitated behavior. Progressive lethargy, uncontrollable shivering, and coma will follow if no treatment is given. The result is death, unless the victim (who usually does not understand the situation) is treated, and it is not unusual for the victim to resist treatment and even combat the rescuers.

If you suspect a person is hypothermic, find him or her shelter from the wind and rain, and remove any wet clothing.

Place the victim in a sleeping bag without clothes or with dry garments. Be sure to cover the head and neck, and provide insulation from the ground. If the victim is fully conscious, supply quick-energy food and warm (not hot) nonalcoholic drinks. Keep the victim inactive until signs of improvement appear. Allow adequate rest before moving on; do not hesitate to send for help if there is any doubt that the victim should proceed.

Uncontrollable shivering is evidence of advanced hypothermia. This shivering will eventually cease on its own, but that is an indication that the hypothermia is becoming even more severe. In severe cases, only professional treatment offers hope for survival. Reduce exposure to wind and rain, prevent further heat loss, and send for help. Do not try to rewarm in the field.

The prevention of hypothermia is infinitely easier than its treatment and should be a prime concern of hikers during any season. Sources of detailed information on causes, prevention, and current treatment are available through the AMC's Boston or Pinkham Notch headquarters.

GETTING LOST

If you get lost in the Maine woods, it is not necessarily a serious matter. First *stop;* sit down and think. If you are familiar with the territory, you may be able to find your way back to the trail or to a high spot to survey the area. If you are unsure which direction to take, *stay where you are!* If you have informed someone of your trip plan, then you will probably be found quickly. *Don't panic.* If you have the proper equipment, you can improvise a shelter (near water if possible) and wait for help. Build a fire for warmth and to draw attention. (Be careful to keep the fire under control, of course.) The main thing to remember is to *stay put* and *stay calm.*

SEARCH AND RESCUE

The Department of Inland Fisheries and Wildlife is empowered to conduct search and rescue operations in Maine. All Maine telephone books carry the 800 number of the nearest Warden District.

The text of the relevant sections of Maine law is given below; for more information write to the Commissioner, Department of Inland Fisheries and Wildlife, 221 State St., Augusta, ME 04333.

Title 12, Sec. 7035, No. 4; Powers

Search and rescue. Whenever the commissioner receives notification that any person has gone into the woodlands or onto the inland waters of the State on a hunting, fishing or other trip and has become lost, stranded or drowned, the commissioner shall exercise the authority to take reasonable steps to ensure the safe and timely recovery of that person; except in cases involving downed or lost aircraft covered by Title 6, section 303.

A. The commissioner may summon any person in the State to assist in those search and rescue attempts. Each person summoned shall be paid at a rate set by the commissioner with the approval of the Governor and shall be provided with subsistence while engaged in these activites.

B. The expenses of the department in search and rescue efforts shall be paid from the General Fund. The Joint Standing Committee of the Legislature having jurisdiction over Inland Fisheries and Wildlife shall report out a bill during each regular session requesting General Fund monies for the full cost of the search and rescue.

C. The commissioner may enter into written agreements with other agencies or corporations, including com-

mercial recreational areas, allowing partial search and
rescue responsibility within specified areas.

D. The commissioner may terminate a search and rescue
operation by members of his department when, in his
opinion, all reasonable efforts have been exhausted.

Any person who has knowledge that another person is
lost, stranded or drowned in the woodlands or inland waters
of the State shall notify the Warden Service Division of the
Department of Inland Fisheries and Wildlife.

Sec. 7036, No. 4; Prohibited Acts

Failure to notify. Except as otherwise provided through
written agreement, a person is guilty of failure to report a
lost, stranded or drowned person if he has knowledge that a
person is lost, stranded or drowned in the woodlands or inland waters of the State and fails to give notice of the inci-
dent by quickest means to the Warden Service Division of the
Department of Inland Fisheries and Wildlife.

FIRES AND FIRE CLOSURE

The following is a summary of regulations that govern
building fires in various areas:

1. In Acadia National Park and in state parks, regulations permit fires at designated places only. In Acadia
National Park, consult a park ranger before building
any fire.

2. In the White Mountain National Forest, permits are no
longer required, but hikers who build fires are still
legally responsible for any damage they may cause.

3. In other areas:

a. In *organized* territory (i.e., within the boundaries
of a township with its own local civil government),
fires may be kindled on private land only with written permission from the landowner.

b. In *unorganized* territory (i.e., where the local government function is performed by state or county authorities; a Maine Forestry District), a permit for outdoor cooking and warming fires may be obtained free of charge from any MFS Ranger.

c. Fires may be built without a permit at the following places:

   (1) MFS authorized campsites and lunch grounds
   (2) State Highway Commission roadside picnic areas
   (3) Appalachian Trail shelter sites
   (4) Baxter Park and Recreation campgrounds and campsites (but see park regulations and discuss with rangers)
   (5) State Park and Recreation Commission campsites and picnic areas

d. Specific and detailed information on fire permits may be obtained from any MFS Ranger or the forest service's Augusta office.

During periods when the danger of fires is high, the governor, through proclamation, may prohibit all outdoor fires or may close the woods altogether. These prohibitions include MFS campsites.

We cannot stress enough the importance of care in using fire in the woods. Hikers as a group have compiled a fine record, but a forest fire traced to the carelessness of a hiker could result in the closing of much land and many trails.

CAMP TRIP LEADERS' PERMITS

Those who lead summer camp trips in Maine should be aware of a law, passed by the Maine Legislature in 1969, that regulates issuing permits for camp trip leaders. The text of the legislation is given below; for more information write to the Commissioner, Department of Inland Fisheries and Wildlife, 221 State St., Augusta, ME 04333.

Title 12, Sec. 2054; Permits for Camp Trip Leaders

Boys' and girls' summer camps located in Maine and duly licensed by the Department of Health and Welfare or located in another state and duly licensed in a similar manner if the laws of said other state so require, having trips other than on water adjacent to the location of the main camp, shall have a counselor as a party member who is a holder of a camp trip leader's permit. Said camp trip leader's permits, as approved and granted by the commissioner, shall be good only for the period of June 15th through September 15th of the year issued, shall be good only for a children's camp sponsored trip and specifically shall not entitle the holder to be in charge of any group other than from said boys' and girls' camp, nor does it grant to said holder any rights to hunt or fish. A counselor to hold such camp trip leader's permit must be 18 years of age. The fee for said permit shall be $5 for counselors of Maine camps and $10 for counselors of camps from other states.

POLICIES OF LANDOWNERS IN NORTHERN MAINE

Maine's economy depends very much upon its woodlands. These lands are owned by a large number of small-lot owners and by a small number of companies that own large areas. These private holdings include many of Maine's mountains; generally, owners allow recreational use of their land.

The opening of the Allagash Wilderness Waterway and improved highways and roads leading to northern and northwestern Maine have increased the flow of hikers, hunters, fishermen, canoeists, and others to the forest country. At the same time, continuing technological advances in logging have led to greater use of trucks to haul lumber and pulpwood. The timberland owners constantly extend their system of private roads, many of which are open to the public. These roads offer access to many areas that used to be difficult to reach. In 1971 the North Maine Woods, an association of landowners, was established to control recreational use of the area west of ME 11 and north of a line that starts several miles north of Baxter State Park and runs around Telos and Caucomgomoc lakes and then west to the Canadian border. The line extends north along the border to Estcourt, south to St. Francis, southwest to Fish River, south into T8 R6, and west toward Baxter State Park. The Katahdin Ironworks/Jo-Mary (Gulf Hagas) area is also under the association's management. The MFS has transferred control and management of most of its forest campsites in this area to North Maine Woods, which operates traffic control centers on the major private roads into the area. Users must register at the control centers and pay fees, which vary somewhat from year to year and are at times higher for out-of-state residents. There are also fees for use of campsites within the controlled area.

The landowners have established some basic rules for their roads. Speed limits are posted. *Trucks always have the right of way* on these private roads. Do not leave unattended cars that block passage on any road; the road could suddenly be needed to fight a forest fire.

Each landowning company has particular rules, and prior permission is often needed to use a company's roads. For instance, some companies do not allow trailers or RVs on their roads, and others limit length and width. Anyone coming from a distance to enter an area should check ahead of time with the companies concerned.

For a map showing the locations of control centers and for the latest regulations and information, write to North Maine Woods, P.O. Box 421, Ashland, ME 04732 (207-435-6213).

The Paper Industry Information Office, 133 State Street, Augusta, ME 04330 (207-622-3166), offers some maps of company-owned lands in northern Maine and in other areas of the state and information regarding public use of privately held lands.

MAINE'S MOUNTAINS IN WINTER

For those who are properly prepared, winter hiking and climbing in Maine offers challenge and satisfaction. The general comments in the *AMC White Mountain Guide*'s section on winter climbing apply equally well to winter climbing in Maine. An added factor in Maine winter climbing is that unplowed access roads frequently lengthen a trip. Many trips that take only a day in the summer may take two or more in the winter and require camping.

Snowshoes are a must. (The bear paw type is best for climbing.) Climbers should also carry crampons if they are likely to travel on ice or "boiler plate" snow. Other required gear includes an ice ax or ski pole if you are climbing on open slopes. For brisk snowshoeing, a light shell over a wool shirt is usually sufficient, even in very cold weather. At rest or above timberline, you will usually need an insulated parka and wind pants, and perhaps a face mask and goggles also. Be sure to carry spare pairs of wool socks and warm mittens and an extra hat. Ordinary leather boots are inadequate. Waterproof insulated boots are recommended, and they should not be too tight.

Deep snow can make route-finding difficult. In steep areas or when snow is not compacted, hiking time is much longer than in summer. Be prepared to make an early start and to return after dark using artificial light. Trips should be planned carefully.

The trail descriptions given in various sections of this guide usually apply in the winter, with the qualifications that unplowed roads may add distance and trail markers may be hidden. Winter hikers should avoid high peaks and steep rocky slopes unless they have a lot of experience.

Any hikers climbing the higher and longer routes in winter should be fully aware of the danger of low temperatures and high winds. This danger is infinitely greater in winter than in summer. The wind-chill chart in this guide gives some indication of how cold it can be. Hikers should plan their trips with such weather in mind.

SKIING

A number of Maine's downhill ski areas are mentioned briefly in the text. To locate them easily, refer to the index under *Skiing*.

In summer, ski trails offer routes that, because of their width and their usually zigzag course on the steeper slopes, are likely to have better views than do regular summer trails. On the other hand, ski trails are less shady, the footing may be poor and rough, and some of them cross swampy places.

BUSHWHACKING IN THE MAINE MOUNTAINS

This guide deals mainly with mountains in Maine that have trails, but it does include a few peaks where hikers must bushwhack for short distances. It leaves out countless other bushwhacking sites, ranging from rather low hills to mountains approaching 4000 ft. The AMC Maine Mountain Guide Committee feels that such areas should remain without trails so that interested hikers can gain experience in bushwhacking. Some of the mountains are close to existing roads and trails, but many others are accessible only by water or long approach walks. Various topographic maps will show many of these named and unnamed trailless peaks.

WIND CHILL CHART

Estimated Wind Speed in MPH	Actual Thermometer Reading (°F)											
	50	40	30	20	10	0	-10	-20	-30	-40	-50	-60
	Equivalent Temperature (°F)											
calm	50	40	30	20	10	0	-10	-20	-30	-40	-50	-60
5	48	37	27	16	6	-5	-15	-26	-36	-47	-57	-68
10	40	28	16	4	-9	-21	-33	-46	-58	-70	-83	-95
15	36	22	9	-5	-18	-36	-45	-58	-72	-85	-99	-112
20	32	18	4	-10	-25	-39	-53	-67	-82	-96	-110	-124
25	30	16	0	-15	-29	-44	-59	-74	-88	-104	-118	-133
30	28	13	-2	-18	-33	-48	-63	-79	-94	-109	-125	-140
35	27	11	-4	-20	-35	-49	-67	-82	-98	-113	-129	-145
40	26	10	-6	-21	-37	-53	-69	-85	-100	-116	-132	-148

(wind speeds greater than 40 mph have little additional effect)

LITTLE DANGER (for properly clothed person)

INCREASING DANGER

GREAT DANGER

Danger from freezing of exposed flesh

Only people who are fully experienced in route-finding, using a compass, and map reading should try to bushwhack the higher and more distant mountains. Bushwhackers can encounter a variety of problems and should take extra care to carry sufficient food, clothing, shelter, compasses, first aid equipment, and similar supplies. Bushwhacking is much more time consuming than ordinary hiking, and hikers should be prepared to spend the night out if necessary.

Since most trailless mountains are located on private property, hikers should obtain permission from an authorized person prior to starting out. They should also be extra careful to leave word with a responsible party of their routes and destinations.

Bushwhackers should *not* mark their routes. The usual markers, such as rags and tapes, deteriorate rapidly. Missing markers may mislead those who subsequently attempt to follow them. Markers destroy the concept of a mountain without trails. If you plan to take the same route out that you take in and you want to mark it to save time on the return, please remove your markers as you leave.

MAPS

Extra copies of the maps at the back of this guide may be purchased separately from the AMC, 5 Joy St., Boston, MA 02108. Elevations of mountaintops and other points can be found on the maps. Remember, though, that a map cannot indicate the condition of a trail. This is a function of the text. Never assume the existence of a usable route merely because there is a dotted line on the map. Consult both the text and the map.

Other Maps, Guides, and Literature

Among many maps and books covering the mountainous areas of Maine, the following may be particularly valuable.

USGS topographic quadrangles have been published for all of Maine. The 7.5-minute series is replacing the old 15-minute series. In this book, the text indicates the quadrangle available for a given mountain. An index map showing all USGS maps is available at many sporting goods stores and bookstores throughout the state. The index map and individual maps are also available from the Branch of Distribution, USGS, 1200 So. Eads St., Arlington, VA 22202.

Booklets on Maine's *Public and Reserved Lands* and *Outdoors in Maine* are available from the Department of Conservation's Maine Forest Service, at State House Station 22, Augusta, ME 04333.

DeLorme Publishing Company (Main Street, Box 298, Freeport, ME 04032) publishes *The Maine Map and Guide*, an accurate and regularly updated map of Maine. *The Maine Atlas and Gazetteer*, by the same publisher, provides detailed sectional maps indicating roads, trails, and significant topographic features (no contour lines).

The 1988 edition of the *Guide to the Appalachian Trail in Maine* contains further information about the Appalachian Trail and maps (7) for the entire Appalachian Trail in Maine. Copies are available at many retail outlets and from the Maine Appalachian Trail Club, PO Box 283, Augusta, ME 04330.

The Length and Breadth of Maine, by Stanley B. Attwood, has an exhaustive list of all of the state's geographical features—mountains, lakes, and streams—that have names. The listing includes elevations, areas, and distances. This book is available from the University of Maine Press, Service Bldg., University of Maine at Orono, Orono, ME 04469.

The AMC's journal, *Appalachia*, periodically publishes material on the mountains of Maine, and the *AMC Maine Mountain Guide* contains references to some of these articles.

COOPERATION

The AMC earnestly requests that those who use the trails, shelters, and campsites in public lands know the rules and follow them, especially those pertaining to fires. The same consideration should be shown to private landowners.

The New England Trail Conference advises that trails should not be blazed or cut on private property without the consent of the owners and definite provision for maintenance. Trails should not be cut or marked on public lands without the approval of the park or forest officials.

The main purpose of this book is to furnish accurate details, both in the text and on the maps; so we will gratefully accept corrections from any source. If you find inaccuracies, signs missing, obscure places on the trails, or a map that needs correcting, please send a report to Maine Mountain Guidebook Committee, Appalachian Mountain Club, 5 Joy St., Boston, MA 02108.

ACKNOWLEDGMENTS

The Maine Mountain Guidebook Committee appreciates the help received during the preparation of this book from members of the AMC and many others. Publication of this book would not have been possible without their assistance.

Maine Mountain Guidebook Committee

Editor
Paul W. Wentworth

Judith A. Marden
Lester Kenway
Lois Winter
Arthur Martineau
Soren Christensen
Richard Foote
Elliot Bates
Mark Stoffan
Tim Perry
Keith Chapman
Robert J. Lovejoy
James Mitchell
Stephen Alberg
Joe Rankin
Richard Dufour
Stephen Clark

Abbreviations

The following abbreviations are used in the trail descriptions.

min.	minute(s)
hr.	hour(s)
mph	miles per hour
in.	inch(es)
ft.	foot, feet
yd.	yard(s)
mi.	mile(s)
m.	meter(s)
km.	kilometer(s)
est.	estimate
AMC	Appalachian Mountain Club
AT	Appalachian Trail
BSP	Baxter State Park
CTA	Chatham Trail Association
FR	Forest Route
GNPC	Great Northern Paper Company
MATC	Maine Appalachian Trail Club
ME	Maine
MFS	Maine Forest Service
NH	New Hampshire
NPS	National Park Service
US	United States
USFS	United States Forest Service
USGS	United States Geological Survey
WMNF	White Mountain National Forest

AMC
Maine
Mountain
Guide

SECTION 1

Katahdin Area

Katahdin, the highest mountain in Maine at 5267 ft., is about 80 mi. north of Bangor, between the East and West branches of the Penobscot River. It is as wild and alluring as any mountain in the East. The name, in Indian dialect, means *greatest mountain*. It lies within Baxter State Park (BSP), created by a gift of former Governor Percival P. Baxter in 1931. By the time of his death in 1969, Governor Baxter had extended the grant to over 200,000 acres. A condition of his gift—there are variant wordings and differing interpretations by Governor Baxter and others—is that the area "shall forever be left in its natural wild state, forever be kept as a sanctuary for wild beasts and birds and forever be used for public forest, public park and public recreational purposes." Since 1921, the mountain and most of the neighboring summits have been part of a state game preserve.

KATAHDIN

Katahdin, an irregularly shaped mountain mass, rises abruptly from comparatively flat country to a gently sloping plateau above the treeline. It culminates on its southeastern margin in an irregular series of low summits. The southern two are the highest. These peaks are 0.3 mi. apart, and Baxter Peak (5267 ft./1605 m.), to the northwest, is the higher of the two. From the southeastern South Peak (5240 ft./1597 m.), a long, curved, serrated ridge of vertically fractured granite, known as the Knife Edge, hooks away to the east and northeast. About 0.7 mi. from South Peak, this ridge ends in a rock pyramid called Chimney Peak. Immediately beyond Chimney Peak and separated from it by a sharp cleft, is a broader rock peak, Pamola (4902 ft./1494 m.). It is named for the Indian avenging spirit of the mountain. To the

1

north, the broad rock mass of Hamlin Peak (4751 ft./1448 m.) dominates the plateau or tableland, which ends in the series of low North (Howe) Peaks (4734 to 4612 ft./1443 to 1406 m.). Refer to the Katahdin map in this guide.

Katahdin was first climbed in 1804 by a party of eleven, including Charles Turner, Jr., who wrote an account of the ascent. There may have been unrecorded ascents during the next fifteen years, but we know the mountain was climbed again in 1819 and 1820. After this date, ascents became more regular.

The tableland, nearly 4 mi. long, falls away abruptly from 1000 to 2000 ft. on all sides. After that the slope becomes more gentle. Great arms stretch out to embrace glacial cirques, known locally as basins. The Great Basin, with its branch, the South Basin, is the best known. In the floor of the latter, at an altitude of 2910 ft., Chimney Pond lies flanked by impressive cliffs and bordered by dense spruce forest. It fills about eight acres and is a base for many varied mountain climbs. North of the Great Basin, but still on the eastern side of the mountain, is the North Basin (floor altitude 3100 ft.), whose high, smooth-ledged sides surround a barren, boulder-strewn floor. The nearby Little North Basin has few visitors. On the western side of the tableland, the little-known Northwest Basin lies at about 2800 ft., and farther south there is a broad valley known as the Klondike. Klondike Pond rests in a small glacial arm of this valley, just below the plateau. At 3435 ft., it is 0.3 mi. long, deep, narrow, and remarkably beautiful.

From the peaks at its northern and southern ends, the tableland slopes gradually toward the center, known as the Saddle. From the eastern escarpment of the Saddle, the land falls off gently toward the dense scrub that carpets the northwestern edge. Many avalanches have scored the walls of the tableland, but only two of these are now climbing routes—the Saddle Slide at the western end of the Great

Basin and the Abol Slide on the southwestern flank of the mountain.

Katahdin's isolated position makes for an exceptional view that takes in hundreds of lakes, including Moosehead; the many windings of the Penobscot; and to the south, the hills of Mount Desert and Camden. Mount Washington seems to lie in a direct line behind Mount Abraham and is not visible.

Katahdin is the northern terminus of the Appalachian Trail, which includes the Hunt Trail on Katahdin itself. The great mountain lies on the southeastern side of a scattered group of smaller mountains, many of which offer interesting climbs and good views, particularly of Katahdin. The text describes these mountains following the description of Katahdin and covers them in a clockwise direction— west, north, and then northeast.

West of Katahdin, the following mountains form an elbow-shaped range: the Owl, Barren Mountain, Mount O-J-I, Mount Coe, South Brother, North Brother, and Fort Mountain. Sentinel Mountain and the striking Doubletop Mountain offer fine views from the west side of Nesowadnehunk Stream. Mullen Mountain and Wassataquoik Mountain are in the remote area between Fort Mountain and Wassataquoik Lake. Sprawling Traveler Mountain is the principal mountain in the northern section of the park. The South Branch Ponds and campground sit at its western base. Turner Mountain is to the northeast of Katahdin and offers magnificent views of it.

In all, there are at least forty-six mountain peaks in the park. Eighteen of them exceed 3500 ft.

Camping facilities that accommodate about seven hundred persons are available at nine different public campgrounds, from which most trails are accessible (see the Katahdin/Baxter map). The campgrounds are: Roaring Brook, Abol, Katahdin Stream, Nesowadnehunk (Sourdna-

hunk), Daicey Pond, South Branch Pond, Trout Brook
Farm, Russell Pond, and Chimney Pond. Russell Pond and
Chimney Pond are accessible only by trail; park roads serve
the other seven. All the campgrounds have lean-tos (except
Trout Brook) and tent sites (except Chimney Pond); some
have bunkhouses; only Daicey Pond has cabins. All these
sites offer only the most basic facilities. There are no hot
showers, grocery stores, or gasoline stations, and the water
is untreated.

There are areas for groups of twelve or more at Avalanche
Field, Foster Field, Nesowadnehunk Field, and Trout Brook
Farm. Backcountry campsites for smaller hiking parties are
at Davis Pond, Pogy Pond, Wassataquoik Stream, Wassata-
quoik Lake Island, Little Wassataquoik Lake, Little East,
Webster Stream, Long Pond, Middle Fowler Pond, Lower
Fowler Pond, Upper South Branch Pond, Billfish Pond,
Round Pond, Littlefield Pond, Matagamon Lake, and Web-
ster Lake. Park headquarters in Millinocket handles all
reservations for park facilities. Visitors can rent canoes at
South Branch Pond, Russell Pond, and Daicey Pond. Campers and visitors supply their own food and cooking utensils.

In recent years, use of the facilities at BSP has increased
considerably. At the same time, park authorities have begun
limiting the number of campers in the park. During most of
the summer, the campgrounds are completely full. *Reservations are strongly recommended and are the only way to
guarantee space. Reservations must be confirmed and paid
for in advance; the park accepts no phone reservations.* The
address is Reservation Clerk, Baxter State Park, 64 Balsam
Drive, Millinocket ME 04462 (207-723-5140). When allotted
spaces have been filled, no more overnight campers are allowed in the park. To avoid unnecessary driving and disap-
pointment, campers without reservations should call the
reservation clerk before starting a long trip to the park.

If park facilities are filled, campers can try a number of

private sporting camps and campgrounds in the area around the park. The MFS maintains several campsites in the general area.

The park is open to the public twelve months a year at nominal usage fees. Nearly all of the 180 mi. of trails are blue-blazed. The only exception is the white-blazed Appalachian Trail. Remember that at various points on the tableland of Katahdin, and particularly near its summit, local variation in declination makes the compass somewhat unreliable.

Roads to the park run through Millinocket, Patten, and Greenville. These routes are shown on the official Maine Highway Map (or any other general highway map). Roads in the BSP area are indicated on the Katahdin/Baxter map with this guide. To reach the southern and eastern entrances to the park from points to the south, follow I-95 north to the Medway exit, and then go west on ME 157 to Millinocket and the park area; or continue on I-95 to Sherman Mills, and then follow ME 11 to Patten and ME 159 west past Shin Pond to the northern portion of the park. The approach through Greenville to the southern entrance is rougher, longer, and more time consuming than the other, but it is very interesting and offers good views of the Katahdin area.

Currently, the park has four entrances. As they enter or leave the park, all visitors must stop at the entrance gate house to register and to pick up or leave passes. Visitors can also find out about the status of hiking trails on the mountains and get other information at the gatehouses.

The southernmost gate house is just north of Togue Pond, about 18 mi. from Millinocket. Immediately past the gate house, the road forks. The right fork leads 8.1 mi. to Roaring Brook Campground and trails to Chimney Pond and Russell Pond. The left fork leads to Abol Campground (5.7 mi.); to Katahdin Stream Campground (7.7 mi.); and to Nesowadnehunk Field and Campground (16.8 mi.).

The second control point is on **Matagamon (First Grand)** Lake on the approach road to the northeastern part of the park. It is 24 mi. from Patten and ME 11. Follow ME 159 west from Patten past Shin Pond. Trout Brook Farm Campground is 2.6 mi. to the west on the perimeter road. South Branch Pond Campground is 9.6 mi. Drive west, at first, on the perimeter road and then south about 2.5 mi. on a well-marked turnoff.

There is a third control point on the park's western boundary at Nesowadnehunk Campground. It is 58 mi. from Greenville or 51 mi. from Millinocket to Nesowadnehunk Gate over rough, privately owned logging roads. There is a fourth entrance at Telos Gate, 10 mi. north of Nesowadnehunk Campground. Inquire from BSP headquarters about route and road conditions before starting out.

You can reach most campgrounds and other facilities in the park from the perimeter road. To meet the terms of former Governor Baxter's deeds of trust, the roads are unpaved and relatively unimproved. The perimeter road extends 50.5 mi. from Togue Pond Gate House to Matagamon Gate House. It is a very narrow, winding, dirt or gravel road. Except in a few places, the dense foliage along the road restricts the view. A trip to the park is not really worthwhile unless you plan to hike and camp.

From the Togue Pond Gate House, the perimeter road first leads northwest and then generally north. It skirts the southern and western flanks of Katahdin. During the first 5 mi. of the drive, the mountain is briefly visible a few times. After passing Abol and Katahdin Stream Campgrounds, the road reaches Foster Field, where you can see Doubletop, O-J-I, and other mountains in the range west of Katahdin. After that the views are very restricted all the way to the Matagamon Gate House. Most of the perimeter road follows the routes of old logging roads. For clarity and consistency, the older, more colorful, road names have been dropped in favor of the term *perimeter road*.

People planning to camp, hike, and use the facilities in the park should know the rules and regulations, which are revised annually. They can be obtained by writing to Baxter State Park, 64 Balsam Dr., Millinocket ME 04462. The latest versions of the most important rules are summarized below.

Camping is allowed only at authorized campgrounds or campsites. A responsible adult at least 18 years old must accompany groups that include five or more persons under 16 years of age; there must be one adult for each five minors. Larger camping groups may be restricted to authorized group-camping areas. The rules *prohibit bringing pets* into the park and also limit the entry and use of larger recreational vehicles. They also prohibit airplanes, motorboats and motorcycles, trail bikes, and other all-terrain vehicles. Currently, snowmobiles may be operated only on the perimeter road of the park. They may not be used on the South Branch Pond Road or the Roaring Brook Road, except by authorized park personnel.

Warning. Increased use of BSP in recent years has resulted in more accidents; several people have died on the mountain. The upper summits are very high and are rugged and bare above the timberline, and the park is fairly far north. As a result, the weather and trail conditions can change very quickly, even in the middle of summer. The weather on Katahdin is similar to that on Mount Washington, but longer access routes can make conditions even more dangerous in many cases.

Hikers planning to go to higher elevations should take plenty of food, water, and warm clothing. No hired packers serve the park; hikers who do not want to carry their own packs should make needed arrangements before arriving. The trails on many of the routes are among the steepest and most difficult in New England. Hikers should be in good physical condition if they plan to climb the higher and more distant summits; those who are not in good shape should limit their activities accordingly. *Do not* leave the trails (unless bushwhacking is suggested in this guide), particularly on Katahdin or during severe weather or limited visibility.

Hikers entering the park via the AT must register at the first campground, Daicy Pond.

Hunt Trail

The white-blazed Hunt Trail, the route of the Appalachian Trail up Katahdin, climbs the mountain from the southwest. The trail leaves from Katahdin Stream Campground. From the treeline to the tableland this trail is steep and rough. Heed the warnings in the previous paragraphs. The trail was first cut in 1900 by Irving O. Hunt, who operated a sporting camp on Sourdnahunk Stream.

The trail follows the north side of Katahdin Stream. At 1.1 mi. from the campground it passes the trail to the Owl on the left, crosses Katahdin Stream, and shortly after that a trail leaves left to Katahdin Stream Falls. The trail steepens through the spruce and at 2.7 mi. reaches two large rocks that form a cave, which will shelter four people. There is a *spring,* undependable in dry periods, 50 yd. down the trail from the cave.

The trail passes through a growth of small spruce and in 0.2 mi. emerges on the bare, steep crest of the southwestern shoulder, called the Camel's Hump. There cairns mark the trail, which goes on to wind among gigantic boulders. The trail then traverses a broad shelf and climbs steeply 0.5 mi. over broken rock to the open tableland (at 3.7 mi.), where two slabs of rock mark the "Gateway." The trail continues east, following a worn path and paint blazes, until it reaches Thoreau Spring (at 4.2 mi.), where there is *water* except in dry seasons. (At the spring, Baxter Peak Cutoff goes off to the left and reaches the Saddle in 0.9 mi. This trail avoids the summit and is the best route in stormy weather for traveling between Thoreau Spring and the Saddle.) (To the right, the Abol Trail descends 2.8 mi. to Abol Campground.) From the spring, the Hunt Trail climbs moderately northeast for 1 mi. to Baxter Peak, with its commanding panoramas and surprising view of the South Basin.

Hunt Trail
Distances from Katahdin Stream Campground

to Owl Trail junction: 1.1 mi. (45 min.)

to cave: 2.7 mi. (2 hr. 55 min.)

to the Gateway: 3.7 mi. (4 hr. 25 min.)

to Thoreau Spring, and junctions with Abol Trail and Baxter Peak Cutoff: 4.2 mi. (4 hr. 35 min.)

to the Saddle (via Baxter Peak Cutoff): 5.1 mi. (5 hr. 30 min.)

to Baxter Peak: 5.2 mi./8.4 km. (5 hr. 20 min.)

to Chimney Pond Campground (via Baxter Peak, the Knife Edge, and Dudley Trail): 7.6 mi./12.2 km. (7 hr. 45 min.)

to Chimney Pond Campground (via Baxter Peak Cutoff and Saddle Trail): 6.8 mi./10.9 km. (6 hr. 30 min.)

Abol Trail

The Abol Trail is believed to be the oldest route up the mountain, and evidence exists that the first recorded ascent took place near this trail. It follows a great slide up the southwestern side of Katahdin.

Caution. This trail is *dangerous* because of its steepness and the great amount of loose rock and gravel in the slide. Climb and descend with great care.

The trail leaves the perimeter road at Abol Campground. It crosses through the campground and at 0.2 mi. enters an old tote road and reaches the south bank of a tributary of

Abol Stream. It continues along the south bank of the stream for 0.6 mi. The trail then bears right (northeast) away from the brook and leads sharply right. It reaches a gravel wash of old Abol Slide (1.3 mi.) and climbs the slide, reaching a more recent slide at 1.9 mi. Beyond this point the slide is steeper and becomes entirely bare. Huge boulders and increasing steepness mark the latter part of this climb. On the tableland, paint blazes lead 0.1 mi. to Thoreau Spring and the Hunt Trail. Go right on the Hunt Trail and continue northeast up gentle slopes to the summit of Katahdin. Except in dry seasons, there is water at Thoreau Spring. It is possible to make a long but rewarding circuit using the Hunt and Abol trails. You can either leave cars at the Abol and Katahdin Stream campgrounds or walk the 2 mi. between them on the perimeter road. Going up by the Abol Trail is best.

Abol Trail

Distances from Abol Campground

to foot of old Abol Slide: 1.3 mi. (1 hr. 20 min.)

to tableland: 2.6 mi. (3 hr. 15 min.)

to Thoreau Spring and Hunt Trail junction: 2.8 mi. (3 hr. 20 min.)

to Baxter Peak (via Hunt Trail): 3.8 mi./6 km. (4 hr. 5 min.) (*descending*, 2 hr. 45 min.)

to Katahdin Stream Campground (via Hunt Trail, including summit): 9 mi./14.5 km. (*est.* 9 hr.)

Roaring Brook Campground

This campground, at about 1480 ft., is on the south bank of Roaring Brook at the northern terminus of Roaring Brook Road. It is about 8.1 mi. from Togue Pond Gate House. Trails to Chimney Pond and Russell Pond start here. Closer by are Sandy Stream Pond (where hikers often see moose) and South Turner Mountain.

Distances from Roaring Brook Campground

- *to* Chimney Pond (via Chimney Pond Trail): 3.3 mi./5.3 km. (2 hr. 20 min.) (*descending,* 1 hr. 40 min.)
- *to* Baxter Peak (via Chimney Pond and Dudley trails and Knife Edge): 5.7 mi./9.2 km. (6 hr. 5 min.) (*descending,* 4 hr. 40 min.)
- *to* Baxter Peak (via Chimney Pond and Saddle trails): 5.5 mi./8.9 km. (4 hr. 35 min.) (*descending,* 3 hr. 15 min.)
- *to* Baxter Peak (via Taylor Trail and Knife Edge): 4.3 mi./6.9 km. (5 hr. 15 min.) (*descending,* 3 hr. 10 min.)
- *to* Hamlin Peak (via Chimney Pond, North Basin Cutoff, and Hamlin Ridge Trails): 4.5 mi./7.2 km. (4 hr. 15 min.)
- *to* North Basin (via Chimney Pond, North Basin Cutoff, and North Basin trails): 3.3 mi./5.3 km. (2 hr. 35 min.) (*descending,* 1 hr. 50 min.)
- *to* Russell Pond (via Russell Pond Trail): 7 mi./11.3 km. (3 hr. 45 min.)
- *to* South Turner Mountain summit (via Russell Pond and South Turner Mountain trails): 2 mi./3.2 km. (1 hr. 50 min.)

Helon N. Taylor Trail

A lot of this trail follows the route of the old Leavitt Trail. It provides a direct route from the Roaring Brook Campground to Pamola and follows the exposed Keep Ridge. This route provides the best sustained views of any trail starting from a road in the park, but it also exposes the hiker to the weather. *Be careful.* Avoid this trail in bad weather, particularly if you plan to go all the way to Baxter Peak via the Knife Edge. The Taylor Trail does not have dangerous footing, but it does require almost continuous climbing over rocks and boulders, so it is fairly tiring.

The trail, relocated in 1980, begins on the Chimney Pond Trail 0.1 mi. west of Roaring Brook Campground. It climbs

0.5 mi. through mixed growth to a ridge crest. It then levels off for a short period, passing through scrub and a boulder field. After that it climbs steeply through small birch, enters an old flat burn, and drops to the small Bear Brook, one of the branches of Avalanche Brook. This stream offers the only *water* on the trail.

After Bear Brook, the trail ascends steeply through scrub, a fine stand of conifers, and a boulder field with wide views in all directions. It climbs over and between boulders to Keep Ridge and then along the open ridge, with a spectacular view of the Knife Edge opening up ahead, to the summit of Pamola.

Helon N. Taylor Trail
Distances from Roaring Brook Campground
    to start (via Chimney Pond Trail): 0.1 mi. (5 min.)
    to Pamola summit: 3.2 mi./5.2 km. (3 hr. 20 min.)
       (*descending*, 2 hr. 15 min.)
    to Baxter Peak (via the Knife Edge): 4.3 mi./6.9 km.
       (5 hr. 15 min.) (*descending*, 3 hr. 10 min.)
    to Chimney Pond Campground (via the Knife Edge and
       Cathedral Trail): 6 mi./9.7 km. (4 hr. 55 min.)

Chimney Pond Trail

The Chimney Pond Trail begins at the ranger's cabin at Roaring Brook Campground. Following the old Basin Ponds tote road, it climbs west along the south bank of Roaring Brook. After 0.6 mi., it bears gradually away from the brook and climbs more steeply. A brook, the outlet of Pamola Pond, crosses at 1 mi. At 1.9 mi., the trail bears left; 150 ft. to the left is the site of the old Basin Ponds Camp, GNP Camp No. 3, 1921–1936. The trail then bears right and enters an overgrown clearing at 2 mi. At that point Lower Basin Pond comes into view.

The trail follows the southern end of Lower Basin Pond and continues along its southwestern shore. At 2.2 mi. the trail goes left uphill into the woods. At 2.3 mi. the North Basin Cutoff goes off to the right. Stay left to continue on the Chimney Pond Trail. At 2.7 mi. it follows the side of a depression known as Dry Pond, which holds water in the spring and after heavy rains. At 3.0 mi. the North Basin Trail to Hamlin Ridge and North Basin leaves on the right, and at 3.2 mi. there is a cabin on the left. The trail then goes downhill slightly to end at the shore of Chimney Pond.

Chimney Pond Trail
Distances from Roaring Brook Campground
- *to* brook crossing: 1 mi. (35 min.)
- *to* North Basin Cutoff junction: 2.3 mi. (1 hr. 20 min.)
- *to* Dry Pond: 2.7 mi. (1 hr. 55 min.)
- *to* North Basin Trail junction: 3 mi. (2 hr. 10 min.)
- *to* Chimney Pond Campground: 3.3 mi./5.3 km. (2 hr. 20 min.)

Chimney Pond Campground
Magnificently located on Chimney Pond (2910 ft.), this campground is an excellent base for climbing to the highest summits and the tableland area. Because of this campground's heavy use and fragile ecology, the park authority enforces several restrictions. No open fires are allowed; campers must use portable stoves. In addition, campers may not set up tents; overnight visitors must sleep in the bunkhouse or lean-tos. Early reservations are a must at this popular site.

Distances from Chimney Pond Campground
- *to* Roaring Brook Campground (via Chimney Pond Trail): 3.3 mi./5.3 km. (1 hr. 40 min.)
- *to* North Basin (via Chimney Pond and North Basin trails): 1.2 mi./1.9 km. (45 min.)
- *to* Hamlin Peak (via Chimney Pond, North Basin, and

Hamlin Ridge trails): 2 mi./3.2 km. (2 hr. 30 min.)
(*descending*, l hr. 45 min.)

to Davis Pond Lean-to (via Saddle and Northwest Basin
trails): 4.4 mi./7.1 km. (3 hr. 30 min.) (*returning*, 3 hr.
45 min.)

to Baxter Peak (via Dudley Trail and Knife Edge): 2.4
mi./3.9 km. (3 hr. 45 min.) (*returning*, 3 hr.)

to Baxter Peak (via Cathedral Trail): 1.7 mi./2.7 km.
(2 hr. 30 min.) (*descending*, 1 hr. 45 min.)

to Baxter Peak (via Saddle Trail): 2.2 mi./3.5 km. (2 hr.
15 min.) (*descending*, 1 hr. 35 min.)

to Baxter Peak (via Chimney Pond, North Basin, Hamlin
Ridge, and Saddle trails): 4.2 mi./6.8 km. (3 hr. 55
min.) (*descending*, 3 hr. 5 min.)

to Katahdin Stream Campground (via Saddle Trail, Baxter Peak Cutoff, and Hunt Trail): 6.8 mi./10.9 km.
(5 hr.)

Dudley Trail

The Dudley Trail leads from Chimney Pond to Pamola. It
runs from the ranger's cabin east across the outlet of the
pond, bears right, climbs over huge boulders, and reenters
the woods, where the route is well blazed. On the rocks,
cairns mark the trail clearly.

At 0.3 mi. from the pond, a side trail to the left marked
"Pamola Caves" leads past ledges, often streaming with water, and climbs to some caves that are about 0.8 mi. from the
Dudley Trail. In the caves, hikers must worm their way
through small winding passages to reach three remarkably
straight, spacious corridors. At the junction of the Dudley
Trail and the trail to the caves, there is a *spring* 30 ft. straight
ahead.

The Dudley Trail continues nearly due east from the junction, reaches a major cleft in the cliffs, and then climbs rapidly
south. The soft granite has eroded into curious forms, and the

trail becomes more difficult. Emerging above the timberline, the trail is marked by cairns, blue paint blazes on the rocks, and a well-worn path where it traverses patches of heath and low spruce. The trail bears slightly right (southwest) nearly to the edge of the South Basin. Then it heads south again and on up the long north slope of Pamola. The route's boulders rival the ones on the Hunt Trail, but the constantly changing view of the Great Basin below enhances the climb. After 30 min. among boulders, the going gets smoother and Index Rock (1 mi.) rises ahead. The trail passes just to the right of this landmark and continues less steeply 0.3 mi. to the peak of Pamola (4902 ft.). To reach Baxter Peak and points beyond, continue along the Knife Edge (see below). At Pamola, the Taylor Trail from Roaring Brook Campground comes in over Keep Ridge from the east.

Descending, the left-hand (western) line of cairns should be followed from the summit of Pamola. Stay near the edge of the South Basin and pass just to the left of Index Rock. At 1 mi. from Pamola, the side trail to Pamola Caves goes to the right and the Dudley Trail descends to the left.

Dudley Trail
Distances from Chimney Pond Campground
> *to* side trail to Pamola Caves: 0.3 mi. (15 min.)
> *to* Pamola Caves (via side trail): *est.* 1.1 mi. (1 hr.)
> *to* Pamola summit: 1.3 mi./2.1 km. (2 hr.) (*descending,* 1 hr. 30 min.)
> *to* Baxter Peak (via the Knife Edge): 2.4 mi./ 3.9 km. (3 hr. 45 min.) (*descending* back to Chimney Pond, 3 hr.)

The Knife Edge
This narrow serrated ridge tops the southern wall of the South Basin. Cliffs plummet down on the north, and the walls on the south are only slightly less steep. In places, the ridge narrows to only 2 or 3 ft. This is probably the most

spectacular mountain trail in the East. The narrowness of
the ridge, combined with the dizzying height and sheer cliffs,
gives a sense of extreme exposure.

From the summit of Pamola follow the cairns that lead
southwest. The trail drops abruptly into the sharp cleft at the
top of the Chimney, then climbs the equally steep rock tower
of Chimney Peak. From there the route is fairly obvious. It
traverses the "Sawteeth," finally climbing South Peak and
continuing along the rocks of the summit ridge to Baxter
Peak. *Caution.* The Knife Edge is *dangerous in a strong
wind. Do not leave the trail.* In recent years, several climbers
have had accidents while trying to take unmarked "short-
cuts" to the bottom.

The Knife Edge
Distance from Pamola summit
   to Baxter Peak: 1.1 mi./1.8 km. (1 hr. 45 min.)

Cathedral Trail
The three immense Cathedral Rocks extend from the sum-
mit ridge and partly separate the South Basin from the Great
Basin.

A sign a few feet west of the ranger's cabin at Chimney
Pond marks the start of this route to Baxter Peak by way of
Cathedral Rocks. The trail climbs through a small tangled
spruce forest and passes into an old evergreen forest. At 0.3
mi., it goes by Cleftrock Pool, on the right. At 0.4 mi., by a
large cairn, the trail turns right toward the Cathedrals,
crosses a "bridge" of rock covered with low growth, climbs
steeply through boulders to a high point, and from there
continues through low trees.

In 1967, a slide wiped out part of the next section of the
trail, but with care, it is still easy to follow the route. Cairns
mark the way around to the right, although ice sometimes
sweeps them away. The trail goes around to the right, then up

the steep side of the first Cathedral (0.8 mi.). The climb of the second Cathedral (0.9 mi.) is interesting and offers spectacular views of the Chimney and the Knife Edge. The route continues up the ridge to the top of the third Cathedral at 1.1 mi. At 1.2 mi., the trail forks. The right (northwest) fork is the Cathedral Cutoff and leads 0.2 mi. to the Saddle Trail. The Cathedral Trail bears left (southwest) 0.2 mi. over large boulders to the Saddle Trail (1.4 mi.), which it joins 0.8 mi. above the Saddle.

It is better to climb up via the Cathedral Trail than to descend by it. For one of the best circuits of the upper part of Katahdin, go up the Cathedral Trail to Baxter Peak; then either return to Chimney Pond via the Saddle Trail or take the Knife Edge to Pamola and return to Chimney Pond via the Dudley Trail or go on to Roaring Brook Campground via the Taylor Trail.

Cathedral Trail
Distances from Chimney Pond Campground
- *to* second Cathedral: 0.9 mi. (1 hr. 30 min.)
- *to* Saddle Trail junction: 1.4 mi. (2 hr. 20 min.)
- *to* Baxter Peak (via Saddle Trail): 1.6 mi./2.6 km. (2 hr. 30 min.)
- *to* Chimney Pond Campground (via Saddle Trail): 3.9 mi./6.3 km. (4 hr. 5 min.)
- *to* Chimney Pond Campground (via the Knife Edge and Dudley Trail): 4.1 mi./6.6 km. (4 hr. 15 min.)
- *to* Roaring Brook Campground (via the Knife Edge and Taylor Trail): 6 mi./9.7 km. (5 hr. 40 min.)

Saddle Trail
Climbers have taken this general route out of the basin since the Saddle Slide occurred in 1899. Before that they used an older slide just north of the present one.

The Saddle Trail is the easiest route up Katahdin from

Chimney Pond. From the ranger's cabin, the worn trail climbs a rocky path through dense softwoods. Beyond this stand, the trail swings to the right (north) and becomes smoother and flatter as it continues through an evergreen forest. It crosses a brook at 0.8 mi., then climbs steeply over large boulders. At 0.9 mi. the trail bears left up the Saddle Slide and passes through stunted birches. At 1 mi. it emerges from scrub, and there is a scramble for 0.2 mi. up the loose, open slope of the slide. (Be careful of loose rocks.) At 1.2 mi. the trail suddenly reaches the top of the slide and the level, open tableland at the Saddle between the summits of Baxter Peak and Hamlin Peak. Go left (south) to reach Baxter Peak. The Northwest Basin Trail, to the right, leads to Caribou Spring, the Hamlin Ridge Trail, the North (Howe) Peaks Trail, the Northwest Basin, and all points on the northern end of the mountain. About 250 yd. northwest of the head of the slide, there is *water* (unreliable) at Saddle Spring, which flows among the rocks near the edge of the scrub.

The Saddle Trail to Baxter Peak continues south over gentle slopes. Cairns mark the well-worn path.

At 1.7 mi. the trail passes a large boulder. The northern end of the Cathedral Cutoff, which leads to the Cathedral Trail, is on the left (east); on the right (west) is the eastern end of the Baxter Peak Cutoff, which leads southwest along the base of the summit 0.9 mi. to Thoreau Spring and the Abol and Hunt trails. At 2.0 mi. the Cathedral Trail from Chimney Pond enters on the left. The Saddle Trail continues on to Baxter Peak at 2.2 mi.

Saddle Trail
Distances from Chimney Pond Campground
to Saddle Slide: 0.9 mi. (40 min.)
to the Saddle and Northwest Basin Trail junction: 1.2 mi. (1 hr. 25 min.)
to Cathedral Trail junction: 2 mi. (1 hr. 55 min.)

> *to* Baxter Peak: 2.2 mi./3.5 km. (2 hr. 15 min.)
> *to* Chimney Pond Campground (via Cathedral Trail): 3.9 mi./6.3 km. (4 hr.)
> *to* Chimney Pond Campground (via the Knife Edge and Dudley Trail): 4.6 mi./7.4 km. (4 hr.)
> *to* Roaring Brook Campground (via the Knife Edge and Taylor Trail): 6.5 mi./10.5 km. (5 hr. 25 min.)

Baxter Peak Cutoff

This trail makes it possible to go from one side of Katahdin to the other without climbing over the summit, saving 0.7 mi. of distance and about 600 ft. of elevation. It is wise to take this route in bad weather.

The trail leaves the Saddle Trail 1.7 mi. from Chimney Pond. It runs southwest over the open tableland along the base of Baxter Peak and ends at Thoreau Spring, which is on the Hunt Trail, 4.2 mi. from Katahdin Stream Campground. These two trails form the shortest route between Chimney Pond and Katahdin Stream Campground (6.8 mi.)

Baxter Peak Cutoff
Distances from Chimney Pond Campground

> *to* start of cutoff (via Saddle Trail): 1.7 mi. (1 hr. 45 min.)
> *to* Thoreau Spring (Hunt Trail/Abol Trail junction): 2.6 mi./4.2 km. (2 hr. 15 min.)
> *to* Abol Campground (via Abol Trail): 5.3 mi./8.5 km. (5 hr.)
> *to* Katahdin Stream Campground (via Hunt Trail): 6.8 mi./10.9 km. (5 hr. 30 min.)

North Basin Trail

From Chimney Pond follow the Chimney Pond Trail toward the Basin Ponds. At 0.3 mi. the North Basin Trail starts on the left (north) (sign). The trail runs through spruce forest to a junction with Hamlin Ridge Trail on the left (west) at 0.7 mi. Then it passes across the foot of Hamlin Ridge to a junction, at 0.9 mi., with the North Basin Cutoff Trail. Signs and a large cairn mark this junction. The North Basin Trail continues to the lip of the North Basin, and then it reaches Blueberry Knoll, a few feet higher than the floor of the basin, where there is a sweeping view of both North Basin and South Basin, as well as the landscape to the east. From Blueberry Knoll, it is possible to bushwhack to the boulder-strewn floor of the North Basin, with its two little ponds. The northern wall is a tremendous sheer cliff.

North Basin Trail
Distances from Chimney Pond Campground
- *to* start (via Chimney Pond Trail): 0.3 mi. (10 min.)
- *to* North Basin Cutoff junction: 0.9 mi. (30 min.)
- *to* Blueberry Knoll: 1.2 mi. (45 min.)
- *to* North Basin Ponds (via bushwhack): 1.4 mi./2.3 km. (55 min.)
- *to* Roaring Brook Campground (via North Basin Cutoff and Chimney Pond Trail): 3.9 mi./6.3 km. (2 hr. 35 min.)

North Basin Cutoff
This trail from the Basin Ponds to Hamlin Ridge and the North Basin forks right (sign) 2.3 mi. from Roaring Brook Campground on the Chimney Pond Trail. It traverses an area of second-growth spruce, runs past several active beaver ponds, then climbs steeply through old growth to a junction with the North Basin Trail (0.7 mi.). Turn left (southwest) to reach Hamlin Ridge, or right (northeast) to reach Blueberry Knoll and the North Basin.

North Basin Cutoff
Distances from Roaring Brook Campground
- *to* start (via Chimney Pond Trail): 2.3 mi. (1 hr. 20 min.)
- *to* North Basin Trail junction: 3 mi. (2 hr. 15 min.)
- *to* Blueberry Knoll (via North Basin Trail): 3 mi./4.8 km. (2 hr. 25 min.)
- *to* Hamlin Ridge Trail (via North Basin Trail): 3.2 mi./5.2 km. (2 hr. 15 min.)
- *to* Chimney Pond Campground (via North Basin and Chimney Pond trails): 3.9 mi./6.3 km. (2 hr. 45 min.)

Hamlin Ridge Trail

The trail climbs, largely in the open, up Hamlin Ridge, which separates the North and South basins. The views are magnificent. From Chimney Pond Campground, follow the Chimney Pond Trail 0.3 mi. to the North Basin Trail, then follow the North Basin Trail for 0.4 mi., to the start of the Hamlin Ridge Trail. The trail reaches the treeline after a climb of about 20 min. Then, after a short stretch of boulder-strewn slope, it rises to the backbone of the ridge. The trail follows the open ridge to Hamlin Peak, and from there it goes on 0.2 mi. west across the open tableland and through a boulder field to Caribou Spring, which usually has *water* in a spring on the right side of the trail near a large cairn. To the right from Hamlin Peak, the North (Howe) Peaks Trail runs along the headwall of North Basin and reaches the North Peaks in just under a mile.

Hamlin Ridge Trail
Distances from Chimney Pond Campground
- *to* start (via Chimney Pond and North Basin trails): 0.7 mi. (20 min.)
- *to* Hamlin Peak: 2 mi. (2 hr. 30 min.)
- *to* Caribou Spring: 2.2 mi./3.5 km. (2 hr. 40 min.)

North (Howe) Peaks Trail

This trail offers a route up the northern slope of Katahdin from the Russell Pond area. It leads first over the North (Howe) Peaks. (The official name is Howe Peaks, after Burton Howe, a lumberman who organized a trip that Percival Baxter made to Katahdin in 1920.) The trail continues to Hamlin Peak, from which connecting trails lead to other points on the mountain. The lower end of the North Peaks Trail runs through dense, mixed growth of small trees. The central section follows a brook up into a large ravine between Russell Mountain on the left (east) and Tip Top on the right (west). Then it climbs the ravine's headwall. Be careful above the treeline when visibility is poor, especially descending. There is plenty of *water* nearly to the treeline and usually at Caribou Spring.

The trail leaves the Northwest Basin Trail 1.2 mi. southwest of Russell Pond Campground. At 1.5 mi. the trail crosses to the south bank of Wassataquoik Stream and climbs a short, steep slope to the top of a little horseback ridge at the mouth of a brook. When it leaves the ridge (1.6 mi.) the trail continues along an old road. Then it becomes a narrow path through thick, young spruce and reaches a brook at 2.7 mi. It crosses the brook about 90 yd. farther on.

At the foot of a steep rise the trail bears right (west) away from the west bank of the brook and gradually curves left (south) on a steep climb. At 2.9 mi. it recrosses to the east bank of the brook near the foot of a lovely waterslide, where the brook runs over sloping ledges. The path parallels the waterslide for a short distance before curving to the left away from the brook and climbing through majestic old trees, which become smaller at the top of the headwall. At 4.4 mi. the trail crosses a spring brook—the last place where there is sure to be *water*. At 4.6 mi. the trail becomes a trench in dense scrub, and at 4.9 mi. it reaches the open northern tableland.

Cairns lead up to a minor peak (4182 ft./1275 m.), then down its southern slope and across a level stretch covered with dead scrub. At 5.2 mi. the trail starts its final steep climb to the North Peaks. At 5.6 mi. it reaches the easternmost (4612 ft.) of the high, rocky knobs that make up the summit ridge. (*Caution*. Be careful here in fog. Dangerous cliffs drop off 50 or 60 ft. away, to the southwest (left). The trail follows the line of the ridge southwest over intervening knobs to a large cairn on the highest peak (4734 ft.), at the southwestern end of the ridge (6.3 mi.). From this point the views out over the country to the north are spectacular. The trail, well-cairned, descends slightly and crosses the tableland.

At 6.5 mi. the trail forks. The North Peaks Trail follows the left (southeastern) fork and climbs gradually to Hamlin Peak, where it ends at 6.9 mi. The right fork is the Hamlin Peak Cutoff that leads to Caribou Spring and the Northwest Basin Trail.

North (Howe) Peaks Trail
Distances from Russell Pond Campground

to start (via Northwest Basin Trail): 1.2 mi. (35 min.)
to waterslide: 2.9 mi. (2 hr. 5 min.)
to tableland: 4.9 mi. (4 hr. 5 min.)
to first (easternmost) North Peak: 5.6 mi. (4 hr. 55 min.)
to second North Peak: 6.3 mi. (5 hr. 15 min.)
to Hamlin Peak Cutoff junction: 6.5 mi. (5 hr. 25 min.)
to Hamlin Peak: 6.9 mi./11.1 km. (5 hr. 40 min.)

Hamlin Peak Cutoff

Following a good path along the contour, this trail runs from the North Peaks Trail, at a point in the col between the North Peaks and Hamlin Peak, to the Northwest Basin Trail at Caribou Spring. By traveling north-south along the table-land, it avoids the climb over Hamlin Peak.

Hamlin Peak Cutoff
Distance from North Peaks Trail junction
> **to** Northwest Basin Trail junction, Caribou Spring: 0.3
> mi./0.5 km. (8 min.)

Northwest Basin Trail

This route climbs from the Russell Pond area to the Saddle through wild and secluded Northwest Basin, with its virgin trees, glacial sheepback rocks, five ponds, waterfalls, and interesting central ridge. The lower end of the trail follows the route of the old Wassataquoik Tote Road.

The trail begins at Russell Pond Campground. It leads southwest from Russell Pond following the Russell Pond Trail for 0.1 mi. It then diverges right and crosses a dam at the foot of the Turner Deadwater at about 0.3 mi. From there it goes on through the woods until it joins the route of the old Wassataquoik Tote Road, at about 0.5 mi. At 1.2 mi. the North Peaks Trail leaves left. With Wassataquoik Stream on the left, the trail stays on the tote road and climbs gradually, crossing Annis Brook about 2.5 mi. from Russell Pond. After passing over a section of corduroy road, the trail crosses a small brook that drains the eastern slope of Fort Mountain. It continues through thick woods and crosses Wassataquoik Stream at 3.6 mi. (*Caution*. Be very careful in high water.)

The trail climbs steadily, soon approaching Northwest Basin Brook. It runs along the brook bed for 300 ft. at about 4.4 mi. (Proceed carefully here; the rocks are very slippery and cairns may be swept away by freshets.) Above the junction of the outlets from the first two ponds, Lake Cowles and Davis Pond, the trail leads steeply up to the northern shore of Lake Cowles. It then turns left and crosses the outlet of Lake Cowles at 4.7 mi. Where it climbs to a heath-covered glacial sheepback rock, the path is becoming overgrown with blueberry bushes but is not hard to follow. From the sheepback there are enjoyable views of the entire basin. The trail continues down to the Davis Pond Lean-to, at 5.1 mi. The shelter, rebuilt in 1987, is located on the north side of Davis Pond.

From the Davis Pond Lean-to, the Northwest Basin Trail passes the so-called disappearing pond. (The fourth pond is 0.3 mi. below and on the outlet of Davis Pond; the fifth is hidden deep in the woods between the outlets of Lake Cowles and Davis Pond.) The trail first goes southwest and then south as it climbs through a steep and rough area up the basin wall.

The trail emerges from the scrub and at 6.2 mi. reaches a large cairn that marks a small peak (4401 ft.) near the western end of the Northwest Plateau. The Northwest Plateau reaches toward the west and is a flat extension of the northern tableland. It lies west of the North Peaks and separates the Northwest Basin from the Klondike Pond Ravine. Its lower slopes push their way far out into the Klondike. At 6.4 mi. an obscure, unmaintained route leads right (south) to the head of a slide down into the Klondike Pond Ravine. The Northwest Basin Trail climbs very gradually across the Northwest Plateau, passing through a belt of scrub at 6.8 mi. Then it continues more to the south across open tableland to Caribou Spring, at 7.3 mi. At the spring, the Hamlin Peak Cutoff leads sharply left to the North Peaks Trail, and the Hamlin Ridge Trail climbs left (east) to Hamlin Peak.

The Northwest Basin Trail descends south toward the Saddle, which it reaches at 8.3 mi. To get to Chimney Pond, descend east on the Saddle Trail.

Keep in mind that poor trail or weather conditions, heavy packs, and different levels of physical conditioning in hiking parties will increase the times given here.

Northwest Basin Trail
Distances from Russell Pond Campground
to North Peaks Trail junction: 1.2 mi. (35 min.)

to Annis Brook crossing: 2.5 mi. (1 hr. 30 min.)

to Wassataquoik Stream crossing: 3.6 mi. (2 hr. 15 min.)

to Davis Pond Lean-to: 5.1 mi. (3 hr. 15 min.)

to peak of Northwest Plateau: 6.2 mi. (4 hr. 50 min.)

to Hamlin Ridge Trail and Hamlin Peak Cutoff junction, Caribou Spring: 7.3 mi./11.8 km. (5 hr. 35 min.)

to the Saddle and Saddle Trail junction: 8.3 mi./13.3 km. (6 hr.)

Klondike Pond Ravine

This ravine contains a long, narrow pond that drains into the Klondike. The great slabs of the central gully form the most spectacular route down into the ravine. Rock fields forming an island in dense scrub on the northeastern headwall offer a rough but safe approach to them. (*Caution*. Be careful on the slabs, and avoid wet places on the steeper ones.) At the foot of the headwall, follow the brook 200 yd. to the head of Klondike Pond, where there are impressive views of the ravine.

This trail is *not* officially maintained, and fire poses great danger in this remote area. Therefore, hikers *must* get permission to enter from park officials.

An unmaintained, seldom-used route leaves the Northwest Basin Trail on the left (south) 0.9 mi. northwest of Caribou Spring (about halfway between the belt of scrub and the peak of the Northwest Plateau). This route continues to the rim of the ravine, and after a short drop, it enters the head of a recent slide. From the bottom of the slide, bear slightly right through brush to reach the head of the pond. The dense scrub and the cliffs discourage any other entry into the ravine from above.

It is possible to hike from Chimney Pond to Klondike Pond and back in one day by starting early, but it makes for a long day.

Russell Pond Trail

This trail runs from Roaring Brook Campground northward between Katahdin and Turner Mountain to Russell Pond Campground. It is the principal approach to the Russell Pond area.

After leaving Roaring Brook Campground, the trail crosses Roaring Brook. At 0.2 mi. it turns left (northwest) (sign). To the right the South Turner Mountain Trail leads to Sandy Stream Pond and South Turner Mountain. In the next half mile the Russell Pond Trail crosses several brooks while gradually climbing the low height-of-land between Sandy Stream Pond and Whidden Pond. The trail descends and passes to the east (right) of the latter, where there is an extensive view of the basins and peaks on the east side of Katahdin. At 1.1 mi. the Sandy Stream Pond Trail comes in on the right. At 1.4 mi. an opening yields good views; after this point the trail moves into denser forest. Between 2.3 mi. and 3.1 mi., it crosses several brooks, and at 3.3 mi. it reaches a junction on the right with the Wassataquoik Stream Trail, which leads 2.5 mi. to the two Wassataquoik Stream Lean-tos and rejoins the Russell Pond Trail at 3.9 mi. At 3.4 mi. the Russell Pond Trail crosses the Wassataquoik South Branch and soon crosses another brook.

The trail, now on the western side of the valley, passes under an overhanging rock at 3.8 mi. Moving away from Wassataquoik Stream, it passes several brooks and springs and climbs gently for nearly 2 mi. to a spruce grove. Then the trail gradually descends, with the impressive, high, forested slopes of Russell Mountain on the left. At 6.3 mi. it crosses the main branch of Wassataquoik Stream. At 6.5 mi. it crosses the old Wassataquoik Tote Road with the abandoned clearing for New City Camps on the right. A trail on the right leads 1.4 mi. to the two lean-tos on Wassataquoik Stream. Immediately beyond the tote road, the Russell Pond

Trail crosses Turner Brook (North Branch of the Wassata-quoik).

At 6.9 mi. the Northwest Basin Trail to the Saddle leaves on the left (west). Soon after, the trail reaches Russell Pond.

Russell Pond Trail
Distances from Roaring Brook Campground
- *to* Sandy Stream Pond Trail junction: 1.1 mi. (30 min.)
- *to* Wassataquoik Stream Trail junction: 3.3 mi. (1 hr. 40 min.)
- *to* Wassataquoik Tote Road junction: 6.5 mi. (3 hr. 10 min.)
- *to* Northwest Basin Trail junction: 6.9 mi. (3 hr. 40 min.)
- *to* Russell Pond Campground: 7 mi./11.3 km. (3 hr. 45 min.)

Wassataquoik Stream Trail

Some once called this old route the Tracy Horse Trail or Wassataquoik South Branch Trail. It has been reopened and runs from the Russell Pond Trail along the South Branch of Wassataquoik Stream to the main branch of Wassataquoik Stream. It leaves the right side of the Russell Pond Trail about 3.3 mi. north of Roaring Brook Campground, just before that trail crosses South Branch. It leads to the junction with the main stream and continues along the south bank of the main stream for about 200 yd.

The park authority maintains two lean-tos at the site of the old Hersey Dam (where you can still see spilling at the crossing). Reservations for them may be made as for any campsite.

To reach Russell Pond Campground from the lean-tos, cross to the north side of Wassataquoik Stream upstream from the lean-tos (no bridge) and look for a blue-blazed trail along the old Wassataquoik Tote Road. In the downstream direction, this trail leads 1.6 mi. to a junction with the Grand

Falls Trail at Inscription Rock. In the upstream direction, it leads 1.4 mi. to a junction with the Russell Pond Trail just south of the Turner Brook crossing. Turn right on the Russell Pond Trail to reach the campground, which is about 0.4 mi. away.

Wassataquoik Stream Trail
Distances from Roaring Brook Campground

to start of trail to lean-tos (via Russell Pond Trail): 3.3 mi. (1 hr. 40 min.)

to lean-tos: 5.8 mi. (3 hr.)

to Russell Pond Campground (via Russell Pond Trail): 7.6 mi./12.2 km. (3 hr. 45 min.)

RUSSELL MOUNTAIN (2801 ft./854 m.)

This mountain is the most northern extension of Katahdin. Its broad, trailless summit area is devoid of recognizable characteristics and so flat and full of boulders that you have to search for the summit cairn. But the summit offers excellent views in all directions. To reach it, bushwhack west from the Russell Pond Trail about 4.5 mi. north of Roaring Brook Campground. Since there is no trail to the mountain and conditions change from year to year, check with the ranger at Russell Pond Campground for the latest information.

Russell Pond Campground

On the southwestern shore of Russell Pond (1333 ft.) in the heart of the wilderness north of Katahdin, this campground is a convenient and interesting hiking base. The wildlife in this remote area is especially intriguing. Facilities include tent sites, lean-tos, and a bunkhouse. The Wassataquoik Lake Cabin and the lean-tos on Wassataquoik Stream, Pogy

Pond, and Little Wassataquoik Pond are administered from this campground.

Russell Pond Campground
Distances from Russell Pond

- *to* Roaring Brook Campground (via Russell Pond Trail): 7 mi./11.3 km. (3 hr. 45 min.)
- *to* Hamlin Peak (via North Peaks Trail): 6.9 mi./11.1 km. (5 hr. 40 min.) (*descending*, 3 hr. 50 min.)
- *to* Davis Pond Lean-to (via Northwest Basin Trail): 5.1 mi./8.2 km. (3 hr. 15 min.) (*descending*, 2 hr. 45 min.)
- *to* Wassataquoik Lake (via Wassataquoik Lake Trail): 2.4 mi./3.9 km. (1 hr. 15 min.)
- *to* Little Wassataquoik Lake (via Wassataquoik Lake Trail): 5.2 mi./8.4 km. (3 hr. 10 min.)
- *to* dam at Nesowadnehunk Lake (via Wassataquoik Lake Trail): 11.4 mi./18.4 km. (6 hr. 15 min.)
- *to* Lookout Ledges (via Pogy Notch and Grand Falls trails): 1.3 mi./2.1 km. (50 min.)
- *to* Grand Falls (via Grand Falls Trail): 2.8 mi./4.5 km. (1 hr. 30 min.)
- *to* South Branch Pond Campground (via Pogy Notch Trail): 9.7 mi./15.6 km. (4 hr. 40 min.)
- *to* Wassataquoik Stream Lean-tos (via Wassataquoik Stream Trail): 1.8 mi./2.9 km. (1 hr.)

Wassataquoik Lake Trail

This trail connects the Russell Pond Campground with the Wassataquoik Lake area and continues on to the west to the perimeter road and the foot of Nesowadnehunk Lake. Most of the first part of this route was a logging road prior to 1878, and there is evidence it was cut out before 1845. The area was logged several times afterward. The west end of the trail follows a fairly new logging road built after the park was created. The former owners retained cutting rights for a period after they sold the property to Governor Baxter.

The trail leads north off the Pogy Notch Trail opposite lean-to No. 4 at the northwestern corner of Russell Pond. At 0.6 mi. from Russell Pond take the left fork (the right fork leads to Deep Pond). At 1.7 mi. the trail crosses a dam between two of the Six Ponds. It then crosses a brook at 2.2 mi., and at 2.3 mi. it takes the left fork (the right fork leads to the dam at the foot of Wassataquoik Lake) to a point near the dam (2.4 mi.). On an island near the eastern end of the pond there is a cabin. To reach the island, you can make arrangements at Russell Pond to use a canoe.

To reach the head (western) end of the lake (4.2 mi.), follow the trail along the rocky southern shore. The views are magnificent. About halfway along the southern shore of Wassataquoik Lake, a trail leads left (south) uphill to Green Falls, one of the most beautiful spots in the park. Above the falls, the hiker can pick out a route through a stand of virgin spruce to the summit of Wassataquoik Mountain (2984 ft./910 m.).

Near the head of Wassataquoik Lake, at an old grassy clearing, the trail leaves the lake and leads nearly due north on an old road. After crossing the outlet stream from Little Wassataquoik Lake several times, it reaches the lake itself. Then it follows along the northern shore to the lake's western end (about 5.2 mi.) The trail heads west from the lake toward a col between Wassataquoik Mountain and Lord Mountain. Shortly after leaving the lake, the trail passes the Little Wassataquoik Lake Lean-to. The trail climbs to the col and then descends into the Trout Brook drainage area. From the col, the trail follows an old logging road for about a mile and a half before it leaves the road and turns left at about 6.5 mi. Wet in places, it crosses a brook several times, and at about 7.6 mi. it crosses the South Branch of Trout Brook. Soon after crossing the brook, the trail enters an old logging camp

clearing. From here, a tote road that is easy to follow leads
for about 4 mi. through a valley between Center Mountain
and Strickland Mountain. It reaches a col and then descends
to the perimeter road. Turn left for the dam at the foot of
Nesowadnehunk Lake.

Wassataquoik Lake Trail
Distances from Russell Pond Campground
- *to* start (via Pogy Notch Trail): 0.2 mi. (5 min.)
- *to* Deep Pond side trail junction: 0.6 mi. (20 min.)
- *to* dam at Six Ponds: 1.7 mi. (50 min.)
- *to* side trail to dam at foot of Wassataquoik Lake: 2.3 mi.
  (1 hr. 10 min.)
- *to* Green Falls (via side trail): *est.* 3.3 mi. (1 hr. 45 min.)
- *to* Little Wassataquoik Lake: 5.2 mi. (3 hr. 10 min.)
- *to* left turn off old logging road: 6.5 mi. (3 hr. 50 min.)
- *to* tote road junction: 7.5 mi. (4 hr. 30 min.)
- *to* Nesowadnehunk Lake (via tote road): 11.4 mi./18.4
  km. (6 hr. 15 min.)

Grand Falls Trail

This trail leads from Russell Pond Campground to several
interesting locations in the Wassataquoik Valley. The first
part coincides with the Pogy Notch Trail.

From the campground, follow the Pogy Notch Trail
around the western shore of the pond. The Wassataquoik
Lake Trail leaves to the left soon after the start of the route.
At 0.2 mi. the Pogy Notch Trail continues north (left) at a
junction. The Grand Falls Trail takes the right fork, passes
the ranger station, and continues to the next junction (0.4
mi.), where the trail to Lookout Ledges leaves to the left
(north). The Grand Falls Trail continues ahead on the right
through woods and over relatively level ground toward Wassataquoik Stream. As it nears the Wassataquoik, a side trail

to the right leads 50 ft. to the bank of the stream and Inscription Rock, a huge boulder with a notice about logging in the area that was inscribed in 1883. A 1.6-mi. segment of the Wassataquoik Tote Road, from Inscription Rock to the Wassataquoik Stream Lean-tos, was reopened in 1983, so it is now possible to loop back to Russell Pond via the Wassataquoik Stream Trail and the Russell Pond Trail. From this junction, the main trail soon reaches the bank of Wassataquoik Stream near the Grand Falls of the Wassataquoik. These falls drop steeply through high granite walls and are impressive, particularly in high water. The ruins of a logging dam lie just upstream.

Grand Falls Trail
Distances from Russell Pond Campground
- *to* Lookout Ledges Trail junction: 0.4 mi. (10 min.)
- *to* Inscription Rock (via side trail): *est* 2.5 mi. (1 hr. 20 min.)
- *to* Grand Falls: *est.* 2.8 mi./4.5 km. (1 hr. 30 min.)

Lookout Ledges Trail
This high outlook (1730 ft./527 m.) offers views from Traveler Mountain around to Katahdin and is easy to reach from Russell Pond Campground. Follow the Pogy Notch and Grand Falls trails for 0.4 mi. and turn left at the junction. The trail climbs moderately and steadily for nearly a mile to the ledges.

Lookout Ledges Trail
Distances from Russell Pond Campground
- *to* start (via Pogy Notch and Grand Falls trails): 0.4 mi. (10 min.)
- *to* Lookout Ledges: 1.3 mi./2.1 km. (50 min.)

THE OWL (3736 ft./1139 m.)

This mountain is the first summit in the long, high range that runs west from Katahdin. Its southern face is especially steep.

The Owl Trail

The blue-blazed Owl Trail leaves the Hunt Trail 1.1 mi. from Katahdin Stream Campground. The trail goes left from the Hunt Trail just before a crossing of Katahdin Stream and then follows the north bank of a tributary. It turns *sharp* right (southeast) and crosses the tributary at 1.6 mi. (last source of *water*). The trail climbs gradually through dense spruce and fir and follows the western spur toward the summit. At 2.9 mi. the trail rises steeply through a ravine and then across the upper part of the Owl's prominent cliffs. At 3.2 mi. the trail reaches the first outlook. After a more gradual climb, it reaches the summit at 3.3 mi. Views in all directions are outstanding, especially the ones into the Klondike and across to the tremendous "wind-rows" in Witherle Ravine and on Fort Mountain.

The Owl Trail
Distances from Katahdin Stream Campground
to start (via Hunt Trail): 1.1 mi. (45 min.)
to first outlook: 3.2 mi. (2 hr. 35 min.)
to the Owl summit: 3.3 mi./5.3 km. (2 hr. 40 min.)

BARREN MOUNTAIN
(3580 ft. and 3681 ft./1091 m. and 1122 m.)

A high wooded ridge, Barren Mountain has two well-defined summits and several lower humps. A blowdown that occurred in 1974 eliminated possible approaches from the south and southwest.

One route goes up the southeast slide of O-J-I and then southeast into the col and up the Barren summit ridge. Scrub growth near the summits of O-J-I and Barren makes this route slow. It is also possible to climb from the Owl-Barren ravine, but blowdowns make this approach very difficult.

MOUNT O-J-I (3410 ft./1039 m.)

Mount O-J-I got its name from three slides on the southwestern slope that suggested the three letters. After a major storm in 1932, however, the slides began to enlarge and the letter shapes have become distorted. A fourth large slide that can be climbed came down in 1954 and is south of the so-called south slide.

Two of the other slides, the north and south slides, offer routes up the mountain. They are connected, which allows a circuit of the mountain in either direction. However, descending the smooth, steep granite slope on the north slide can be very dangerous, particularly in wet weather; so it is better to climb up by the north slide and return by the south slide.

The trail leaves the perimeter road at Foster Field directly opposite the road to Kidney Pond and immediately crosses a brook. At 0.4 mi. the trail forks. Go left to reach the north slide. (The right fork leads to the south slide.) The trail follows an old road and immediately crosses two small brooks. At 1.1 mi. the road ends in a small open area covered with slide gravel and cut by a stream bed that is usually dry. (About 45 yd. north of this point watch for a huge boulder off the trail on the left. The boulder is approximately 73 ft. long, 48 ft. wide, and 25 ft. high.) From the small open area, the trail parallels the stream bed without crossing it and leads directly (approximately 200 yd.) to a large open wash at the foot of the north slide and then to the top of the lower ledges. Many sections of this route traverse smooth granite, sometimes covered by gravel; so *be careful,* particularly if the rock is wet. Climb to the head of the slide and then go through brush to the summit ridge. There the trail heads to the western summit, where a trail leads left to the Old Jay Eye Rock, a fine observation point. From the summit ridge a trail leads right to the south slide.

To follow the south slide route, go right at the fork 0.4 mi. from Foster Field. The route follows an old road and at 1.8 mi. continues on a narrow trail. As the gravel wash from the slide becomes noticeable on the forest floor, the trail bears right and soon reaches the open wash (2 mi.). Climb to the head of the slide and through brush and scrub to the summit ridge. Then go northwest to the summit (2.9 mi.).

Another route is to approach the mountain by climbing the Mount Coe slide. The O-J-I Link Trail, cleared in 1983, runs 0.5 mi. from the Mt. Coe slide across the col to a junction with the O-J-I south slide trail 0.2 mi. from the summit.

Mount O-J-I
Distances from perimeter road at Foster Field

to fork in trail: 0.4 mi. (10 min.)
to foot of north slide (via left fork): 1.2 mi. (45 min.)
to O-J-I summit (via north slide): 2.7 mi./4.3 km. (3 hr.)
to foot of south slide (via right fork): 2 mi. (1 hr. 10 min.)
to O-J-I summit (via south slide): 2.9 mi./4.7 km. (3 hr. 15 min.)
to perimeter road (via north slide-south slide circuit): 5.6 mi./9 km. (6 hr.)

MOUNT COE (3764 ft./1147 m.)

This peak, just north of Mount O-J-I, has excellent views into the Klondike and is well worth the challenge of the climb.

Follow the Marston Trail to the sign 1.2 mi. from the perimeter road. Turn right, and follow the trail 0.2 mi. to the bottom of the Mount Coe slide. The climb is steady but moderate at first, then steep. At 2.6 mi. the trail bears left and begins to climb the left center of a wide slide area at 2.8 mi. (The O-J-I Link Trail leads right 0.5 mi. to the O-J-I South Slide Trail. It is 0.7 mi. to the summit of O-J-I via this trail.) At 3.1 mi. the trail enters scrub growth. At 3.3 mi. you will reach the summit.

An extension of the Mount Coe Trail, cleared in 1983 and further extended in 1987, rejoins the Marston Trail at a point 0.8 mi. from the summit of North Brother.

The trail descends the east ridge of Mount Coe and proceeds toward South Brother. At 4.2 mi. pass two clearings with fine views of Mount Coe. At 4.4 mi. the South Brother Side Trail leads right 0.3 mi. to the summit of South Brother. At 5.1 mi. reach the junction with the Marston Trail. Ahead it is 0.8 mi. to the summit of North Brother. To the left it is 2.9 mi. to the perimeter road.

Mount Coe
Distances from perimeter road, at Slide Dam

 to start of Mount Coe Trail (via Marston Trail): 1.2 mi. (50 min.)

 to foot of Mount Coe slide: 1.4 mi. (1 hr.)

 to start of scrub: 2.9 mi. (3 hr. 40 min.)

 to Mount Coe summit: 3.3 mi./5.3 km. (4 hr.) (*descending*, 2 hr.)

 to junction South Brother Side Trail: 4.4 mi. (4 hr. 45 min.)

 to junction Marston Trail: 5.1 mi./8.2 km. (5 hr. 15 min.)

THE BROTHERS (North 4143 ft. and South 3930 ft./1263 m. and 1198 m.)

North and South Brother are open peaks that offer splendid views in several directions. (*Caution.* Early in the season, in late May and the first half of June, climbers should expect to find deep snow from the head of the slide all the way to the ledges at the summit of North Brother—a distance of 1.5 mi.)

Marston Trail

The Marston Trail, the best approach for exploring the area, was relocated in 1987.

The trail leaves the perimeter road at Slide Dam, 5.9 mi. north of Katahdin Stream Campground and 3.6 mi. south of Nesowadnehunk Campground. The trail starts from the road, nearly opposite the picnic shelter, and follows the northern bank of Slide Brook to an open, sandy area. At 0.2 mi., the trail bears left into a wooded area and over a slight rise into the drainage area of a second brook. The trail, climbing steadily, follows this brook closely for the next mile. At 0.8 mi., it crosses, and there are several more crossings in the next 0.4 mi. before the trail reaches the junction with the Mount Coe trail at 1.2 mi.

The Marston Trail leads to the left and climbs gradually through extensive blowdown. A small pond with fine views is reached at 2 mi. At 2.1 mi. the pond's outlet is reached (last *water*). The trail then climbs steeply, passing several viewpoints. The trail levels off at 2.7 mi. and reaches the upper junction with the Mount Coe Trail at 2.9 mi. To the left, it is 0.8 mi. to North Brother. To the right, the Mount Coe Trail leads (1 mi. to South Brother via the South Brother Side Trail) 5.1 mi. to the perimeter road. After crossing this fairly level valley, it passes a *spring* at 3.1 mi. and then climbs steeply. At 3.6 mi. the trail leaves the scrub and continues among open boulders, reaching the summit of North Brother at 3.7 mi. Note particularly the view of the west slopes of Katahdin and, in the opposite direction, of the Nesowadnehunk Lake region and the interesting valley of Little Nesowadnehunk Stream.

Marston Trail
Distances from perimeter road at Slide Dam
- *to* Mount Coe Trail first junction: 1.3 mi. (50 min.)
- *to* Pond: 2.0 mi. (1 hr. 10 min.)
- *to* Mount Coe Trail, second junction: 2.9 mi. (2 hr.)
- *to* North Brother summit: 3.7 mi./6 km. (3 hr.) (*descending*, 2 hr.)

FORT MOUNTAIN (3861 ft./1177 m.)

This mountain, with its 0.5-mi. summit ridge, is northeast of North Brother. A high saddle connects the two. The best and easiest route to Fort Mountain is a trail leading left into the bush from the summit of North Brother. The trail is rough, unmarked, and obliterated in sections by blown-down trees, and keeps to the southern side of the North Brother-Fort ridge most of the way. It emerges on the north-western end of the Fort ridge. The distance is less than 1 mi.

Before trying to take this route, keep in mind that it comes at the end of a very tiring climb to North Brother.

Fort Mountain
Distances from perimeter road at Slide Dam
- *to* North Brother summit (via Marston Trail): 3.7 mi. (3 hr.)
- *to* Fort Mountain northwestern summit: *est.* 4.7 mi./7.6 km. (4 hr.) (*descending*, 2 hr. 45 min.)

Daicey Pond Campground

When the BSP Authority terminated the private leases still existing in the park in the late 1960s it decided to continue operations on a modified scale at the former Twin Pines Camps at Daicey Pond. There are ten cabins for rent. Users must provide their own cooking equipment. Canoes may be

rented. To reach Daicey Pond, follow the perimeter road for
2.7 mi. beyond Katahdin Stream Campground and turn left
(south). It is 1.5 mi. to the camps, which have beautiful views
of the western side of Katahdin and the mountains to the
west. From a canoe on the pond, you can get an excellent
view of Doubletop.

The Appalachian Trail passes within a short distance of
the campground and skirts the shore opposite the camp for
0.3 mi. Hikers entering the park from the south along the
Appalachian Trail must register at Daicey Pond. Katahdin
Stream Campground is 1.9 mi. northeast on the Appalachian Trail. South of Daicey Pond, the Appalachian Trail
passes an old dam on Nesowadnehunk Stream and Little and
Big Niagara Falls. All are worth seeing and are within 1.3 mi.
of the campground. The Appalachian Trail then leads out of
the park to the West Branch of the Penobscot (see the MATC
Guide to the Appalachian Trail in Maine for details).

Daicey Pond is a good starting point for the climb to Sentinel Mountain. Trails also lead to the Kidney Pond area, and
a lovely trail of about 1 mi. leads from the canoe landing on
Daicey Pond, across from the cabins, to Lost Pond.

SENTINEL MOUNTAIN (1837 ft./560 m.)

This low mountain rises over the northern bank of the
West Branch of the Penobscot River and offers the finest
view of the western side of Katahdin. From Kidney Pond
Road, skirt the western side of Kidney Pond, or paddle
across it to the canoe landing (Sentinel Landing) on the
southern side of the cove on the right (west).

From Daicey Pond, cross Nesowadnehunk Stream and
branch left (west) from the trail to Kidney Pond at a point
300 yd. from that pond. The trail goes around the southwestern side of the pond to Sentinel Landing, which is about 0.7

mi. from Daicey Pond. (*Caution.* Be careful to avoid several branch trails that are almost as clear as the main trail; some of them lead from a landing that the main trail passes before it gets to Sentinel Landing.)

From Sentinel Landing, the blue-blazed trail to Sentinel Mountain leads southwest. At 0.3 mi. (sign) the trail bears right onto a section that was relocated to avoid beaver flow. At 0.7 mi. you will have to cross Beaver Brook on stepping stones. The trail climbs the northeastern side of the mountain along a brook, which crosses the trail at 1.1 mi. and furnishes water nearly to the open summit ledges. The trail reaches the ledges at 2.2 mi. Follow the ledges to the right (north) to the actual summit (2.3 mi.).

From the actual summit at the western end of the summit ridge, the trail continues back along the southern side of the ridge, with an outlook over the West Branch, to form a loop. It rejoins the main trail about halfway between the first ledges and the true summit.

Sentinel Mountain Trail
Distances from Sentinel Landing

to Beaver Brook crossing: 0.7 mi. (20 min.)
to second brook crossing: 1.1 mi. (40 min.)
to Sentinel summit: 2.3 mi./3.7 km. (1 hr. 30 min.)

DOUBLETOP MOUNTAIN
(North Peak 3488 ft./1063 m.)

Doubletop's steep, slide-scarred eastern slopes make it easy to identify from many points in the Katahdin region. The views from its two peaks are impressive and are particularly helpful to anyone planning to climb South Brother, Mount Coe, O-J-I, or Barren Mountain or to hike into the Klondike.

Doubletop Mountain Trail, Southern Approach

To approach Doubletop from the south, take the road to Kidney Pond, which intersects the perimeter road at Foster Field. Follow it for 0.8 mi. across a bridge over Nesowadnehunk Stream. There is parking for several cars in a gravel pit on the right immediately after a bridge crossing.

From the bridge, the Doubletop Mountain Trail starts on the right and follows the general course of Nesowadnehunk Stream for about 0.5 mi. Then it crosses Slaughter Pond Brook, bears left, climbs slowly, and leads more or less directly to the eastern side of Deer Pond. It follows the old Deer Pond Trail to the Slaughter Pond Tote Road, which leads to the old Camp 3 clearing (at about 1.3 mi.).

At the far end of the Camp 3 clearing, the trail to Doubletop forks right (north), leaving the clearing near its northwest corner.

[*Watch carefully*; this turn is hard to see. Straight ahead (west) an old road continues to Slaughter Pond. Turn right (north) before reentering the woods or leaving the clearing.] The trail follows an old road northwest up a valley and crosses a stream four times. The stream and the trail run together for a while, which makes the route extremely wet and muddy. The trail passes close under the cliffs on Squaw's Bosom, the peak west of Doubletop, and then turns northeast at about 2.3 mi. Just after crossing the headwaters of the stream, it reaches uncut spruce woods and passes a spring at 3.1 mi. Turning north again, the trail climbs the saddle west of Doubletop. Then it slabs up a steep timbered slope on the western side of the mountain to South Peak (4 mi.), which is above the timberline. The trail continues from South Peak 0.2 mi. to North Peak. From North Peak the trail descends and leads north to Nesowadnehunk Campground.

Doubletop Mountain Trail, Southern Approach
Distances from Kidney Pond road
- *to* old Camp 3 clearing: 1.3 mi. (45 min.)
- *to* spring in spruce woods: 3.1 mi. (2 hr. 15 min.)
- *to* South Peak: 4 mi. (3 hr. 20 min.)
- *to* North Peak: 4.2 mi./6.8 km. (3 hr. 30 min.)
- *to* Nesowadnehunk Campground: 7 mi./11.3 km. (6 hr. 30 min.)

Doubletop Mountain Trail, Northern Approach

The approach from the north leads south from the last lean-to at Nesowadnehunk Campground. Initially it parallels Nesowadnehunk Stream, which lies to the east. For the first mile, it follows a fairly level course, and then it turns southwest and ascends gradually in the valley of the brook draining the area between Veto Mountain on the Northwest and Doubletop on the Southeast. After about 1.5 mi. the trail swings generally south once more to follow the northern ridge of Doubletop as it climbs more steeply and steadily to North Peak.

Doubletop Mountain Trail, Northern Approach
Distances from Nesowadnehunk Campground
- *to* North Peak: 3.1 mi. (2 hr. 45 min.)
- *to* South Peak: 3.3 mi. (3 hr.)
- *to* Kidney Pond road: 7 mi./11.3 km. (6 hr. 30 min.)

Nesowadnehunk Campground

This campground on Nesowadnehunk Stream, although beautiful, is not a major hiking center. It is the base for the approach to Doubletop from the north. It is also a control point for entering the park from the west. Fishermen find this campground a convenient base.

MULLEN MOUNTAIN (3450 ft./1052 m.)

This rock-capped peak is north of the Brothers and south of Wassataquoik Mountain. The climb starts in the vicinity of Mullen Pond. Virgin spruce cover the northern slope, and the hiking is smooth.

A route, the old Mullen Brook Tote Road, up Mullen Brook to Mullen Pond provides an approach from the Russell Pond area. (This route is not official—check for permission and trail conditions with the Russell Pond Campground ranger.) The old Mullen Brook Tote Road leaves the Northwest Basin Trail on the north, opposite from where the Northwest Basin Trail joins the old Wassataquoik Tote Road, about 0.5 mi. from Russell Pond. The old Mullen Brook Tote Road is overgrown and hard to see from the Northwest Basin Trail. Beavers have dammed ponds along the route, so the trail skirts them and is often difficult to follow. Soon after leaving the Northwest Basin Trail, the route follows the edge of a swamp and then turns sharply left, skirts another swamp, crosses a brook, and returns to the Mullen Brook Tote Road. The tote road climbs gradually and then more steeply to Mullen Pond, about 3.5 mi. from the Northwest Basin Trail. To bushwhack to the summit, from the eastern shore of the pond turn left (south) and pass through open spruce woods to a collar of thick dwarf birches just below the open, rocky summit.

Mullen Mountain
Distances from Russell Pond Campground
- *to* old Mullen Brook Tote Road junction (via Northwest Basin Trail): 0.5 mi. (25 min.)
- *to* Mullen Pond: *est.* 4 mi. (2 hr. 15 min.)
- *to* Mullen Mountain summit: *est.* 5 mi./8 km. (4 hr. 30 min.)

WASSATAQUOIK MOUNTAIN (2984 ft./910 m.)

Hikers can climb this broad, wooded mountain from the southern shore of Wassataquoik Lake. (See the description of Wassataquoik Lake Trail for the approach to the start of the route.) The trail up Wassataquoik is not officially maintained. It starts west of the outlet brook of Green Falls, crosses the brook, and climbs steeply east of the falls. After several more crossings, it leaves the brook and climbs on up the mountain. Near the top, it is obscured by raspberry bushes and debris from a fire in 1959. From the southern and more precipitous edge of the summit, there is a good view of Mullen Mountain and the country beyond.

Wassataquoik Mountain
Distances from Russell Pond Campground

   to start of trail to Green Falls (via Wassataquoik Lake Trail): *est.* 3.2 mi. (1 hr. 35 min.)

   to Green Falls: *est.* 3.3 mi. (1 hr. 45 min.)

   to Wassataquoik summit: *est.* 5 mi./8 km. (4 hr.)

STRICKLAND MOUNTAIN (2400 ft./732 m.)

It is best to climb this low, wooded summit from Camp Phoenix on Nesowadnehunk Lake. Camp Phoenix, on the eastern side of Nesowadnehunk Lake, is an enclave of privately owned land surrounded by BSP and the lake. From the eastern side of barnyard in the rear of the camps, cross the perimeter road and follow logging roads over the gentle slope to where it starts to get steeper. Beyond, there are no trails, but you can hike through mostly open, pleasant woods to the summit, from which there are good views toward Center Mountain and the Brothers. Take a compass bearing on Camp Phoenix before descending.

BURNT MOUNTAIN (1793 ft./547 m.)

There is a fire tower on this low summit in the northwestern section of the park. Trees are gradually blocking what were once excellent views from the summit. Burnt Mountain Trail begins at the Burnt Mountain picnic area, 13.8 mi. west of Matagamon Gate or 8.8.mi. north of Nesowadnehunk Gate.

Burnt Mountain Trail
Distances from Burnt Mountain picnic area
>   to Burnt Mountain summit: 1.3 mi./2.1 km. (50 min.)

South Branch Pond Campground
This campground is at the eastern end of the Lower (northern) South Branch Pond (981 ft.). The South Branch Ponds have perhaps the most spectacular surroundings of any in Maine, except the ones near Katahdin. They lie in a deep valley between Traveler Mountain to the east and the South Branch Mountains (Black Cat Mountain) to the west. The campground, the usual base for hiking in the Traveler area, has choice views of Traveler's peaks and ridges, of the pond, and of the South Branch Mountains. Facilities include open-front shelters, tenting space, a bunkhouse, and rental canoes.

South Branch Campground
Distances from South Branch Campground
>   to Middle Fowler Pond: 4.0 mi./6.5 km. (2 hr. 30 min.)
>   to North Traveler summit (via North Traveler Trail): 2.5 mi./4 km. (2 hr. 20 min.)
>   to Peak of the Ridges (via Pogy Pond and Center Ridge trails): *est.* 3.5 mi./5.6 km. (2 hr. 50 min.)

to southern end of Upper South Branch Pond (via Pogy
     Notch Trail): 1.9 mi./3.1 km. (1 hr.)

to Russell Pond Campground (via Pogy Notch Trail): 9.7
     mi./15.6 km. (4 hr. 40 min.)

Pogy Notch Trail

This trail leads from South Branch Pond Campground
around the eastern shores of the ponds, then south through
Pogy Notch. It passes west of Pogy Pond and continues
southwest to Russell Pond Campground. The trail offers
fairly easy access to the center of the park and the trails on
Katahdin, and nice views enhance the hike.

From South Branch Pond Campground enter woods on
the trail toward the eastern shore of the pond. The North
Traveler Trail diverges left at 0.2 mi. At 1.0 mi. the trail
reaches the delta of Howe Brook and the Howe Brook Trail,
which leaves to the west. Soon it enters some woods, where it
follows a brook route at first and then bears right (south)
away from the brook. At 1.3 mi. the trail climbs over the end
of the cliff between the Lower and the Upper South Branch
Pond. The Center Ridge Trail goes left at 1.4 mi. The Pogy
Notch Trail descends and passes an old campsite at the
southeastern corner of the upper pond. The South Branch
Mountain Trail comes in on the right at the old campsite (1.9
mi.). The Pogy Notch Trail continues south, passing through
an alder swamp and beaver works at 2.8 mi. It crosses several
brooks and rises and falls moderately in the next 0.5 mi. At
3.3 mi. the trail forks. Straight ahead is the old route to Traveler Pond; the Pogy Notch Trail turns right, climbs gradually, and passes through Pogy Notch.

Bear left at 3.9 mi. into a sparsely grown old burn. The
trail then crosses a beaver canal and descends into the Pogy
Pond watershed. It crosses a brook several times while passing out of the notch area and descending toward Pogy Pond.

Then it crosses several other brooks and reaches the head of
Pogy Pond at 6.0 mi. (There are clear views of Traveler,
Turner, and Katahdin mountains from the shore of the
pond.)

The trail bears right, uphill, and at 6.1 mi. a side trail to
the left leads in 0.2 mi. to the Pogy Pond Lean-to. The main
trail descends nearly to the pond (6.2 mi.), then bears right,
away from the pond. (Be careful you don't take a wrong turn
onto a short spur trail to the west, and watch carefully for
blazes, which are scarce in this area.) The main trail rises
gradually, then descends through an old burn, traverses a series of shallow rises, and bears right. At 6.7 mi. the trail
drops into the gully of the western tributary of Pogy Brook.
It crosses the brook and climbs up the opposite slope. Then
it runs through a swampy hollow, climbs a rocky rise, and
descends gradually to cross another brook (7.3 mi.). Immediately after the brook the trail bears right and climbs gradually through sparse mixed growth. It crosses a beaver
meadow, reaches a rough boulder field at 7.8 mi., and descends through it. The trail descends toward Russell Pond,
and at 9.4 mi. the trail to Grand Falls and Lookout Ledges
leaves to the left. Just before Russell Pond Campground, the
Wassataquoik Lake Trail leaves to the right.

Pogy Notch Trail
Distances from South Branch Pond Campground
- *to* North Traveler Trail junction: 0.2 mi. (5 min.)
- *to* Howe Brook Trail junction: 1 mi. (30 min.)
- *to* Center Ridge Trail junction: 1.4 mi. (45 min.)
- *to* South Branch Mountain Trail junction: 1.9 mi. (1 hr.)
- *to* Pogy Pond: 6 mi. (3 hr.)
- *to* Grand Falls Trail junction: 9.3 mi. (4 hr. 30 min.)
- *to* Russell Pond Campground: 9.7 mi./15.6 km. (4 hr. 40 min.)

SOUTH BRANCH (BLACK CAT) MOUNTAIN
(north summit 2599 ft. and south summit 2585 ft./792 m. and 788 m.)

South Branch Mountain (Black Cat Mountain on USGS maps) is across the ponds from Traveler Mountain. It offers extraordinary views of Traveler Mountain (as well as the region immediately to the west), and the climb can help hikers pick out routes up Traveler Mountain.

South Branch Mountain Trail

The South Branch Mountain Trail runs from South Branch Pond Campground over both summits and down to the Pogy Notch Trail, which it joins at the southern end of the upper pond.

The trail (blue blazes) starts at the northwestern corner of Lower South Branch Pond, across the outlet brook from the canoe rack (sign). The trail parallels a small brook, staying from 100 to 200 yd. away from it, for 0.3 mi. and then follows a ridge for 0.8 mi. to nearly flat lookouts with vistas of the ponds and the Traveler range. After contouring for 0.3 mi., the trail turns abruptly right and climbs more steeply to the northern peak.

The southern peak is 0.5 mi. farther—an easy hike along the high saddle connecting the two summits. The trail from the south peak was relocated in 1983. It descends over gentle meadows and rock fields to open ledges on the south side of the mountain. At about 3 mi. it swings eastward and descends through mixed forests. There is a short, steep climb of about 0.1 mi., then the trail rejoins the old trail at about 4 mi. At 4.3 mi. it passes a side trail to the upper South Branch Lean-to and at 4.5 mi. it crosses a brook with beaver works before joining the Pogy Notch Trail at the southern end of the upper pond. Turn left (north) for South Branch Pond

Campground and right (south) for Pogy Notch and Russell Pond Campground.

South Branch Mountain Trail
Distances from South Branch Campground
- *to* lookouts: 1.1 mi. (45 min.)
- *to* South Branch Mountain northern peak: 2 mi. (2 hr.)
- *to* South Branch Mountain southern peak: 2.5 mi./4 km. (2 hr. 15 min.)
- *to* Pogy Notch Trail junction: *est.* 4.5 mi. (4 hr.)
- *to* South Branch Campground (via Pogy Notch Trail): *est.* 6.4 mi./10.3 km. (5 hr.)

TRAVELER MOUNTAIN (3541 ft./1079 m.)

Traveler Mountain is a great starfish-shaped mountain with four high ridges sprawling out south, west, northwest, and north, and four shorter spurs between them.

Fires have ravaged the mountain, the last one in 1902, so that while the lower parts support hardwoods of some size, the upper slopes are mostly bare, and good for climbing. The bareness of these higher slopes makes for a uniform landscape that can be highly confusing in fog or darkness. Although the mountain's altitude is quite a bit lower than Katahdin's, the routes up Traveler from the South Branch Pond Campground are longer, partially without trails, and equally exposed; so treat the mountain with respect, start early, and allow a full day for the climb. Estimate time, distance, and the roughness of the terrain generously.

There are four main routes up Traveler from South Branch Pond Campground. Three of them follow trails for part of the climb. The following sections describe the routes in order, from north to south.

North Traveler Trail

From South Branch Pond Campground follow the Pogy Notch Trail 0.2 mi. to the North Traveler Trail, which diverges left. The North Traveler Trail climbs through open woods to the crest of North Ridge, which it follows over bare ledges in places. The view improves until the trail enters birch woods. After that the trail passes through lovely alpine meadows and fine old woods that alternate with steep ledges. At about 1.6 mi., in one of the wooded sections, a side trail leaves left to a good *spring*. After emerging from the last section of woods, the trail continues in the open up the ridge to the summit at 3144 ft./958 m. The views are impressive.

North Traveler Trail
Distances from South Branch Pond Campground
to start (via Pogy Notch Trail): 0.2 mi. (5 min.)

to side trail to spring: *est.* 1.7 mi. (1 hr. 30 min.)

to North Traveler summit: 2.5 mi./4 km. (2 hr. 20 min.)

Howe Brook Trail

The Howe Brook Trail begins at the southeastern corner of Lower South Branch Pond, where the rocky, fan-like delta of Howe Brook merges with the pond. This inlet is 1 mi. south along the Pogy Notch Trail from the campground. The trail follows the route of the brook to the first chutes and potholes. (Howe Brook is noted for its many pools, rock- and water-formed potholes, slides, and chutes, which continue for quite a distance up the valley.) The trail crosses the brook a number of times before it ends at a beautiful waterfall.

Howe Brook Trail
Distances from South Branch Pond Campground
to start (via Pogy Notch Trail): 1 mi. (30 min.)

to waterfall: *est.* 3 mi./4.8 km. (1 hr. 45 min.)

Center Ridge Trail

This route starts at the foot of Center Ridge at the northeastern corner of the upper pond, 1.4 mi. south on the Pogy Notch Trail from South Branch Pond Campground. The Center Ridge Trail runs to the Peak of the Ridges. Diverging left (east) from the Pogy Notch Trail, it climbs steadily through woods and then across open ledges. There are excellent views of the Howe Brook valley and North Traveler. After climbing over many rocky knobs, the trail reaches the Peak of the Ridges (about 3200 ft./975 m.) where it ends. There the route up Pinnacle Ridge comes in on the right.

Center Ridge Trail
Distances from South Branch Pond Campground
   to start (via Pogy Notch Trail): 1.4 mi. (45 min.)
   to Peak of the Ridges: *est.* 3.5 mi./5.6 km. (2 hr. 50 min.)

Loop Route over Traveler and North Traveler

Only strong parties can make a circuit of Traveler Mountain. Climbers who attempt this trip, which takes at least twelve hours, should be well supplied with food and water and should carry a good compass. It is possible to follow the route by ascending North Traveler first, but the description goes in the other direction.

Climb to Peak of the Ridges on the Center Ridge Trail. To climb Traveler, continue northeast along the ridge from Peak of the Ridges to the point where you can see clearly down into the meadow in the col on the way to Traveler. From there, use binoculars to carefully study the animal yards and rock slides on the way to Traveler summit. There are three animal yards. An almost straight line of animal trails going up the slope (east) connects them to the meadow. You should keep a little to the right of the center of each animal yard to find the path to the next one above. Near the top of the third yard, turn almost 90° to the right (south) and look for an exit out onto the rock slide. There is at least one that is almost completely open. Traverse horizontally and possibly drop down a little to get around the end of the heavy brush. Keep close to the brush and angle up as soon as possible. There are several breaks in the trees through which you can angle up until you come out into the open below one of the western peaks of Traveler. Continue up toward the peak. The rock slope is somewhat loose but stable enough for safe passage. Traveler's summit is about 1.7 mi. from the Peak of the Ridges.

To reach North Traveler from Traveler, first go as far northeast as possible in the open (there is a cairn on the last outcrop). From there take a compass bearing on the several outcrops visible on the way to North Traveler. Study the areas between these outcrops and between them and the one you are on. The trees are so thick it is necessary to follow a compass bearing carefully to come out on the first outcrop. (The strongest member of the party might want to break through the trees guided by the compass carrier following 5 to 10 yd. behind.) The trees are so dense that you may not be able to see the next outcrop from the first one. Correct the compass bearing based on your earlier observation and go down into the trees again. Follow the compass to come out on the next outcrop. The next leg of the bushwhack will also have to be on a compass course, and then you will be able to stay in the open until you pass over the top of a subsidiary northern peak of Traveler. Then you should take a compass bearing for a spot just above the evergreen growth in the col between there and North Traveler. Lucky climbers may find animal trails that will make hiking easier, but be careful not to go too far to the right (northeast) and get into the evergreen growth. By staying to the left you will also avoid a deep cut at the bottom of the col.

Hard bushwhacking will continue up the slope of North Traveler. Again you should watch the compass and, at the same time, take advantage of animal trails. Be careful again not to get too far off course, and you will come out into the open and be able to continue to the top of North Traveler. The distance is a very tiring 3 mi. from the Traveler summit.

From North Traveler, descend to South Branch Pond Campground via the North Traveler Trail.

Loop Route over Traveler and North Traveler
Distances from South Branch Pond Campground
to Center Ridge Trail (via Pogy Notch Trail): 1.4 mi. (45 min.)
to Peak of the Ridges: 3.5 mi. (2 hr. 50 min.)
to Traveler summit: *est.* 5.2 mi. (4 hr.)
to North Traveler summit: *est.* 8.2 mi. (10 hr.)
to South Branch Pond Campground (via North Traveler Trail): *est.* 10.7 mi./17.2 km. (12 hr.)

Pinnacle Ridge Route

This is the most spectacular of the four routes up Traveler, but there is no trail beyond the Pogy Notch Trail. From the southern end of the south pond, follow the Pogy Notch Trail about 0.8 mi. to a knoll where the slide on the Pinnacle is plainly visible. Turn left (east) through pleasant woods and across older slides, and you will reach the Pinnacle slide. Climb up on the left to avoid the cliffs above. From the top of the Pinnacle, a steady climb through open brush brings you to the Peak of the Ridges. The distance from the Pogy Notch Trail to the Peak of the Ridges is about 2 mi.

Do not descend the Pinnacle Ridge. If you are caught by bad weather as you climb up on the upper slope, there is an emergency way off via the so-called Escape Route down the broad gully between Pinnacle and Center ridges. It gets climbers off the exposed ridge quickly and allows them to follow the little stream and skirt the low cliffs near the bottom to the Pogy Notch Trail near the southern end of the upper pond.

Pinnacle Ridge Route
Distances from South Branch Pond Campground

to turn off Pogy Notch Trail: *est.* 2.7 mi. (1 hr. 25 min.)

to Peak of the Ridges: *est.* 4.7 mi. (3 hr.)

to Pogy Notch Trail (via Center Ridge Trail): *est.* 5.8 mi. (3 hr. 35 min.)

to South Branch Campground (via Pogy Notch Trail): *est.* 7.2 mi./11.6 km. (4 hr. 20 min.)

Trout Brook Farm Campground

The newest campground in BSP, Trout Brook Farm is on the site of an old farm that served logging operations. The campground is on the north side of the perimeter road, about 27 mi. west of Patten and 2.6 mi. west of Matagamon Gate House. It is 4.7 mi. east of the Crossing Lunchground, where the perimeter road crosses Trout Brook and where the road to South Branch Campground leads south. Trout Brook Farm has only tent sites. It is a starting point for many trips in the park, including canoe trips and hikes to Traveler Mountain and other outlying mountains and hikes along the new trail system in the northern and northeastern sections of the park. Trails north of Trout Brook Campground are, for the most part, not on the map that accompanies this book. In addition to a handout, *Outlying Campsites,* available from BSP, hikers are referred to *A Guide to Baxter Park and Katahdin*, by Stephen Clark, and to *DeLorme's Map and Guide of Baxter State Park and Katahdin* (DeLorme Publishing Co., PO Box 298GS, Freeport, ME 04032).

Webster Lake and Freezeout Trails

Combined, these trails make a delightful two- or three-day circuit, which is the longest linear backpacking trip in the park. The many tent sites along the route permit flexibility in planning the trip. Although it does not involve mountain travel, it offers streams and ponds and access to good fishing areas.

The Webster Lake and Freezeout trails traverse a section of the park known as the Scientific Forest Management Area. This 28,000-acre parcel was specifically designated by Governor Baxter as an area to be managed by the "most modern methods of forest controls," and further as a "showplace for those interested in forestry" and forest management operations.

Caution. Ask at Park Headquarters or any facility in the northern end of the park for locations of the latest timber-harvesting operations. If you run into any equipment working in the woods, don't get too close. Questions and comments are invited; write the Park Forester at Park Headquarters.

The Webster Lake Trail leaves the perimeter road at the Black Brook Farm site, 8.8 mi. west of Trout Brook Farm. It leads northwest along the route of the old Wadleigh Tote Road until it reaches the east bank of Thissell Brook, which it follows for some distance. Then it turns northeast to the shore of Webster Lake. The Webster Lake Trail ends there at its junction with the Freezeout Trail.

The Freezeout Trail parallels the entire length of Webster Stream, which under the right conditions can be a challenging white water experience (see the *AMC River Guide: Maine*).

The trail leaves the Webster Lake Trail at the southern shore of Webster Lake. It follows the shore around to the outlet, where there is a good tent site. From here, the trail generally descends toward Matagamon Lake, paralleling Webster Stream. It sometimes bears away from the stream, but it always returns. At 5.2 mi. it passes Webster Stream Lean-to and at 9.5 mi. it passes Little East Branch Lean-to, opposite the confluence of the East Branch of the Penobscot and Webster Stream. (Make arrangements to use lean-tos and tent sites with park officials in Millinocket or at one of the campgrounds.) From there, the trail makes a sharp right turn onto the remains of the old Burma Road, an improved tote road last used in 1950. Follow it for the remaining distance to Trout Brook Farm.

Webster Lake and Freezeout Trails
Distances from perimeter road, Black Brook farm site

to Freezeout Trail junction (via Webster Lake Trail): 7.2 mi. (3 hr. 50 min.)

to Webster Lake outlet tent site (via Freezeout Trail): 8.1 mi./13.1 km. (4 hr.)

to Webster Stream Lean-to: 13.4 mi./21.6 km. (6 hr. 45 min.)

to Little East Branch Lean-to: 15.9 mi./25.6 km. (8 hr.)

to Trout Brook Farm Campground: 21.8 mi./35.1 km. (10 hr. 55 min.)

FOWLER PONDS AREA

In conjunction with the development of Trout Brook Farm Campground, some new official routes have been opened to several lakes in the area south of the perimeter road, west of Horse Mountain, and northeast of the South Branch Ponds area. Between Barrell Ridge and Billfish Mountain are the three Fowler Ponds; in the next valley to the northeast are Billfish and Round ponds (which drain to the east) and High and Long ponds (which drain into Fowler

Brook). Further north, at the head of Littlefield Brook, is Littlefield Pond. For years, fishermen kept routes to these ponds open from the perimeter road to the east and north. Official campsites are on the northern shore and outlet of Lower Fowler Pond and at the outlet and southern end of Middle Fowler Pond. See the ranger at Trout Brook Farm or South Branch Pond Campground for camping and trail information. The Clark guide and the BSP handout mentioned above under *Trout Brook Farm* would be most useful.

The Fowler Brook Trail leads south from the perimeter road about 2 mi. west of Trout Brook Farm Campground. It generally follows Fowler Brook and leads to the northern end of Lower Fowler Pond.

A second trail leaves the southern side of the perimeter road 1 mi. west of the entrance to Trout Brook Farm Campground. It leads generally south for about 1.8 mi., after which it forks. (The left fork is a side trail leading to High and Long ponds.) After crossing a second brook, the main trail climbs a crest and reaches a second junction. The trail to the left goes to the Middle Fowler Pond outlet and its campsites; to the right, the trail reaches the northeastern shore of Lower Fowler Pond at about 2.5 mi.

A third route leaves south from the perimeter road on the west side of Littlefield Brook, about 0.9 mi. east of the Trout Brook Farm Campground entrance. It leads south 1.5 mi. up the valley of Littlefield Brook to Littlefield Pond.

In 1982, a new route was opened from Littlefield Pond to High Pond via Billfish and Round ponds. There are new tent sites at Littlefield, Billfish, Round, and Long ponds.

In 1987 a new route was opened from South Branch Pond to Middle Fowler Pond. It is considered to be an extension of the Middle Fowler Pond Trail.

The trail leaves the north end of the campground and follows the Ledges Trail for the first 0.3 mi. The trail climbs gradually, following a small brook until open ledges are reached at 1.7 mi. From here the trail proceeds through the gap between Big Peaked and Little Peaked mountains. The trail then traverses the north slope of Traveler Mountain and provides occasional views. At 3 mi. the Barrell Ridge Side Trail leads 0.3 mi. to the open summit of Barrell Ridge. The summit has very fine views, expecially of Traveler Mountain. From this point the trail descends, and it reaches Middle Fowler Pond at 4 mi. (sign). To the left it is 3.3 mi. to the perimeter road via the Middle Fowler Pond and Fowler Brook trails. To the right it is 0.2 mi. to the south campsite on Middle Fowler Pond.

Fowler Ponds Area
Distances from perimeter road
> to Lower Fowler Pond, northern end (via Fowler Brook Trail): 1.5 mi./2.4 km. (1 hr.)
> to Lower Fowler Pond, northeastern shore (via High and Long ponds): *est.* 2.5 mi./4 km. (1 hr. 15 min.)
> to Littlefield Pond: *est.* 1.5 mi./2.4 km. (45 min.)

Distance from South Branch Pond
> to Middle Fowler Pond: 4 mi/6.4 km. (2 hr. 30 min.)

HORSE MOUNTAIN (1589 ft./484 m.)

In the northeastern corner of BSP, this mountain rises above the western shore of First Grand (Matagamon) Lake. There is an abandoned MFS fire tower on the summit, which is easy to reach from the perimeter road.

The trail leaves the southern side of the perimeter road 2.5 mi. west of the bridge over the East Branch of the Penobscot and just west of the Matagamon Gate House. It rises at an easy rate and near the top turns sharp right (west) to the summit and tower.

Horse Mountain
Distance from perimeter road
  to Horse Mountain summit: 1.4 mi./2.3 km. (1 hr. 5 min.)

TURNER MOUNTAIN (north summit 3323 ft. and south summit 3122 ft./1013 m. and 952 m.)

This mountain northeast of Katahdin is low compared with the great mountain. However, Turner offers magnificent views of Katahdin, particularly of the basins. You can approach South Turner from Roaring Brook Campground. The hike involves a moderate climb up the southwestern slide. North Turner is trailless. The two summits are over 2 mi. apart and are separated by a deep saddle.

South Turner Mountain Trail
This trail starts out across Roaring Brook at Roaring Brook Campground and coincides with the Russell Pond Trail. (At 0.2 mi. the Russell Pond Trail goes left.) The Sandy Stream Pond Trail goes straight to Sandy Stream Pond. At 0.4 mi. it turns right, crosses the outlets, and continues around the southeastern shore of the pond. (This section is often wet and muddy during rainy seasons.) Along the trail near the southeastern shore of the pond, a number of side paths lead left to the shore. Moose frequent the pond. The trail follows the right fork at 0.7 mi. (the left fork is the Sandy Stream Pond Trail, which leads northwest 0.9 mi. to Whidden Pond and a junction with the Russell Pond Trail 1.1 mi. north of Roaring Brook Campground.) The South Turner Mountain Trail enters a small boulder field at 0.9 mi. and follows cairns and paint blazes on the rocks as it climbs. At 1.1 mi. it turns left and rises steeply. At 1.5 mi. it passes a side trail right to a spring, bears left and continues. At 1.8 mi. the trail leaves the scrub and starts over open ledges. It follows cairns and paint blazes to the summit at 2 mi.

South Turner Mountain Trail
Distances from Roaring Brook Campground
- *to* start (via Russell Pond Trail): 0.2 mi. (5 min.)
- *to* Whidden Pond Trail junction: 0.7 mi. (20 min.)
- *to* South Turner summit: 2 mi./3.2 km. (1 hr. 50 min.)

MOUNT CHASE (2440 ft./849 m.)

This mountain north of Patten has an abandoned MFS fire tower. There are extensive views from the summits. Looking northeast from Katahdin, it is the very prominent mountain in the distance. Refer to the USGS Island Falls Quadrangle, 15-minute series.

The approach road diverges left (west) from ME 11 6.5 mi. north of Patten, 1.5 mi. north of the Penobscot-Aroostook border, and 9.5 mi. south of Knowles Corner. Unless the approach road has been rebuilt since this edition was prepared, hikers have to park beside ME 11 or beside the approach road no more than 0.5 mi. from its start. Follow the approach road to the west for 2.3 mi. from ME 11.

The trail leaves the right (northern) side of road, proceeds first west and then almost due north, following a jeep road to the warden's cabin, which it reaches in about 0.8 mi. Beyond the cabin, the trail climbs steadily north to the summit. *There is no water* on the trail. The fire tower, used as an emergency transmitter by the Boy Scouts' Matagamon Wilderness Camp, is locked and boarded up.

Mount Chase
Distances from ME 11
- *to* start (via approach road): *est.* 2.3 mi. (1 hr. 10 min.)
- *to* fire warden's cabin: *est.* 3.1 mi. (1 hr. 50 min.)
- *to* Mount Chase summit: *est.* 3.8 mi./6.1 km. (2 hr. 35 min.)

Aroostook

Aroostook County, with an area of 6453 square miles, sprawls along Maine's northern and northeastern boundary. It is larger in area than Connecticut and Rhode Island combined. Aroostook's greatest north-south dimension is about 120 mi. and its greatest east-west dimension is 104 mi.

The mountains of Aroostook County are widely scattered. There are no ranges or compact mountain areas except two small clusters of hills—the DeBoulie Mountain region west of Eagle Lake and east of the Allagash territory, and the hills west of Bridgewater and around Number Nine Lake. Solitary Mars Hill (1660 ft.), which rises from almost level country near the county's eastern boundary, is probably the best known mountain. Peaked Mountain (2260 ft./689 m.), a trailless summit in the wilderness west of Ashland, is the county's highest.

See the introduction to this guide for information on the North Maine Woods Association and its control policies in the western part of Aroostook County.

NUMBER NINE MOUNTAIN (1638 ft./499 m.)

This peak is west of Bridgewater in the small group of mountains around Number Nine Lake. The lake has an interesting MFS campsite. Refer to the USGS Howe Brook quadrangle, 15-minute series.

At the southern end of Bridgewater turn west off US 1 onto Boutford Road. This road runs west, northwest, and then west again into a wilderness area. At about 11 mi. take the left fork (south) toward Number Nine Lake (1084 ft.), which is less than 1 mi. farther. The road crosses the outlet and follows the eastern shore. An increasingly obscure road diverges left (east) and climbs 1 mi. to the summit, where there is a radar installation and an abandoned MFS fire tower.

Number Nine Mountain
Distance from US 1 in Bridgewater
  to Number Nine Lake: *est.* 12 mi.
Distance from lake outlet
  to Number Nine summit: 1.5 mi./2.4 km. (1 hr. 15 min.)

MARS HILL (1660 ft./506 m.)

This monadnock rises abruptly from an almost level area of farms and woodland in the eastern section of the town of the same name. Refer to the USGS Mars Hill quadrangle, 15-minute series.

The mountain runs north-south for 3 mi. and parallels the Canadian border, which is about 1 mi. to the east. The southern peak is the highest and is being developed as a recreation area (with picnicking and tenting) by the Mars Hill Junior Chamber of Commerce. There is also a ski area on the mountain. A rough road climbs up this peak, rising slightly more than 1000 ft. in 1.6 mi. The views from the summit extend across the potato fields in all directions to other mountains in the county and on to Katahdin to the southwest and across the St. John River valley into New Brunswick to the east.

From Mars Hill village, take US 1A north for 0.5 mi. Then turn right (east) on the road marked "Ski Area" (Boynton Road). The pavement ends 0.6 mi. from US 1A. Turn right and then take the first left (toward Mars Hill and the ski area, which are easy to see). There is parking in the field near the access road. The access road is too rough for cars. It rises easily to the summit, crossing the ski trail, a tow path, and several land-clearing operations along the way.

Mars Hill
Distance from start of access road
   to Mars Hill summit: 1.6 mi./2.6 km. (1 hr. 15 min.)

QUAGGY JOE (1213 ft./370 m.)

Quaggy Joe (also called Quoggy Joe and Quaquajo) dominates Aroostook State Park from the southwestern corner of Presque Isle. The 577-acre state park offers swimming, boating, camping, and picnicking. A side road runs west to the park from US 1 (sign) 4 mi. south of Presque Isle and 10.5 mi. north of Mars Hill village. Refer to the USGS Presque Isle quadrangle, 15-minute series.

The mountain, which rises 600 ft. above Echo Lake, has two peaks. On the higher, southern peak there are two radio transmitters and an aircraft beacon. The slightly lower, northern peak has better views to the northwest and east.

The trail to the summit starts from the playground area and soon joins the Quaquajo Trail and climbs quickly to the northern peak. From the northern peak a trail leads south to the true summit on the southern peak.

Quaggy Joe
Distance from parking area
   to summit of northern peak: 0.8 mi./1.3 km. (40 min.)
   to summit of southern peak: 1.5 mi./2.4 km. (1 hr. 5 min.)

DEBOULIE MOUNTAIN (1981 ft./604 m.)

DeBoulie Mountain is the highest of a small cluster of mountains in the wilderness south of St. Francis and southwest of Eagle Lake. Refer to the USGS Fish River Lake quadrangle, 15-minute series.

The views from the MFS fire tower on DeBoulie's summit

take in Long, Eagle, and Square lakes. From one spot, Quebec Province can be seen beyond the strip of New Brunswick that runs north of Fort Kent. Other mountains in the area include Black Mountain (1901 ft.) to the east, and Gardner Mountain (1817 ft.) and Whitman Mountain (1810 ft.) to the south. Interspersed between the mountains are small but picturesque lakes and ponds.

In 1975 the state of Maine, through a land exchange, took ownership of 15,000 acres on and around the mountain.

Approach the DeBoulie area from the east. Turn west off ME 11 just north of the bridge over the Fish River between Eagle Lake and Winterville (sign). The road follows the northwestern shore of St. Froid Lake for 2 mi. and passes a state fish hatchery 3 mi. from ME 11. Only high-clearance vehicles can continue beyond the fish hatchery.

The foot trail to the fire tower starts 18 mi. from ME 11, follows the north shore of Deboulie Pond at the end of the road and is clearly marked at all main junctions. The actual climb up the mountain from DeBoulie Pond (1128 ft.), near the western end of the rock slide, is quite steep.

DeBoulie Mountain
Distance from end of auto road at DeBoulie Pond
   to DeBoulie summit: *est.* 3.5 mi./5.6 km. (2 hr. 10 min.)

HEDGEHOG MOUNTAIN (1594 ft./486 m.)

This mountain is in T 15 R 6 just off ME 11 between Winterville and Portage. (T and R stand for *township* and *range*. The state of Maine uses this system to designate unincorporated areas.) The mountain, which runs north-south, falls off steeply on its eastern side. Refer to the USGS Winterville quadrangle, 15-minute series.

The two trails up Hedgehog start on the west side of ME 11, 3.5 mi. south of Winterville and 12.8 mi. north of Portage at the warden's camp. There are also a picnic site, camp-site, a good *spring*, and a parking area at the start. Both trails begin behind the warden's cabin. The trail on the right is the steeper of the two and only a little shorter; the trail to the left is better cleared to the summit and is easier to follow going down. The summit views are good from the tower but not from the ground because of new growth.

Hedgehog Mountain
Distance from warden's cabin
   to Hedgehog summit (via left fork): 0.6 mi./1 km. (30 min.)

ROUND MOUNTAIN (2174 ft./654 m.)

This mountain is west of Ashland and south of the American Realty Road, which serves as an access road. There is a MFS fire tower on the summit. Peaked Mountain (2260 ft.), 2 mi. to the southwest, is the highest point in Aroostook County, but there is no trail up it. Refer to the USGS Mooseleuk Lake quadrangle, 15-minute series.

At the western end of the bridge over the Aroostook River in Ashland, turn west off ME 11 onto a paved road. In 0.6 mi. go straight ahead on American Realty Road, which is private but open to the public for a fee at a tollgate about 6 mi. west of Ashland. The road runs west and, about 14 mi. from ME 11, it goes over a pass (1280 ft.) between Greenlaw Mountain and Orcutt Mountain. Then it descends and crosses Machias (Aroostook) River in another 2 mi. It reaches the start of the trail to Round Mountain about 22 mi. from ME 11 and about 0.3 mi. west of the line between T 11 R 8 and T 11 R 9.

The trail starts out south, crosses the outlet of Rowe Lake, and runs along the southwestern shore. Beyond, it passes to the west of Round Mountain Pond and skirts the northwestern base of the mountain before arriving at the warden's camp. The trail then climbs steadily to the summit.

Round Mountain
Distances from American Realty Road

to warden's camp: *est.* 3.3 mi. (1 hr. 40 min.)

to Round Mountain summit: 4 mi./6.4 km. (2 hr. 20 min.)

HORSESHOE MOUNTAIN (2084 ft./635 m.)

Horseshoe Mountain is part of the Rocky Brook Range, which has some surprisingly rugged terrain for this part of the state. Refer to the USGS Mooseleuk Lake quadrangle, 15-minute series.

The road to the trail leaves the left side of the American Realty Road (see the preceding section) about 41 mi. west of Ashland and 2.5 mi. before the Upper McNally Pond Campsite (MFD Campsite #45). About 1 mi. from the American Realty Road, the road to the trail turns sharply left up over a hill. The trail begins on the right at this corner, where there is a small sign on a tree.

At first the trail is a road that leads in about 0.3 mi. to a fire warden's cabin. The trail passes directly behind the cabin, and after another 200 yd. it reaches a side trail on the right. (The side trail goes 0.8 mi. to the very picturesque Horseshoe Pond.) About 0.5 mi. from the cabin the main trail gets increasingly steeper and in another 0.5 mi. it reaches the summit. The summit is flat, and there is a 50-ft. steel fire tower from which you can view the landscape in all directions. The Katahdin area is 40 mi. to the south.

Horseshoe Mountain

Distances from road

> *to* fire warden's cabin: 0.3 mi.
> *to* Horseshoe summit: 1.3 mi./2.1 km. (1 hr. 10 min.)

PRIESTLY MOUNTAIN (1900 ft./579 m.)

Priestly Mountain, in northern Piscataquis County, near the Aroostook boundary, rises west of the Allagash River about 60 mi. west of Ashland. Its summit bears a steel fire tower.

Drive to a point on the Churchill Dam Road about 7.5 mi. before the American Realty Road (see the section on Round Mountain) 67 mi. west of Ashland and west and south of Umsaskis Lake. Refer to the USGS Umsaskis Lake quadrangle, 15-minute series.

The trail (small sign on a tree) leaves the west side of Churchill Dam Road (left when going northwest from Churchill Dam) on a hill. At first it is an old road and flat. It runs generally southwest for 1.3 mi. and crosses Drake Brook, the outlet of Priestly Lake. The trail turns south near the northwestern side of Priestly Lake. About 0.3 mi. from the brook it reaches a fire warden's cabin, where it turns abruptly right (west) uphill to the right of the cabin. It then rises moderately for 0.5 mi. to the summit. The fire tower has a long stretch of excellent views, particularly of the Allagash Wilderness Waterway.

Priestly Mountain

Distances from Churchill Dam Road

> *to* fire warden's cabin: 1.5 mi.
> *to* Priestly summit: 2 mi./3.2 km. (1 hr. 25 min.)

SECTION 3

Mount Desert Island

Mount Desert Island is connected to the mainland about 10 mi. southeast of Ellsworth by a short bridge and causeways. The island is about 16 mi. long and 13 mi. wide, roughly heart-shaped, and is divided into east and west sides by Somes Sound. Somes Sound is often described as the only true fjord on the East Coast. A mountain chain of seventeen peaks runs through the island from the southwest to the northeast. (Elevations are from 200 to about 1500 ft.) The southerly thrust of glacial action and resultant deep valleys may require descent almost to sea level to go from one peak to the next. Acadia National Park was first created in 1919. Including the sections on Schoodic Point and Isle au Haut, it now has an area of approximately 35,000 acres.

Climbing and walking on Mount Desert Island are very rewarding. Over 100 mi. of trails are maintained and marked, providing a unique network of mountain, lakeshore, and seaside paths. A 50-mi. system of graded dirt roads (known as the carriage paths), barred to automobiles, permits pleasant walking even in wet weather. These roads furnish easy snowshoeing and cross-country ski routes and clear horseback trails. The National Park Service (NPS) encourages their use and has tailored some for bicycle riding. The fine-grained gravel surface on the carriage roads around Eagle Lake and Witch Hole Pond makes them suitable for bicycles with small-diameter tires. Other carriage roads tend to have a softer, looser surface suitable for nonmotorized mountain bikes.

The traveler on Mount Desert Island should be prepared for the changeable weather of the northern New England seashore. Changes can be swift, but because the maximum elevation, Cadillac Mountain, is only 1530 ft., problems will generally involve discomfort and not danger. The trails are all within a few miles of roads or houses. The terrain is often sharp and precipitous, so the climber who explores off marked trails risks uncomfortable going and even dead ends at cliffs and ravines. The hiker can find paths of any desired degree of difficulty, from the mildest lakeside path to the Precipice Trail on Champlain Mountain, where ladder rungs driven into rock are a welcome aid. (Novice hikers should consult a park ranger for specific advice on how difficult a trail to attempt.) In the event of heavy fog, the hiker must make certain to locate the next cairn before leaving the last when above treeline. Most of the summits are bare.

There are camping facilities within the National Park. A complete selection of hotels, motels, tourist homes, and private campgrounds is available on the island. Park campsites, shown on the map, are at Blackwoods (by Ticketron reservation from June 15–Sept. 15; first-come, first-serve for the rest of the year) and Seawall (first-come, first-serve from late May to late September). For detailed park campground information, write: Acadia National Park, P.O. Box 177, Bar Harbor, ME 04609 (or phone 207-288-3338). If park campgrounds are filled you will be referred to private campgrounds on the island.

Acadia National Park Visitor Center, on ME 3 at Hulls Cove near Bar Harbor, offers current information, including an NPS map and descriptive material. Of particular interest will be "Acadia's Beaver Log" (summer and fall only), which announces guided naturalist walks, hikes, and boat cruises. The villages of Bar Harbor, Northeast Harbor, and Southwest Harbor maintain offices that provide help to visitors. The Thompson Island Information Center, located at the entrance to Mount Desert Island, is jointly operated by the National Park Service and the island-wide Chambers of Commerce.

Public excursion boats for local trips depart from the town dock areas of Bar Harbor, Northeast Harbor, Southwest Harbor, and Bass Harbor. Bar Harbor is the western terminus of a ferry (autos carried) that departs in the early morning for Yarmouth, Nova Scotia. Round trip, this ferry takes a long day with no appreciable time for sightseeing in Yarmouth.

Most of the larger lakes are public water supplies, but freshwater swimming is available at a public beach, maintained by the NPS, at the south end of Echo Lake. The NPS also offers Sand Beach—a saltwater beach with fine sand and traditionally cold Maine sea bathing.

The following descriptions do not cover *all* the trails on the island. Some areas, around Northeast Harbor for example, are honeycombed with local woodland paths. Those selected for detailed treatment here give access to all of the preferred summits and are well marked, except as noted. For the most part, you can reach the individual summits in comfortable half-day walks. Longer or more strenuous excursions can be planned easily by including as many peaks as desired. To simplify reference, the island is divided into an eastern district and a western district to conform with Acadia National Park nomenclature. The NPS maintains all trails described, and markings include signs, cairns, painted arrows, and red metal markers. In addition to the map in this guide, refer to the USGS Mount Desert and Bar Harbor Quadrangles, 15-minute series.

For those inclined toward easier walking, the NPS provides seaside walks and carriage roads. The surf during stormy weather is especially magnificent. A few of the outstanding shore walks are listed below:

Great Head Trail (Eastern District)

The Great Head trail is a scenic short walk that passes largely along cliffs directly above the sea. From the Sand Beach parking area, cross Sand Beach to the east end. Near the seaward end of the interior lagoon, look for a trailhead post and a series of granite steps ascending a high bank. The trail quickly reaches a huge millstone, where the trail turns sharp right (south), switchbacking up the cliff. The path continues to the extremity of the peninsula, then turns northeast along the cliff to the high point, Great Head (145 ft.), where there are the ruins of a stone teahouse. The trail descends northwest to a junction at which the right path leads north toward Schooner Head Rd., and the left path returns more quickly to the east end of Sand Beach. The path that leads north reaches an abandoned service road in about 0.3 mi. Turn left on the road, and follow it south for about 0.3 mi. to the east side of Sand Beach.

Great Head Trail
Distances from east side of Sand Beach

> *to* south end of peninsula (via millstone): 0.5 mi.
>
> *to* teahouse ruins: 0.8 mi.
>
> *to* junction with Schooner Head Road/Sand Beach paths: 1.3 mi.
>
> *to* start (via service road): 1.6 mi./2.6 km. (55 min.)

Ocean Trail (also called Shore Path)
(Eastern District)

Park at the large Sand Beach parking area. From the parking area, follow the asphalt trail about 50 ft. toward the beach. Where the stairway descends to the left, turn right to begin the Ocean Trail. As of publication date, the trailhead was *not* marked. The trail leads uphill several hundred yards, crosses through a small paved parking area, and continues to Otter Point, paralleling Park Loop Rd. 1.8 mi. The Ocean Trail offers spectacular shoreline scenery and follows a level grade. Of interest en route are Thunder Hole, Monument Cove, and the Otter Cliffs.

Ocean Trail
Distance from Sand Beach
  to Otter Point: 1.8 mi./2.9 km. (55 min.)

Ship Harbor *(Western District)*

This is reached by ME 102A, 6 mi. south of Southwest Harbor. The parking area is marked with a small sign that says "Ship Harbor Nature Trail." A self-guiding nature trail of less than a mile leads to the mouth of the harbor and the rocky seacoast.

Bass Harbor Light *(Western District)*

Turn left off ME 102A about 1.5 mi. west of Ship Harbor where the road swings due north. Drive south for 0.5 mi. to the light (a short, easy walk).

EASTERN DISTRICT
(EAST OF SOMES SOUND)

CHAMPLAIN MOUNTAIN
(1058 ft./322 m.) AREA

Champlain Mountain is the easternmost summit on the island. Its east face is sharp, with the Precipice Trail climbing on ladder rungs in some parts. The Bear Brook Trail offers easier access up the north ridge. From the west and the Sieur de Monts Spring area, the Beachcroft Path traverses Huguenot Head en route to the summit. To the south is the Bowl (415 ft.), a delightful mountain pond, and the Beehive (520 ft.), a sharp promontory above Sand Beach. A pleasant excursion is possible following any route up Champlain and proceeding to Sand Beach via the Bowl and the Beehive. Gorham Mountain (525 ft.) is another summit south of the Beehive.

Precipice Trail

This trail starts from the Precipice Trail parking area on Park Loop Rd. at the foot of Champlain Mountain. Following a rugged talus slope full of big boulders, the trail ascends northwest about 0.4 mi. Here, the right fork runs under the east face of the mountain to connect with the Bear Brook Trail 0.5 mi. from the summit on the north ridge. From the fork, the Precipice Trail climbs southwest, rising steeply to a point directly west of the parking area. The direction is now west-northwest. Along this section of the trail, ladders and iron rungs help hikers negotiate precipitous vertical drop-offs. The final 500 ft. to the summit follow gentle slopes and ledges. People afraid of heights should *not* climb the Precipice Trail. In addition, hikers less than 5 ft. tall may have difficulty reaching some handholds. It's most important that Precipice Trail hikers remain on the designated trail. Wandering off the trail can quickly lead hikers onto cliffs that require technical mountain-climbing skills and equipment.

Precipice Trail

Distances from Park Loop Road
> *to* right fork to Bear Brook Trail: 0.4 mi. (15 min.)
> *to* Champlain summit: 0.8 mi./1.3 km. (1 hr. 15 min.)

Bear Brook Trail

This trail starts at the north terminus of the Gorham Mountain Trail, at the south end of the Bowl, and rises along the south ridge of Champlain Mountain to reach the summit in 1.5 mi. The trail then descends 1.1 mi. over the mountain's north ridge to Park Loop Rd. 0.2 mi. east of the entrance to the Bear Brook Picnic Area. This trail is exposed throughout and gives outstanding views of Frenchman's Bay and Schoodic Peninsula on the mainland to the east.

Bear Brook Trail
Distances from Gorham Mountain Trail terminus
to Champlain summit: 1.5 mi. (1 hr. 5 min.)
to Park Loop Road: 2.6 mi./4.2 km. (1 hr. 45 min.)

Beachcroft Trail

This is a convenient route between Champlain Mountain and the area to the west. For the most part the trail is entirely open and can be traveled easily in either direction. It leaves ME 3 close to the north end of the Tarn and begins with a flight of granite steps on the east side of the highway. (There is parking above the north end of the Tarn off the west side of the highway.)

The trail runs southeast, often on carefully placed stone slabs. In switchbacks and stone steps, it rises up and across the west face of Huguenot Head. The trail passes to the south of (not over) the summit at about 0.4 mi. A brief, gradual descent into the gully between Huguenot Head and Champlain Mountain is followed by a sharp ascent up the northwest slope of Champlain Mountain to the summit at 0.8 mi.

Beachcroft Trail
Distance from ME 3
to Champlain summit: 0.8 mi./1.3 km. (55 min.)

Beehive Trail (also called Bowl Trail)

The trail starts opposite the Sand Beach parking area and rises gently for 0.2 mi. Take a sharp right at the sign marked "Beehive." For 0.3 mi., the trail rises abruptly via switchbacks and iron ladders over steep ledges to the summit of the Beehive. This trail is sporty and not for those who are uneasy on precipitous heights. The views of the Frenchman's Bay–Sand Beach–Otter Cliff area are magnificent.

The trail continues down the northwest slope of the Beehive and dips steeply to the south for 0.2 mi. to a junction with the Gorham Mountain and Bowl trails. Take the left fork for 0.5 mi. to return to Park Loop Road.

Beehive Trail
Distances from Park Loop Road
- *to* The Beehive: 0.5 mi. (20 min.)
- *to* Park Loop Road: 1.2 mi./1.9 km. (35 min.)

Gorham Mountain Trail
The trail starts at the Gorham Mountain trailhead parking area on Park Loop Rd. and rises gently over open ledges 0.3 mi. to a junction. The Cadillac Cliffs loop leads right and rejoins the Gorham Mountain Trail 0.5 mi. later, after passing under ancient sea cliffs and by an ancient sea cave. The Gorham Mountain Trail continues 0.3 mi. over easy open granite ledges to where the Cadillac Cliffs loop rejoins the main trail. The main trail continues north over the Gorham Mountain summit, which is open and bare, with some of the finest panoramas on Mount Desert Island. In about another 0.5 mi. there is a junction. For the Bowl, go left 0.2 mi. To reach the Beehive, turn right then left at the next junction, about 0.1 mi. farther. (Continuing straight ahead at this junction will bring you to Park Loop Rd. at Sand Beach.)

Gorham Mountain Trail
Distances from trailhead parking area
- *to* The Bowl: *est.* 1.5 mi. (1 hr.)
- *to* Park Loop Road in Sand Beach Area: *est.* 1.8 mi./2.9 km. (1 hr. 10 min.)

DORR MOUNTAIN (1270 ft./387 m.) AREA

Dorr Mountain lies immediately west of Sieur de Monts Spring. Two routes up the mountain are possible from Sieur de Monts Spring. Trails also ascend from the north and south over the rather long ridges. Both the east and west slopes are sharp. With properly placed cars, a party can have a good climb leaving from Sieur de Monts Spring, traversing Dorr, and continuing west to the summit of Cadillac Mountain (1530 ft.). The route descends to about 1000 ft. between the two summits. There is parking both at the spring and on Cadillac.

Dorr Mountain Trail

Follow the paved walkway from the Nature Center toward the Springhouse. At the rock inscribed "Sweet Waters of Acadia," turn right on a walkway that remains paved for only a few feet. The trail continues, following a series of switchbacks up the northeast shoulder of Dorr Mountain. The first half has many stone steps. At 0.5 mi. the trail is joined by the East Slope Trail, which comes directly up from the north end of the Tarn. At 1.1 mi. there is a junction on the left with a short trail leading to the Dorr Mountain Ladder Trail, which comes directly up from south end of the Tarn. Much of the next 0.4 mi. to the summit is steep and exposed.

Dorr Mountain Trail
Distances from Sieur de Monts Spring

to East Slope Trail junction: 0.5 mi. (30 min.)
to link to Dorr Mountain Ladder Trail: 1.1 mi. (1 hr.)
to Dorr summit: 1.5 mi./2.4 km. (1 hr. 20 min.)

Dorr Mountain Ladder Trail

This trail climbs from the south end of the Tarn up the eastern side of Dorr Mountain. The first half has many stone steps. At 0.3 mi. a short trail that connects with the Dorr Mountain Trail leaves on the right. Much of the next 0.4 mi. to the summit is steep and exposed.

Dorr Mountain Ladder Trail
Distance from south end of the Tarn
   to Dorr summit: 0.6 mi./1 km. (50 min.)

Dorr Mountain North Ridge Trail

This trail begins on the south side of Park Loop Rd. about 2 mi. northwest of Sieur de Monts Spring. It climbs south over the summit of Kebo Mountain (407 ft.), traverses a second hump, and ascends the burned-over ledges of the north ridge to the summit.

Dorr Mountain North Ridge Trail
Distance from Park Loop Road
   to Dorr summit: 2.3 mi./3.7 km. (1 hr. 50 min.)

Dorr Mountain South Ridge Trail

This trail diverges right from the Canon Brook Trail 0.6 mi. from ME 3 at the southern extremity of Dorr Mountain. It rises with moderate grade due north over the south ridge of Dorr Mountain to the summit.

Dorr Mountain South Ridge Trail
Distances from ME 3
   to start (via Canon Brook Trail): 0.6 mi. (25 min.)
   to Dorr summit: 1.2 mi./1.9 km. (1 hr. 5 min.)

Dorr Mountain Notch Trail

This short trail links the summits of Dorr and Cadillac mountains. From the summit of Dorr Mountain, go north on the North Ridge Trail about 0.1 mi. Then go left (west) on the Dorr Mountain Notch Trail, which drops quickly and in another 0.3 mi. reaches junctions with the Gorge Path and the A. Murray Young Path in the valley between the two mountains.

To reach Cadillac summit, follow the trail southwest for 0.5 mi.

Dorr Mountain Notch Trail
Distances from Dorr summit
> *to* Gorge and A. Murray Young paths: 0.4 mi. (12 min.)
> *to* Cadillac summit: 0.9 mi./1.4 km. (40 min.)

A. Murray Young Path

Ascending the narrow valley between Dorr and Cadillac mountains from the south, this trail leaves the Canon Brook Trail 0.7 mi. west of ME 3. It climbs by easy grades to the Gorge Trail near its junction with the Dorr Mountain Notch Trail. From this point there is quick access to the summit of either mountain.

A. Murray Young Path
Distances from ME 3
> *to* start (via Canon Brook Trail): 0.7 mi. (25 min.)
> *to* Dorr Mountain Notch Trail: 1.2 mi. (1 hr.)
> *to* Dorr summit: 1.6 mi./2.6 km. (1 hr. 20 min.)
> *to* Cadillac summit: 1.7 mi./2.7 km. (1 hr. 25 min.)

Jesup Path

A pleasant, level woodland walk, this path begins on Park Loop Rd. opposite the tenth tee of the Kebo Golf Club. However, it follows the west margin of Great Meadow, where it may be flooded as a result of beaver activity. The path passes through pleasant hemlock woods and hardwoods to Sieur de Monts Spring at 0.6 mi. Located here are the Abbe Museum, which has displays of ancient Indian culture; the Wild Gardens of Acadia, a formal garden of native plants; and the Nature Center, with a book sales area and natural history exhibits. The trail terminates 0.3 mi. farther at the north end of the Tarn.

Jesup Path
Distances from Park Loop Road
  to Sieur de Monts Spring: 0.6 mi. (20 min.)
  to north end of the Tarn: 0.9 mi./1.4 km. (30 min.)

The Tarn Trail (Kane Path)
This path leads from the north end of the Tarn, south to the Canon Brook Trail and links the Sieur de Monts Spring area and the southern aspect of Dorr and Cadillac mountains, while avoiding ME 3. At its start, the path runs south directly along the west side of the Tarn along the base of a rocky talus slope. After reaching the south end of the Tarn, the trail continues south and gently upward until its junction with the Canon Brook Trail.

The Tarn Trail
Distance from north end of the Tarn
  to Canon Brook Trail: 1.4 mi./2.3 km. (45 min.)

Canon Brook Trail
From a pullout on ME 3 about 0.5 mi. south of the south end of the Tarn and about 2 mi. north of Otter Creek Village, the Canon Brook Trail runs west to join the Pond Trail in the valley south of Bubble Pond. It gives access (via the Pond Trail) to the Jordan Pond area, as well as to the trails running north to Dorr and Cadillac mountains.

From the highway, the trail descends west to Otter Creek and intersects the Tarn Trail at 0.3 mi. Turn left (south) at the intersection and follow the Tarn Trail in the valley of Otter Creek. After a brief, sharp rise from the valley, the trail reaches a junction with the Dorr Mountain South Ridge Trail, which diverges right at 0.6 mi. The trail descends to a junction with the A. Murray Young Path, which goes right at 0.7 mi. Then the trail runs steeply westward up the south bank of Canon Brook for about 0.5 mi., and then swings away from the brook, ascending to cross the Cadillac Mountain South Ridge Trail at 1.4 mi.

Crossing an open ridge and a small pond known as the Featherbed, the trail swings southwest and begins its descent to the valley, meeting the Pond Trail at the carriage path 0.5 mi. south of Bubble Pond.

Canon Brook Trail

Distances from ME 3

to the Tarn Trail junction: 0.3 mi. (10 min.)

to Dorr Mountain South Ridge Trail junction: 0.6 mi. (25 min.)

to A. Murray Young Path junction: 0.7 mi. (30 min.)

to Cadillac Mountain South Ridge Trail junction: 1.4 mi. (1 hr. 5 min.)

to Pond Trail junction: 2 mi./3.2 km. (1 hr. 25 min.)

CADILLAC MOUNTAIN (1530 ft./466 m.)

This peak is the highest point on the island. There is an automobile road to the summit, which has parking, a small gift shop, and bathrooms. Accessibility by car makes this summit the busiest in the park, and its height offers commanding views.

Trails approach the Cadillac Mountain summit from all four directions. The long South Ridge Trail begins from

Loop A in Blackwoods Campground or directly from ME 3 near the campground. The steep West Face Trail begins at the north end of Bubble Pond. The North Ridge Trail, beginning on Park Loop Rd., can be connected with the Gorge Trail, which ends on Park Loop Rd., creating a loop up and down Cadillac.

Cadillac Mountain South Ridge Trail

A relatively long hike for Mount Desert Island, this trail starts on the north side of ME 3, about 50 yd. west of the entrance to the NPS Blackwoods Campground. It climbs generally north. At 1.0 mi. a short loop trail on the right leads to Eagles Crag, which has good views to the east and southeast. The loop trail rejoins the main trail in 0.2 mi. After leaving the woods, the South Ridge Trail rises gently over open ledges. It crosses the Canon Brook Trail about 2.3 mi. from ME 3, in a slight col at the Featherbed. Continuing in the open, it passes close to a switchback in the Summit Rd. and ends at the summit parking area. (If two cars are available, it is recommended that you follow this trail from the top down, to walk "into the views." To locate the trailhead on the summit, follow the gravel road that leads west from the gift shop.)

Cadillac Mountain South Ridge Trail
Distance from ME 3
>   *to* Cadillac summit: 3.5 mi./5.6 km. (2 hr. 30 min.) (*descending* Cadillac summit to ME 3, subtract 45 min.)

Cadillac West Face Trail

This steep trail, which starts at the north end of Bubble Pond, is the shortest route to the summit. Park Loop Rd. passes north of Bubble Pond. Use the short spur road to reach the pond. The trail rises steeply through woods and over open ledges to a junction with the Cadillac Mountain

South Ridge Trail 0.5 mi. south of the summit. For the summit turn left (north).

Cadillac West Face Trail
Distances from north end of Bubble Pond
> *to* Cadillac South Ridge Trail junction: 0.9 mi. (1 hr. 5 min.)
>
> *to* Cadillac summit: 1.4 mi./2.3 km. (1 hr. 25 min.)

Cadillac North Ridge Trail

This trail ascends Cadillac Mountain in the open for the whole distance. In winter, the North Ridge Trail is often clear of snow when Summit Rd. and trails on other parts of the mountain are blocked. Follow Park Loop Rd. south from the Visitor Center. Take the third left turn (about 3 mi.) following the sign for Sand Beach and Park Loop Rd. Park at a paved pulloff on the north side of the road 0.6 mi. beyond the intersection. The trail starts on the south side of the road. It climbs steadily, always keeping to the east of the automobile road, although it closely approaches switchbacks on two occasions. For much of the distance both sides of the ridge are visible.

Cadillac North Ridge Trail
Distance from Park Loop Road
> *to* Cadillac summit: *est.* 1.8 mi./2.9 km. (1 hr. 30 min.)

Gorge Path

Follow Park Loop Rd. south from the Visitor Center. Take the third left turn (about 3 mi.) following the sign for Sand Beach and Park Loop Rd. The Gorge Path starts from a gravel pullout on the south side of Park Loop Rd., 0.8 mi. beyond the intersection. The trail rises south up the gorge between Cadillac and Dorr mountains for 1.3 mi. to the narrow notch between the two mountains. There are junctions first with the Dorr Mountain Notch Trail and then in a few yards with the A. Murray Young Path. The Gorge Path swings southwest and west and climbs steeply for 0.5 mi. to the summit of Cadillac Mountain.

Descending: The start of the trail at the summit may be difficult to see. Walk counterclockwise along the paved trail on the summit to the interpretive sign about Bar Harbor. Look for cairns and paint marks on the granite indicating the beginning of the trail leading to the gorge. About 0.3 mi. south of Park Loop Rd., where the trail turns somewhat left to cross a brook, avoid an old wood road going straight ahead.

Gorge Path
Distances from Park Loop Road

> *to* Dorr-Cadillac notch: 1.3 mi. (1 hr. 5 min.)
> *to* Cadillac summit: 1.8 mi./2.9 km. (1 hr. 35 min.) (*in reverse direction,* Cadillac summit to Park Loop Road, subtract about 40 min.)

JORDAN POND

This pond (at 274 ft.) is located in the valley between Pemetic Mountain on the east and Penobscot and Sargent mountains on the west. The Bubbles are to the north. The view from the Jordan Pond House across the pond to the Bubbles is justifiably famous.

Jordan Pond Shore Trail

This circuit around Jordan Pond is level most of the way, but crosses a rocky slope with occasional loose boulders. It is 3.3 mi. long; directions here are for traveling the east shore first. Park at the Jordan Pond parking area (off the west side of Park Loop Rd., about 0.1 mi. north of the Jordan Pond House). Follow the boat-launch road to the south shore of the pond.

When you reach the pond, turn right to start the circuit. The trails listed below all diverge to the right, because the route described is counterclockwise around the lake.

Down the west side of the pond returning to the starting point, the trail runs under the sharp Jordan Cliffs and loses the sun early in the day. The trail along the west shore has many wet spots and exposed tree trunks, and the carriage road uphill may be used instead. At the south end of Jordan Pond, the circuit is complete.

Jordan Pond Shore Trail
Distances from Jordan Pond parking area

to Pond Trail (to Canon Brook Trail): 0.1 mi. (5 min.)

to Jordan Pond Carry Trail (to Eagle Lake): 1.0 mi. (30 min.)

to South Bubble Mountain Trail (to gap between North and South Bubble): 1.1 mi. (35 min.)

to Bubble Gap Trail (to Bubble Gap): 1.5 mi. (45 min.)

to Deer Brook Trail (to Penobscot Mountain): 1.6 mi. (50 min.)

to Jordan Pond parking area: 3.3 mi./5.3 km. (1 hr. 40 min.)

THE BUBBLES
(872 ft. and 766 ft./266 m. and 233 m.)

These two finely shaped mounds rise above the north end of Jordan Pond. Formerly covered with heavy evergreen growth, they were swept by fire in 1947.

Trails honeycomb the area, and the best access is from the Bubble Rock parking area about 1.1 mi. south of Bubble Pond on the west side of Park Loop Rd. From the parking area, follow the Bubble-Pemetic Trail west for 0.2 mi. to a junction with the Jordan Pond Carry Trail and the North Bubble Trail.

North Bubble Trail

This trail rises sharply for 0.2 mi. to a junction with the South Bubble Mountain Trail and the Bubble Gap Trail. Then the trail turns to the right (watch carefully for path), continues over the North Bubble summit at 0.4 mi., and on to Eagle Lake, at 1.9 mi. (To complete an excellent loop, take the Eagle Lake Trail along the southwest shore to the junction with the Jordan Pond Carry Trail, which you can follow south back to the start of North Bubble Trail.)

South Bubble Trail

From the junction of the Jordan Pond Carry and North Bubble trails, follow the Jordan Pond Carry Trail south for 0.4 mi. to the Jordan Pond Shore Trail. Turn right (north) and follow the Jordan Pond Shore Trail for less than 0.1 mi. to the start of the South Bubble Trail. The South Bubble Trail traverses South Bubble to the gap between South and North Bubble. There, 0.3 mi. from the Jordan Pond Shore Trail, it meets the North Bubble Trail and the Bubble Gap Trail in the gap between the two summits.

Bubble Gap Trail

This trail also diverges from the Jordan Pond Shore Trail, about 0.4 mi. north of the South Bubble Trail. The Bubble Gap Trail rises 0.2 mi. to a junction with the South Bubble and North Bubble trails in the gap between the two summits.

PEMETIC MOUNTAIN (1248 ft./380 m.) AREA

Pemetic Mountain is located about in the center of the eastern district of the island and offers some of Mount Desert's best views. Trails up the west side are short and relatively steep, while routes from the north and south are more gradual and more wooded. For the trails from the south, climbers park at the Jordan Pond parking area. From the north, there is parking at Bubble Pond, and from the west, at the Bubble Rock parking area located where the Park Loop Rd. crosses the Bubble-Pemetic Trail.

Pemetic Mountain Trail

This trail traverses the length of the mountain north to south. Its views of Jordan Pond, the Bubbles, Sargent Mountain, and Eagle Lake are outstanding.

From the south, the trail leaves the north side of the carriage road in the valley between Day Mountain and the Triad near Wildwood Stables. It climbs north over the Triad (698 ft.) and then descends crossing the Pond Trail. This first mile is through a delightful mixed hardwood-softwood forest. The trail rises under the south shoulder of Pemetic and then goes north over the south ridge to the summit, 2.0 mi. from the start. From the summit to the base of the mountain at the north end of Bubble Pond, the trail travels through spruce and fir forest for most of its length. Check carefully for cairns, particularly on the descent.

Pemetic Mountain Trail
Distances from carriage road

   to Pemetic summit: 2.0 mi. (1 hr. 35 min.)
   to Bubble Pond: 3.3 mi./5.3 km. (2 hr. 15 min.) (*in reverse direction*, Bubble Pond to Pemetic summit: 1.3 mi. [1 hr. 5 min.]; Bubble Pond to carriage road: 3.3 mi./5.3 km. [2 hr. 15 min.])

Pond Trail

This is an easy, pleasant path from the southeast shore of Jordan Pond to the valley south of Bubble Pond, where the Pond Trail meets the west end of the Canon Brook Trail.

The Pond Trail leaves the shore of Jordan Pond, travels east, and crosses Park Loop Rd. at 0.1 mi. There is a small parking area at this crossing. Continuing in heavy woods and by easy grades, the path swings into the valley between the Triad and Pemetic Mountain. It crosses the Pemetic Mountain Trail at 0.8 mi., continues northeast to cross a carriage road at 1.1 mi., and joins the Canon Brook Trail.

Pond Trail
Distances from Jordan Pond
> *to* Pemetic Mountain Trail: 0.8 mi. (25 min.)
> *to* carriage road: 1.1 mi./1.8 km. (40 min.)

Bubble-Pemetic Trail

This trail begins at the Bubble Rock parking area, on the west side of Park Loop Rd. about 1.1 mi. south of Bubble Pond.

The path enters the woods east of Park Loop Rd. and climbs in almost constant cover, sometimes following a streambed, to end at a junction with the Pemetic Mountain Trail about 0.1 mi. north of the summit.

Bubble-Pemetic Trail
Distances from Bubble Rock parking area
> *to* Pemetic Mountain Trail junction: 0.4 mi. (35 min.)
> *to* Pemetic summit (via Pemetic Mountain Trail): 0.5 mi./0.8 km. (40 min.)

SARGENT MOUNTAIN (1373 ft./418 m.)
PENOBSCOT MOUNTAIN (1194 ft./364 m.)

Penobscot Mountain and Sargent Mountain are described together because hikers often include them in the same trip. Both are open summits and they are about 1 mi. apart. Between is Sargent Pond, a pleasant mountain pond. From the south the preferred starting point is Jordan Pond parking area; from here, hikers can climb both Penobscot and Sargent without retracing steps. The longer route up Sargent is from St. James Church on ME 198 via the Giant Slide. The outlying territory to the southwest contains an interesting maze of trails and carriage roads around Bald Peak (974 ft.) and Parkman Mountain (941 ft.) and along small brooks. Ample parking is available at two areas: one is west of ME 198 and about 0.3 mi. north of Upper Hadlock Pond (reservoir, no swimming); and the other, Parkman Mountain parking area, is east of ME 198, about 0.5 mi. north of Upper Hadlock Pond.

Penobscot Mountain Trail

This trail starts from the west side of Jordan Stream (outlet of Jordan Pond) about 0.1 mi. due west of Jordan Pond House and is reached by a short connecting path from the house.

The trail runs west and, after crossing a carriage road, rises abruptly to the south end of Jordan Ridge, about 0.5 mi. from Jordan Pond House. The trail then swings due north, climbing gradually over open granite ledges to the summit of Penobscot Mountain, where it joins the Sargent Pond Trail.

For Sargent Pond and the summit of Sargent Mountain, go left on the Sargent Pond Trail. Sargent Pond (at about 1060 ft.) is a delightful spot nestling between Penobscot and Sargent mountains. You will reach it in only 0.2 mi. From the pond, the Sargent Mountain South Ridge Trail offers easy access to the summit.

Penobscot Mountain Trail
Distances from Jordan Pond House
to Penobscot summit: *est.* 1.5 mi. (1 hr. 10 min.)
to Sargent Pond (via Sargent Pond Trail): *est.* 1.7 mi. (1 hr. 15 min.)

to Sargent Mountain summit (via Sargent Pond and Sargent Mountain South Ridge trails): *est.* 2.5 mi./4 km. (1 hr. 50 min.)

Jordan Cliffs Trail

This exciting and scenic trail leaves the Penobscot Mountain Trail 0.4 mi. west of Jordan Pond House, just northeast of the junction of the Penobscot Trail and the carriage road. Beginning at the carriage road, the trail to Jordan Cliffs heads north and rises up the east shoulder of Penobscot Mountain in gradual pitches to the cliffs at 0.8 mi. The trail then follows along and under Jordan Cliffs, via ladders and handrails, to a junction. Turn left at the junction, following the trail to the summit of Penobscot Mountain. This portion of the trail is spectacular, with views of the Bubbles, Pemetic, and Jordan Pond. (Novice hikers should consult a park ranger before they attempt this trail.)

Jordan Cliffs Trail
Distances from Jordan Pond House

to Jordan Cliffs Trail (via Penobscot Mountain Trail): 0.4 mi. (15 min.)

to Jordan Cliffs: 1.2 mi. (55 min.)

to Penobscot summit: 1.7 mi./2.7 km. (1 hr. 20 min.)

Deer Brook Trail

This is a steep, quick ascent of 0.8 mi. to Sargent Pond from the Jordan Pond Shore Trail at the north end of Jordan Pond. The route is entirely wooded and follows the steep course of Deer Brook. This trail joins the Sargent Pond Trail in the valley between Sargent and Penobscot.

Deer Brook Trail
Distance from Jordan Pond Shore Trail

to Sargent Pond Trail junction: 0.8 mi./1.3 km. (45 min.)

Sargent Mountain South Ridge Trail

This trail starts from the Asticou Trail, just under the south shoulder of Cedar Swamp Mountain. (The Asticou Trail is an old and apparently little-used trail that leaves the east side of ME 198 about 0.4 mi. north of its junction with ME 3, opposite lower Hadlock Pond.)

The Sargent Mountain South Ridge Trail rises over the wooded shoulder and passes just southeast of the summit of Cedar Swamp Mountain. It drops to cross Little Harbor Brook at 1.2 mi. The trail then leaves the woods and rises sharply 0.4 mi. to a junction with the Sargent Pond Trail, which comes in from the right. The trail continues north over open granite ledges to the summit of Sargent, past junctions on the left with the Hadlock Brook Trail at 1.8 mi. and the Maple Spring Trail at 2.1 mi.

Sargent Mountain South Ridge Trail
Distances from start on Asticou Trail
- *to* Sargent Pond Trail: 1.6 mi. (1 hr. 15 min.)
- *to* Hadlock Brook Trail: 1.8 mi. (1 hr. 25 min.)
- *to* Maple Spring Trail: 2.1 mi. (1 hr. 35 min.)
- *to* Sargent summit: 2.4 mi./3.9 km. (1 hr. 45 min.)

Giant Slide Trail

This trail is the approach to the Sargent Mountain area from the northwest. The trail starts at St. James Church, a small stone chapel located on the east side of ME 198, about 0.3 mi. north of the intersection with ME 3 and 1.1 mi. south of the intersection with ME 233. The trail leads east 0.4 mi. to the Acadia National Park boundary and continues through woods up a gradual slope to a carriage road, at 0.7 mi. The trail then turns sharply south and, following Sargent Brook, rises steeply over the tumbled boulders of Giant Slide. At 1.8 mi. from the highway, the Parkman Mountain Trail diverges right and the Sargent Mountain North Ridge

Trail leaves left. The Giant Slide Trail continues through the notch between Parkman Mountain and Gilmore Peak at 2.4 mi. and descends to end at a junction with the Maple Spring Trail at 2.8 mi.

Giant Slide Trail
Distances from the St. James Church on ME 198
   to carriage road crossing: 0.7 mi. (25 min.)
   to Parkman Mountain Trail–Sargent Mountain North Ridge Trail junction: 1.8 mi. (1 hr. 10 min.)
   to Maple Spring Trail junction: 2.8 mi./4.5 km. (1 hr. 45 min.)

Sargent Mountain North Ridge Trail

Leaving the Giant Slide Trail 1.8 mi. from ME 198, this trail ascends east and crosses a carriage road at 0.2 mi. Continuing east and then northeast it rises over slanting pitches another 0.6 mi. to a sharp right (south) turn. The final 0.4 mi. to the summit of Sargent is over open ledges.

Sargent Mountain North Ridge Trail
Distance from Giant Slide Trail
   to Sargent summit: 1.2 mi./1.9 km. (1 hr.)

Hadlock Brook Trail and Maple Spring Trail

These are the principal routes to Sargent Mountain from the west. From the east side of ME 198 just north of Upper Hadlock Pond and opposite the Norumbega Mountain parking area, the Hadlock Brook Trail runs east 0.4 mi. to a junction, where the Maple Spring Trail leaves left and the Hadlock Brook Trail forks right. From here there is little difference between the two trails. They are parallel, wooded, steep, and terminate on the Sargent Mountain South Ridge Trail, south of the summit.

Hadlock Brook Trail and Maple Spring Trail
Distance from ME 198

> *to* Sargent summit (via either route): 2 mi./3.2 km. (1 hr. 35 min.)

Parkman Mountain Trail

The Parkman Mountain Trail starts out with the Hadlock Brook Trail but soon diverges north (left) to lead 1 mi. through woods and over a series of knobs to the summit of Parkman Mountain. The trail crosses a carriage road three times on the way to the summit. At the summit, a trail that leaves right (east) connects with the Giant Slide Trail in the gap between Parkman Mountain and Gilmore Peak. The Parkman Mountain Trail continues north over open ledges, then through woods, crossing a carriage road 0.5 mi. beyond the summit. The trail ends 0.2 mi. farther, at the junction of the Giant Slide Trail and the Sargent Mountain North Ridge Trail.

Parkman Mountain Trail
Distances from ME 198

> *to* Parkman summit: 1 mi. (50 min.)
> *to* Giant Slide Trail–Sargent Mountain North Ridge Trail junction: 1.7 mi./2.7 km. (1 hr. 10 min.)

NORUMBEGA MOUNTAIN (852 ft./260 m.)

Norumbega rises just east of Somes Sound. It is most often climbed from the parking area just north of Upper Hadlock Pond (reservoir, no swimming). You can then descend over the longer south ridge to Lower Hadlock Pond (also a reservoir), and from there walk back to the highway. This summit is more wooded than most, but the blueberries on the north slope make it attractive and appealing in season. The views of Somes Sound and mountains west of the sound are very good.

Norumbega Mountain Trail

The trail leaves the parking lot on the west side of ME 198 about 0.3 mi. north of Upper Hadlock Pond. It ascends quickly and steeply through woods to granite ledges, then swings south to the summit. The trail descends the south ridge through a particularly fine fir-spruce-pine forest to Lower Hadlock Pond. There it turns north, first following the shore of the pond and then Hadlock Brook to Upper Hadlock Pond and ME 198. (Do *not* cross the brook at the north end of Lower Hadlock Pond.)

Norumbega Mountain Trail
Distance from ME 198 north of Upper Hadlock Pond
to ME 198 at Upper Hadlock Pond outlet: 2.5 mi./4 km.
(1 hr. 35 min.)

WESTERN DISTRICT
(WEST OF SOMES SOUND)

ACADIA MOUNTAIN (681 ft./208 m.)

Acadia is the only summit on Mount Desert with an east-west ridge trail along the top. The views of Somes Sound are noteworthy. Some prefer to climb from the west, dropping down to Somes Sound from the east promontory. Flowing into Somes Sound at the base of the mountain is Man o' War Brook, where nineteenth-century frigates renewed their water supplies, taking advantage of the deep-water anchorage close to the shore.

Acadia Mountain Trail

Leave the car at the Acadia Mountain parking area on the west side of ME 102, 3 mi. south of Somesville and 3 mi. north of Southwest Harbor. The Acadia Mountain Trail begins on the east side of ME 102, across the road from the parking area. Go left at the fork 0.1 mi. down the trail.

The trail ascends the west slope, soon leaving woods for open rocks and frequent views. It passes over the highest summit and reaches the east summit, with views of the sound, at about 1 mi. The trail then descends southeast and south very steeply to cross Man o' War Brook. There is a junction about 50 yd. beyond. (Somes Sound is about 100 yd. east from here.) Go west at the junction and proceed past trails to St. Sauveur and Valley Cove, which diverge left in about 100 yd. Go on through a field for 200 yd. to the east end of the Man o' War Brook fire road. Follow the fire road west over gradual grades about 1 mi. back to ME 102, 50 yd. north of the parking area.

Acadia Mountain Trail
Distances from ME 102

  to Acadia Mountain, east summit: *est*. 1 mi. (45 min.)
  to Man o' War Brook: *est*. 1.5 mi. (1 hr.)
  to ME 102: *est*. 2.5 mi./4 km. (1 hr. 30 min.)

ST. SAUVEUR MOUNTAIN (679 ft./207 m.)

This mountain can be climbed from the north via the Man o' War Brook fire road (NPS fire service road from ME 102), from ME 102 on the west, and from the Fernald Cove Rd. on the south. There are good views of Somes Sound from Eagle Cliff, just east of the summit.

St. Sauveur Trail

This trail is an easy route to the summit of St. Sauveur Mountain from the north. Follow the Acadia Mountain Trail description to reach the trailhead. Go right at the fork 0.1 mi. down the trail.

The path runs south through evergreens and over open slopes, rising constantly but not too sharply for 1 mi. to a junction with the Ledge Trail on the right. From there it is 0.3 mi. to the summit, where the St. Sauveur Trail joins the Valley Peak Trail.

St. Sauveur Trail
Distances from ME 102
to Ledge Trail junction: 1 mi. (40 min.)
to St. Sauveur summit: 1.3 mi./2.1 km. (55 min.)

Ledge Trail

This trail begins at St. Sauveur parking area on the east side of ME 102 about 0.2 mi. north of the entrance road to the NPS swimming facilities at the south end of Echo Lake. The parking area is also about 0.2 mi. south of the access road to the AMC Echo Lake Camp (private).

The path enters the woods and rises over ledges to its end. It meets the St. Sauveur Trail 0.5 mi. from the highway and about 0.3 mi. northwest of the summit.

Ledge Trail
Distances from ME 102
to St. Sauveur Trail junction: 0.5 mi. (25 min.)
to St. Sauveur summit: 0.8 mi./1.3 km. (40 min.)

Valley Peak Trail

This trail leaves the west side of the Valley Cove truck road a few yards north of the parking area at Fernald Cove. It rises steeply northwest through shady woods over Valley

Peak (the south shoulder of St. Sauveur Mountain) and skirts the top of Eagle Cliff, with outstanding views of Valley Cove below and the mountains to the east of Somes Sound. On the summit of St. Sauveur, at 0.8 mi., the St. Sauveur Trail comes in on the left. The Valley Peak Trail continues fairly steeply down the northeast shoulder of St. Sauveur to end at a junction with the Acadia Mountain Trail near Man o' War Brook and the east terminus of the Man o' War Brook fire road.

Valley Peak Trail
Distances from the Valley Cove truck road
- **to** St. Sauveur summit: 0.8 mi. (45 min.)
- **to** Acadia Mountain Trail junction: 1.6 mi./2.6 km. (1 hr. 10 min.)

FLYING MOUNTAIN (284 ft./87 m.)

Guarding the entrance to Somes Sound, this low peak offers perhaps the greatest reward on the island for a small effort. The reward for a few minutes' climb to the open top is a fine panorama of the sound, Southwest Harbor, Northeast Harbor, and the islands to the south—the Cranberries, Greening, Sutton, Baker, and Bear.

Flying Mountain Trail
This scenic trail over tiny Flying Mountain leaves the east side of the parking area at the Fernald Cove end of the Valley Cove truck road and rises quickly to the summit. It follows the summit ridge north to a point overlooking Valley Cove, then descends quickly and steeply through spruce woods. At the edge of Valley Cove, the trail follows the shore north over rock slides and under forbidding Eagle Cliff to end at a junction with the Acadia Mountain Trail at Man o' War Brook.

At Valley Cove, the north terminus of the truck road can

be located up the bank about 75 yd. south from the water's edge. For an easy return to the Fernald Cove parking area, follow the road south for about 0.5 mi.

Flying Mountain Trail
Distances from Fernald Cove parking area
- *to* Flying Mountain summit: 0.3 mi. (15 min.)
- *to* Fernald Cove parking area (via truck road from Valley Cove): *est.* 1.2 mi./1.9 km. (45 min.)
- *to* Acadia Mountain Trail junction: 1.5 mi./2.4 km. (1 hr.)

BEECH MOUNTAIN (839 ft./256 m.)

Beech Mountain lies between Echo Lake and Great Pond (Long Pond on some maps). Its summit is easy to reach from either the Beech Cliff parking area or the pumping station area at the foot of Great Pond. Beech Mountain can also be climbed on its southwest flank, beginning at the south end of Long Pond. An added attraction near Beech Mountain is the Beech Cliff–Canada Cliff area just to the east of the Beech Cliff parking area. These rugged cliffs offer spectacular views of Echo Lake.

Canada Cliff Trail

This trail offers access to the top of Beech Cliff. It starts at the Beech Cliff parking area located at the end of the NPS road to the public swimming area on the south shore of Echo Lake. It climbs quickly via switchbacks and ladders to a junction with the Canada Ridge Trail on the left. Follow the Canada Ridge Trail north to the Beech Cliff Trail and proceed out on the top of Beech Cliff for the views of Echo Lake and the ocean and islands to the south. This route also pro-

vides access from the east to Beech Mountain and Great
Pond.

Canada Cliff Trail
Distance from Beech Cliff parking area
> *to* Beech Cliff (via Canada Ridge and Beech Cliff trails):
> 0.5 mi./0.8 km. (30 min.)

Beech Mountain Trail

The trail leaves the northwest side of the Beech Cliff parking area and forks in 0.1 mi. The trail to the right (north) is 1
mi. long and provides a beautiful vista of Great Pond before
climbing to the summit. The trail to the left is 0.6 mi. long
and climbs more steeply to the summit of Beech Mountain,
with its fire tower. The two trails can be combined to form a
scenic loop hike.

From the summit, the Beech Mountain West Ridge and
South Ridge trails depart to the southwest and south, respectively.

Beech Mountain Trail
Distances from Beech Cliff parking area
> *to* Beech Mountain summit (via north fork): 1.1 mi. (45
> min.)
> *to* Beech Cliff parking area (via north fork then south
> fork): 1.8 mi./2.9 km. (1 hr. 15 min.)

Valley Trail

This graded path is a convenient link between the Great
Pond area and the Beech Cliff parking area, which is located
in the notch between Beech Cliff and Beech Mountain. It also
permits a circuit or one-way trip over Beech Mountain, since
it provides direct access to the South Ridge Trail.

The trail enters the woods on the east (right) side of the

service road that skirts the east shore of the south end of Great Pond. The entrance is about 0.3 mi. north of the junction with the road to the pumping station. (Or, park at the pumping station. Take the trail east, go right at a fork in 40 or 50 yd. and cross the service road in about 0.3 mi.)

By easy grades over wooded slopes, the trail runs north briefly and then swings east before entering a series of switchbacks on the south slopes of Beech Mountain. At about 0.3 mi. the South Ridge Trail to Beech Mountain leaves left. Continuing east the Valley Trail soon swings north to maintain altitude as it runs up the valley separating Beech Mountain and Canada Cliff. At about 1 mi. there are remains of the old road to Southwest Harbor and the Canada Ridge Trail comes in from the right. Continue directly ahead (north) 0.2 mi. to the Beech Cliff parking area.

Valley Trail
Distances from service road at Great Pond
- *to* Beech Mountain South Ridge Trail junction: *est.* 0.3 mi. (10 min.)
- *to* old Southwest Harbor road and Canada Ridge Trail junction: 1 mi. (40 min.)
- *to* Beech Cliff parking area: 1.2 mi./1.9 km. (50 min.)

Beech Mountain South Ridge Trail
This well-marked trail diverges left from the Valley Trail about 0.3 mi. east of the service road and ascends the south ridge to the summit.

Beech Mountain South Ridge Trail
Distances from service road at Great Pond
- *to* start (via Valley Trail): *est.* 0.3 mi.
- *to* Beech Mountain summit: *est.* 1 mi./1.6 km. (45 min.)

WESTERN MOUNTAINS

BERNARD MOUNTAIN (1071 ft./326 m.)
MANSELL MOUNTAIN (949 ft./289 m.)

This area has two main summits—Bernard to the west and Mansell to the east. Both summits are wooded, and extensive views are rare. There is access from the north via the Western Trail into Great Notch. From the south, there are many choices: Great Pond Trail, Perpendicular Trail, Sluiceway Trail, or South Face Trail. You can reach all of the south approaches from the parking area at the foot of Great Pond near the pumping station.

Western Trail

This trail's main value is that it provides access to the western mountains from the north. There are no open vistas. To reach the trailhead go about 1 mi. east from ME 102 on the Great Pond (Long Pond) fire road. The fire road crosses just north of Seal Cove Pond and heads toward Pine Hill. The Western Trail starts on the east side of the road about 0.1 mi. beyond the Pine Hill turnaround and parking area.

The trail trends southeast and rises by easy grades to a junction with the Great Pond Trail (left) 1.9 mi. from the fire road. It ends in Great Notch at 2.3 mi. The Great Notch gives access to both western mountain peaks.

Western Trail
Distances from Great Pond fire road
to Great Pond Trail junction: 1.9 mi. (1 hr. 5 min.)
to Great Notch: 2.3 mi./3.7 km. (1 hr. 25 min.)

Great Pond Trail (Long Pond)

This excellent footpath starts at the pumping station at the foot of Great Pond. It follows the west shore of the pond for 1.5 mi., then bears west away from it. Turning south, the

trail passes through a beautiful birch forest and follows
Great Brook to a junction with the Western Trail. With this
route to the Western Trail you can reach the complex of trails
on the mountain and from there complete a circuit back to
the pumping station.

Great Pond Trail
Distance from pumping station
   to Western Trail junction: 2.9 mi./4.7 km. (1 hr. 40 min.)

Perpendicular Trail

This trail, ascending Mansell peak, starts from the Great
Pond Trail on the west shore of Great Pond 0.2 mi. north of
the pumping station. It follows a steep course up the east
slope of Mansell, crossing a rock slide. The trail is very
steep, especially at the start, much of it over stone steps. The
upper portion has an excellent view southeast. At an open
ledge near the top, watch for a sign marked "path," where an
abrupt turn left leads down sharply into woods and marsh
before the trail goes up to the actual summit. The summit is
wooded.

Perpendicular Trail
Distances from pumping station
   to start (via Great Pond Trail): 0.2 mi. (5 min.)
   to Mansell summit: 1.6 mi./2.6 km. (1 hr. 10 min.)

Sluiceway Trail

This trail starts at Mill Field on the western-mountain fire
road. (To reach Mill Field, follow Seal Cove Rd. west from
ME 102 in Southwest Harbor. The pavement ends at the Acadia Park border. Take the first right off the dirt road, bear
right at the first fork, and left at the second fork. The road
ends at Mill Field.) The trail runs north 0.6 mi. to a junction
with the Great Notch Trail. At this junction the Sluiceway

Trail swings northwest and climbs rather steeply, to a junction with the South Face Trail 0.4 mi. farther. To reach Bernard peak, follow the South Face Trail left (south) for 0.2 mi.

Sluiceway Trail
Distances from Western Mountain fire road
> *to* Great Notch Trail junction: 0.6 mi. (25 min.)
> *to* South Face Trail junction: 1 mi. (50 min.)
> *to* Bernard summit (via South Face Trail): 1.1 mi./1.8 km. (1 hr.)

South Face Trail
This trail also starts at Mill Field on the western-mountain fire road. (For directions to Mill Field, see the Sluiceway Trail description.) As do many of the trails on the western mountains, it runs through a magnificent spruce-fir forest and affords fine views of western Mount Desert Island and Blue Hill Bay. It leads west 0.5 mi. and then rises north to Bernard peak at 1.7 mi. and ends in Little Notch at the junction with the Sluiceway Trail 0.2 mi. beyond.

South Face Trail
Distances from western-mountain fire road
> *to* Sluiceway Trail: 1.6 mi. (1 hr. 10 min.)
> *to* Bernard summit: 1.7 mi. (1 hr. 20 min.)
> *to* Little Notch: 1.9 mi./3.1 km. (1 hr. 25 min.)

ISLE AU HAUT

This island, about 5 mi. south of Stonington, was an early landmark for sailors. Samuel de Champlain, a seventeenth-century French explorer, named it High Island. A range of mountains extends for 6 mi., the length of the island. Mount Champlain (543 ft.), near the north end, is its highest summit. Farther south along the ridge are Rocky Mountain (500 ft.), Sawyer Mountain (480 ft.), and Jerusalem Mountain (440 ft.). Near the southwest tip is Duck Harbor Mountain (314 ft.).

The island is reached by mail boat from Stonington (45 min.). The schedule should be checked locally.

About half of the island is within Acadia National Park. The NPS maintains a camping area at Duck Harbor, on the southwest side of the island and about 4 mi. from Isle au Haut village. There are five lean-tos (no tents), which are available by reservation only. The NPS has established daily limits on the number of people allowed to visit Isle au Haut. For the latest information and reservations call the park headquarters on Mount Desert Island (207-288-3338), or write to Acadia National Park, PO Box 177, Bar Harbor, ME 04609.

The 14-mi. road around the island is partly paved. Some sections of the road, however, are very rough and *not* recommended for bike riding. The road passes the foot of Turner Pond (Long Pond on the USGS map), where there is a place to swim.

Numerous trails offer opportunities to explore wild and rocky shoreline, heavily wooded uplands, marshes, and mountain summits. For current hiking information, write to Acadia National Park, stop at the park Visitor Center in Hulls Cove, or pick up a map from the mail-boat operators. From June to September, park rangers will meet the mail boat and provide you with detailed hiking information.

SECTION 4

East of the Penobscot

This section describes the mainland area east of the Penobscot River and south of Aroostook County, between the Penobscot River plain on the west and the coastal rivers, including the Union, Narraguagus, Machias, and St. Croix, on the south and east. In this region the country rolls up into low, mostly widely scattered mountains. Lead Mountain (1475 ft.) and Passadumkeag Mountain (1463 ft.) are the highest, and several others are over 1000 ft. In general, extensive views characterize the mountains, and some have attractive open summits and ledges. This section describes the mountains to the south and west first, and then those to the north and east.

TUNK MOUNTAIN (1157 ft./353 m.)

This mountain is located in T 10 S D (T stands for township). It is northeast of Schoodic Mountain. There is no trail on the upper part, but bushwhacking is fairly easy. Refer to the USGS Tunk Lake quadrangle, 15-minute series.

Take US 1 east from Ellsworth for 6 mi. and bear left on ME 182. At 21.7 mi. from Ellsworth, park at the entrance of a road on the left that is 1 mi. east of the eastern end of Fox Pond and 1.8 mi. west of the outlet of Tunk Lake.

The side road descends to the western shore of Spring River Lake. Cross the beach past tent sites to the northern shore, where a trail leaves north. Vegetation obscures the entrance. At the water's edge cross over some rocks that cover the inlet stream and go into the trees. From there you will be able to see the trail and one rock cairn. Except for the first cairn, the trail is unmarked but is fairly easy to follow to Mud Pond.

The trail leads north, climbing very gradually and then descending to reach Salmon Pond within 15 min. of the start. With the pond in view, the trail forks. (The right fork leads to the shore.) The left fork follows the western end of the pond and then leads away from it and gradually climbs the low ridge that separates Salmon and Mud ponds. With a brook on the left, the trail drops down to Mud Pond, which it reaches in 10 min.

From the western end of Mud Pond, go north, always uphill. You will skirt small cliffs and ledges on the way to the partially wooded summit ridge, which has five peaks. The whole southern face of the mountain consists of cliffs and steep ledges. Views are limited but interesting, particularly the ones of Spring River Lake and the Black Hills.

Tunk Mountain
Distance from entrance of road off ME 182
   to Tunk summit: 1.5 mi./2.4 km. (1 hr. 30 min.)

SCHOODIC MOUNTAIN (1069 ft./326 m.)

Of the small group of mountains northeast of the head of Frenchman's Bay, Schoodic is the most popular for climbing. It is located in T 9 S D. Refer to the USGS Tunk Lake quadrangle, 15-minute series.

A good trail to the abandoned fire tower on the summit starts 2 mi. south of Franklin Village and 4 mi. north of Sullivan. It leaves the east side of ME 200 between two bridges at the foot of a steep hill in East Franklin. Park in the space just north of the north bridge. Take the paved road east and follow the right fork up a hill. At about 0.5 mi., the road (which possibly may be driven to this point) crosses a large brook, the last sure source of *water* on the trail. At about 1 mi. the road crosses a railroad (sign). Turn right and follow the road alongside the railroad for a short distance until it swings away to the left. About 15 min. farther take the well-worn path to the left (cairn), which is a shortcut to a warden's cabin site. The trail then climbs steeply but presents no difficulties. The top of the mountain is bare and flat and offers views in all directions. Those of Mount Desert and Frenchman's Bay are very scenic.

Another, easier approach to the mountain, except during very wet weather, begins in East Sullivan. At the junction of US 1 and ME 183, follow ME 183 north. It crosses railroad tracks at 4.4 mi. At 4.5 mi. turn left on a dirt road, which is rough and no good after long rains. Also, road signs for the tower are not always present at key junctions. At 0.7 mi. from ME 183, continue straight ahead, and at 1.4 mi. take the right fork. Follow it to another fork 1.8 mi. from ME 183 and turn left toward Schoodic Siding, which is 2.5 mi. from ME 183. Park at the siding and walk west on the tracks about 0.5 mi. until, with Schoodic Mountain in view, the railroad curves sharply left. Just before the western end of the curve, the trail to the warden's cabin site leaves on the right and crosses a ditch on railroad ties. Follow the trail up an easy grade for 0.2 mi. to the cabin site and the junction with the trail from ME 200 described in the preceding paragraph. (If the road is impassable, the railroad tracks can be followed for about 2.5 mi. from ME 183.)

Schoodic Mountain
Distances from ME 200

- *to* large-brook crossing: *est.* 0.5 mi. (15 min.)
- *to* railroad tracks: 1 mi. (30 min.)
- *to* warden's cabin site: 2 mi. (1 hr.)
- *to* Schoodic summit: 2.8 mi./4.5 km. (1 hr. 40 min.)

Distances from Schoodic Siding

- *to* warden's cabin site: 0.8 mi. (20 min.)
- *to* Schoodic summit: 1.5 mi./2.4 km. (1 hr.)

BLUE HILL (934 ft./285 m.)

This isolated mountain rises just north of the town of the same name. There is a MFS fire tower on the summit. Refer to the USGS Blue Hill quadrangle, 15-minute series.

Opposite the Blue Hill Fair Grounds, 13 mi. from Ellsworth on ME 172, go right on a road that heads west. An excellent MFS trail leaves this road on the right (north) at a sign 0.8 mi. from ME 172. (You can also reach the start of the trail by turning east from ME 15, 1 mi. north of Blue Hill Village and 11 mi. south of the junction with US 1 between Orland and East Orland. The trail is on the left (north) 0.5 mi. from ME 15.) Not far from the start it branches right and runs through a fine stand of spruce to the summit. Extensive views take in the Mount Desert mountains and Blue Hill Bay.

Blue Hill
Distance from road between ME 172 and ME 15
to Blue Hill Summit: 1 mi./1.6 km. (45 min.)

GREAT HILL (1038 ft./316 m.)

Great Hill appears on the USGS Orland quadrangle, 15-minute series, 1955 edition, as Great Pond Mountain. It is in the town of Orland, northeast of Alamoosook Lake.

Leave US 1 in East Orland 6 mi. east of Bucksport and 14 mi. west of Ellsworth at Toddy Pond Outlet (sign, "Craig Brook National Fish Hatchery"). Take the road to the north for 1 mi. Drive through the hatchery grounds and bear right, then in 0.3 mi. take a right at the gate (sign, "Tunison"). Park the car in the first available space. At about 0.7 mi. on the trail take the left fork. The trail climbs through woods and soon emerges onto spacious open ledges where you can see from Mount Desert to Penobscot Bay. The wooded summit, about 100 ft. higher, with an open ledge, offers views to the northeast and east.

Be careful to note where the trail leaves the woods, so that you can find it again on the way down; there are no markers on the ledges.

Great Hill

Distance from parking area

   to Great Hill summit: 1.8 mi./2.9 km. (1 hr. 15 min.)

BALD MOUNTAIN (1234 ft./376 m.)

This interesting mountain (also known as Dedham Bald Mountain) is in the town of Dedham, and a MFS trail in good condition leads to a tower on the summit. The Bald Mountain Ski Area used to occupy the western side of the mountain. After it closed, the lifts and other equipment were removed. Refer to the USGS Orland quadrangle, 15-minute series.

From US 1A in East Holden, 9 mi. from Bangor and 18 mi. from Ellsworth, turn south onto the paved Upper Dedham Rd.; do *not* take ME 46. In 2.7 mi. take a left at the fire station. Then, 6.3 mi. from US 1A, where the road bears right, look for a sign for the fire tower and park the car on the left. The trail starts at the parking area and is easy to follow. It leads through open fields and over ledges, leading to the tower, which the MFS maintains for communication. From the tower, you can see to the north and northwest from Katahdin to Bigelow, and the nearby ledges on the northern side of the mountain look out over beautiful Phillips Lake, now known as Lucerne-in-Maine. The eastern side offers views of the Mount Desert Island mountains.

An alternative route follows the old ski trail, which is easy to see from the approach road. The ski trail intersects Upper

Dedham Road 0.3 mi. before (north of) the fire tower sign at the parking area.

Bald Mountain
Distance from parking area at fire tower sign
to Bald Mountain fire tower: 0.5 mi./0.8 km. (30 min.)

RIDER BLUFF (813 ft./248 m.)

This bluff in Holden is in the first line of hills east of the Penobscot River plain. It makes a good outlook for viewing the Bangor-Brewer area and the mountains from Katahdin to Bigelow, Sugarloaf, and Abraham. Most people generally hike up the service road for the WLBZ-TV tower on the summit. (During dry weather, cars can usually make it up this road too.) Refer to the USGS Orland quadrangle, 15- minute series.

From US 1A, turn southwest on a blacktop road 8 mi. from Bangor and 1.4 mi. from East Holden. The turn is just southeast of the Holden Town Hall. In 1.3 mi. the blacktop road makes a sharp left turn. Go straight ahead on the private access road. It descends slightly, crosses a small brook, and then turns right (west), and climbs toward the col between Rider Bluff and Hog Hill. About 0.7 mi. from the blacktop road, it turns and climbs more steeply to the summit.

Rider Bluff
Distance from blacktop road
to Rider summit: *est.* 1 mi./1.6 km. (40 min.)

BLACKCAP MOUNTAIN (1022 ft./312 m.)

Five radio and TV masts top Blackcap Mountain, which is in Eddington. Vegetation blocks views, except to the east. Refer to the USGS Orono and Orland quadrangles, 15-minute series.

To reach the summit by car, take ME 46 northeast from US 1A at East Holden. Drive 4 mi. and turn right (sign, "Katahdin Area Council Boy Scout Camp"). From ME 9 in East Eddington, drive southwest on ME 46 0.4 mi.; turn left. The road to the scout camp goes left from the summit road 0.4 mi. from ME 46. Stay right at that, and all other junctions. Continue 1.9 mi. to the end of the road.

Roberts Trail

Hikers can pick up the Roberts Trail either at the summit of Blackcap (near the radio mast with the small green instrument house) or on the scout camp road at the outlet of Fitts Pond, which is opposite a gravel bank near the entrance of the camp 1.5 mi. from the summit road. Other trails also diverge from this point and lead to Burnt Pond and Little Burnt Pond. Blue and white paint blazes and directional arrows mark the Roberts Trail, which crosses the pond outlet on a tripod bridge and climbs steeply to the cluster of radio and TV masts. It continues along the summit ridge over open ledges and through patches of trees to the southern end of the ridge. Then it drops steeply east and northeast to the southern end of Fitts Pond. It crosses a swampy patch to the eastern shore of the pond and runs along the shore. At first it stays close to the shore. Then it goes up on the bluff and returns to the entrance of the boy scout camp. At the southern end of the pond, be careful not to take a wrong turn onto a jeep road that diverges east.

Roberts Trail

Distances from scout camp entrance
  to radio and TV masts: 0.6 mi. (45 min.)
  to southern end of Blackcap summit ridge: 1.4 mi. (1 hr. 10 min.)
  to southern end of Fitts Pond: 2.3 mi. (2 hr.)
  to scout camp entrance: 3.8 mi./6.1 km. (3 hr.)

EAGLE BLUFF (790 ft./241 m.)

With one of the more exposed and scenic views in eastern Maine, this sheer cliff overlooks Mountainy Pond and almost unbroken wilderness. A tote road rises gradually to within 0.8 mi. of the summit, which is bare. The sheer southern side is good for rappelling, friction climbing, and rock climbing. The granite is stable, but not many climbers take advantage of it. Refer to the USGS Orono and Orland quadrangles, 15-minute series.

The trail begins at the Katahdin Scout Camp. (See the preceding section for approach routes.) Park in the lot at the reservation.

From behind the mess hall (the largest building), the trail follows the road, which rises quickly at first. At about 2.8 mi. turn sharply right into a hunting camp. To the left of the camp, an orange-blazed trail climbs steeply, levels off, and then pitches quickly to the summit.

Eagle Bluff

Distance from scout camp
  to Eagle Bluff summit: 3 mi./4.8 km. (2 hr.)

WOODCHUCK HILL (SNOWSHOE MOUNTAIN) (834 ft./254 m.)

A very easy hike in the area northeast of Blackcap Mountain, this mountain offers good campsites at both its summit and its base. Refer to the USGS Orono quadrangle, 15-minute series.

The approach by road is the same as for Blackcap Mountain. Park in the lot at the scout camp. From a small log cabin immediately behind the parking lot on the left, follow the unmarked road, which soon turns into a poorly marked (polka-dot markers) but obvious trail. The trail passes through a campsite beyond Snowshoe Pond and climbs to a Bangor Water District road (paved) at 0.8 mi. On the road, walk 75 ft. to the right to utility pole 66. Then follow irregular blazes or bushwhack for less than 0.5 mi. to the open summit.

Woodchuck Hill

Distance from scout camp

   to Woodchuck summit: *est.* 1.3 mi./2.1 km. (45 min.)

PEAKED MOUNTAIN (1160 ft./354 m.)
LITTLE PEAKED MOUNTAIN

These two summits make a particularly rewarding snowshoeing trip in winter. It is easy to complete the circuit in an afternoon from many points in the surrounding area.

Peaked Mountain

Peaked Mountain, commonly called Chick Hill, straddles the Clifton/Amherst line. A well-marked and popular MFS trail leads to the summit. Refer to the USGS Great Pond quadrangle, 15-minute series.

About 18 mi. from Bangor and 3.5 mi. east of the junction of ME 9 and ME 180, leave ME 9 on the north (left) side on a gravel road. This turn is roughly opposite a Maine Highway Department picnic area. In about 0.7 mi., after passing a small group of houses, park. Follow an old discontinued "Airline" road to the fire warden's camp site (0.2 mi.). There is a dependable *spring* behind the camp site. Continue on the old road, and at about 0.6 mi., as the road levels off, turn right onto a clearly blazed trail. At about 0.9 mi. the trail rises more steeply and on the lower ledge, you can see nearby Little Peaked Mountain to the west. Occasional cairns mark the way to the summit, which offers vistas in all directions and is particularly colorful in fall. The view includes five lakes, the Penobscot River, the Mount Desert mountains to the southeast, and Mount Katahdin to the northwest.

Peaked Mountain
Distance from parking area
  to Peaked Mountain summit: 1.3 mi./2.1 km. (50 min.)

Little Peaked Mountain

The views from Little Peaked Mountain (Little Chick Hill) are also good, except to the north. To reach Little Peaked Mountain, bushwhack uphill to the right of the parking area or from anywhere along the old "Airline" road. Climb through the mixed soft and hardwoods until you reach the ledges on the southwestern side of the mountain.

Another easy route is to take the trail up Peaked Mountain. Just before beginning the climb up the steeper part of the peak, turn right, descend briefly to the col, and bushwhack to Little Peaked Mountain.

LEAD MOUNTAIN (HUMPBACK)
(1475 ft./450 m.)

Lead Mountain is in T 28 M D in Hancock County, just west of the Washington County line. The trail appears on the USGS Lead Mountain quadrangle, 15-minute series.

The trail starts in the yard of the MFS station (283 ft.) in Beddington. The station is 0.1 mi. west of the ME 9 bridge over the Narraguagus River and 1.1 mi. east of the ME 9 and

193 junction. The trail (no sign) starts out as a wide woods road that leads northwest across the field west of the MFS station and enters the woods to the right of a small house. As soon as you enter the woods take the right fork. The remains of a telephone line occasionally border the road, which the trail follows for about 0.5 mi. until it enters a large bulldozed clearing. There the trail leads straight ahead through a marshy area. (Watch carefully, no sign, and you have to avoid the road leading uphill to the right.) The unblazed trail then follows an old telephone line to the summit. At 1.3 mi. a side path leads 200 yd. left to Bear Pond. At 1.5 mi. the trail divides. The left fork goes close to a reliable *spring* 100 ft. to the left of main trail (sign). Then it rejoins the main trail. At 2.5 mi. you will reach the warden's cabin in a col below the summit. The trail continues straight on past the cabin and then bears left (west) to the site of the fire tower, which is on a flat summit area several acres in area. The ledges 200 yd. southwest of the summit are a good lookout.

Descending, remember that where the trail divides, the right fork leads past the *spring*.

Lead Mountain
Distances from MFS station

to side trail to Bear Pond: 1.3 mi. (40 min.)
to warden's cabin: 2.5 mi. (1 hr. 45 min.)
to Lead Mountain summit: 3 mi./4.8 km. (2 hr.)

PEAKED MOUNTAIN (938 ft./286 m.)

Peaked Mountain is in T 30 in Washington County, north of ME 9 and less than 30 mi. east of the mountain near Clifton with the same name. Refer to the USGS Tug Mountain quadrangle, 15-minute series.

A good MFS trail leaves the north side of ME 9 at a sign about 9.8 mi. east of the Narraguagus River and about 14.8

mi. west of Wesley. Park about 100 ft. in on the tote road. Follow the tote road to the fire warden's cabin. Then take the trail, which rises gently and follows a telephone line to an open ledge. The MFS abandoned the fire tower in 1970. Extensive wilderness spreads out below in all directions.

Peaked Mountain
Distance from parking area on tote road
    to Peaked Mountain fire tower (via trail from warden's cabin): 1.3 mi./2.1 km. (45 min.)

WASHINGTON BALD MOUNTAIN
(983 ft./300 m.)

This mountain's MFS fire tower was abandoned in 1970. The mountain is in T 42 M D. Refer to the USGS Wabassus Lake quadrangle and, for the approach, see the Tug Mountain quadrangle, 15-minute series.

The St. Regis Paper Co. maintains a gravel road that leaves the northern side of ME 9, 14 mi. east of the Narraguagus River in Beddington and 10.5 mi. west of Wesley. (The approach road to Sabao diverges left 75 yd. from ME 9.) Take the St. Regis road north to its end (13.1 mi.), where there is room to park four or five cars. At the sign "Trail to Tower," take the old logging road west and follow the forest service telephone line. The trail slopes gently through large trees and some tall grass. A *spring* at 1.5 mi., behind the log cabin on the right, is not always dependable. At 1.7 mi. bear right at the fork; follow the telephone line over the steep pitch to a tower, which was erected in 1935. There is a well sunk in the granite near the warden's cabin.

Trails lead to the third, fourth, and fifth Machias Lakes from the summit but are not recommended. You can see the first, second, third, and fourth Machias Lakes and many mountains from the 65-ft. tower.

Washington Bald Mountain
Distance from end of St. Regis Co. road
to Washington Bald Mountain fire tower (via right fork):
2.2 mi./3.5 km. (1 hr. 30 min.)

PASSADUMKEAG MOUNTAIN
(1465 ft./446 m.)

Passadumkeag Mountain is southeast of Enfield. It runs in a gradual east-west arc for some 5 mi. and rises well above the surrounding countryside, which is particularly flat to the west and southwest. Until 1970 the MFS staffed the fire tower on the highest summit and maintained a good logging road to it. Refer to the USGS Saponac quadrangle, 15-minute series.

Leave West Enfield on ME 155, east from its junction with US 2. After 2.5 mi. go right on ME 188 and follow it to Saponac four corners (green buildings), about 19 mi. from US 2. Turn sharp right onto a gravel road and cross the Passadumkeag River. At 0.4 mi. turn right at the head of a gravel pit. Pass the blue house (a former ranger station) and continue on the increasingly rough road to a fork, which is 1.3 mi. from ME 188. Park at the sign for the tower.

Go left on the road, which occasionally follows a telephone line. The logging road shrinks into a trail that continues southwest and then south up a stream bed. The trail passes through a gap in the mountain ridge and then continues southwest and west along the southern base of the ridge to the warden's cabin (4 mi.). The cabin is now private property. The trail bears right around the cabin and rises steeply in a generally northern direction to the 30-ft. fire tower. From the tower, you can see Brandy Pond to the southeast in T 39 M D, Saponac Lake to the north, West Lakes and Nicatous Lake to the east, and many mountains, including Katahdin. *Springs* are located 0.3 mi. (sign) below the cabin and 200 yd. above the cabin on the trail to the tower.

Passadumkeag Mountain

Distances from parking area
   to private cabin: 4.0 mi. (2 hr.)
   to Passadumkeag fire tower: 4.5 mi./7.2 km. (2 hr. 30 min.)

POCOMOONSHINE MOUNTAIN
(605 ft./184 m.)

Located in Princeton, this mountain rises nearly 500 ft. above Pocomoonshine Lake. Before abandoning it in 1970, the MFS built a road on the back side of the mountain to the tower. Hikers can use this road or the trail described below, but both may be getting overgrown through lack of use. Refer to the USGS Big Lake quadrangle, 15-minute series.

From US 1 in Princeton, turn southwest at the sign for Ed Jones' Camps. At 2.5 mi., turn left at a white farmhouse and follow the driveway to the right of the house. Then drive 0.5 mi. along some wheel tracks through two fields and two open gates to a roomy parking area at the edge of the woods. Take the left fork along the well-worn, shaded trail. The route follows an old MFS telephone line all the way to the summit. At 1.1 mi. you will pass a *spring* (unreliable) on the right, and at 1.5 mi. you should turn right by another *spring* (reliable). Continue along the telephone line and up a steep, rocky pitch in an old stream bed to the summit. There is another good *spring* 0.3 mi. east of the summit.

Pocomoonshine Mountain

Distance from parking area
   to Pocomoonshine summit: 2.1 mi./3.4 km. (1 hr. 15 min.)

SECTION 5

Camden Hills

The Camden Hills, a compact and attractive group of mountains, rise above the western shore of Penobscot Bay in the towns of Camden, Lincolnville, and Rockport. They share many characteristics with the Mount Desert mountains 40 mi. to the east—fine softwood forests, bold cliffs and ledges, and wide vistas of water and mountains. Mount Megunticook (1380 ft.) is the highest of the group and, with the exception of Cadillac Mountain, is the highest point along the Atlantic Seaboard in the United States. A chain of lower summits continues northeast for several miles; Bald Rock Mountain (1100 ft.) is the most conspicuous. Cameron Mountain (811 ft.) is west of Bald Rock and northeast of Maiden Cliff. The summit is private property, a commercial blueberry field. Mount Battie (800 ft.) lies to the south of Megunticook and is only 0.5 mi. by trail from Megunticook St. in Camden. The Megunticook River and Lake separate the main peaks of the group from the hills running to the southwest, which are, from northeast to southwest, Bald Mountain (1272 ft.), Ragged Mountain (1300 ft.), Spruce Mountain (960 ft.), Pleasant Mountain (1064 ft.), and Meadow Mountain (660 ft.). Refer to the USGS Camden, Lincolnville and West Rockport quadrangles, 7.5-minute series, as well as the map included with this guide.

Camden Hills State Park (4996 acres) embraces much of the Mount Megunticook range, plus a large area to the north and northeast and a short stretch on Penobscot Bay north of Camden on US 1. Park facilities include picnic and camping areas. An automobile road (toll) runs to the summit of Mount Battie from the park headquarters. The *water supply* is *not reliable* in many parts of the park, so carry water if you hike there. Most trails are blazed with white paint.

Not in the Camden Hills, but included in this section of

the guide, are several outlying mountains that are to the west of the Penobscot River, south of US 2, and east of the Kennebec River. This section also covers the offshore island of Monhegan.

MOUNT BATTIE (800 ft./243 m.)

This mountain lies to the south of Mount Megunticook. For climbing, it is the most popular of the Camden Hills because its open ledges offer outstanding views and it is close to Camden. For several years after 1897, there was a hotel on the summit. The stone viewing tower that is there now was erected as a war memorial in 1921.

A toll road for cars runs to the summit. Starting at the Camden Hills State Park Headquarters on US 1, it climbs gradually to the Battie-Megunticook col, turns southwest, and finally curves southeast to the top (1.4 mi.).

Mount Battie Trail

This trail, marked with white blazes and cairns, rises steeply over the rocky nose of Mount Battie. Take ME 52 (Mountain Street) from its junction with US 1 in Camden. Then take the fourth right, and then the first left onto Megunticook St. Continue to the end of the street, where there is a small parking area. The trail first climbs northwest and then rises more steeply north through thinning woods. It soon emerges on the open ledges and runs to the summit tower.

Mount Battie Trail
Distance from parking area on Megunticook Street
to Mount Battie Summit: 0.5 mi./0.8 km. (30 min.)

Carriage Road Trail

This trail climbs along the more gradual west and northwest slopes of Mount Battie, via the route of the old carriage road up the mountain. The approach road to the start of the trail is paved at first, with limited parking, and leaves the right (northeastern) side of ME 52 about 1.3 mi. from US 1/ME 52 junction. The road runs north 0.3 mi. to where the Carriage Road Trail forks right, while the Carriage Trail, leading to the Tableland Trail, forks left.

The Carriage Road Trail rises gently on the old carriage road, which is washed out in many places. The trail joins the toll road near the summit parking area.

Carriage Road Trail
Distance from parking area
> **to** Mount Battie summit: 0.8 mi./1.3 km. (35 min.)

Carriage Trail

In conjunction with the Tableland Trail, this trail provides a route up Mount Megunticook from the southwest. To approach the trail, see Carriage Road Trail above.

The trail climbs very gradually. It reaches the Tableland Trail near the Battie-Megunticook col. To reach Ocean Lookout and, beyond that, the true summit of Mount Megunticook, go left on the Tableland Trail. (To the right, the Tableland Trail leads to the Mount Battie summit.)

Carriage Trail
Distances from ME 52
> **to** Tableland Trail junction: 0.8 mi. (30 min.)
> **to** Ocean Lookout (via Tableland Trail): 1.7 mi. (1 hr. 20 min.)
> **to** Megunticook summit (via Tableland and Ridge trails): 2.1 mi./3.4 km. (1 hr. 35 min.)

Nature Trail

This white-blazed trail adds another approach to Mount Battie (besides the toll road for cars) from the east. It leaves the right side of the Mount Battie toll road 200 ft. from the gate house and runs north of the road. It joins the Tableland Trail about 0.5 mi. from that trail's start. Turn left on the Tableland Trail and crossing the toll road at 0.2 mi. continue to Mount Battie. (To the right, the Tableland Trail reaches Ocean Lookout in about 1 mi.).

Nature Trail
Distances from bottom of toll road
- *to* Tableland Trail junction: *est.* 1 mi. (40 min.)
- *to* Mount Battie summit (via Tableland Trail): *est.* 1.5 mi./2.4 km. (50 min.)
- *to* Ocean Lookout (via Tableland Trail): *est.* 2 mi./3.2 km. (1 hr. 30 min.)

MOUNT MEGUNTICOOK (1380 ft./420 m.)

Mount Megunticook is the highest of the Camden Hills. A ridge forms the mountain and runs northwest-southeast for approximately 3 mi. The true summit has no view, but Ocean Lookout, 0.4 mi. to the southeast, takes in the expanse of Penobscot Bay. Several outlooks on the Ridge Trail offer views to the northwest over Megunticook Lake. Maiden Cliff is a prominent bluff near the northwestern end of the mountain.

Mount Megunticook Trail

This trail climbs the eastern slope of the mountain from the Camden Hills State Park Headquarters to Ocean Lookout. The park headquarters, where there is parking, is on the northwest side of US 1, 1.8 mi. northeast of the junction of US 1 and ME 52 in Camden, and 3.8 mi. south of

Lincolnville Beach. The trail starts from the park camping area and climbs first gradually and then steeply. At 1 mi. it reaches Ocean Lookout, where the Tableland Trail from Mount Battie comes up from the left (south). From Ocean Lookout, follow the Ridge Trail northwest about 0.4 mi. to the Mount Megunticook summit.

A 2-mi. snowmobile trail has been cut along the eastern side of Mount Megunticook. It leaves the Mount Megunticook Trail near a water storage tank (sign), which is visible from the start of the Mount Megunticook Trail. It runs around the eastern side of Mount Megunticook and joins the Ski Shelter Trail (see below) near its junction with the Spring Brook Trail. Hikers can complete a 5-mi. loop trip over Mount Megunticook via the Mount Megunticook Trail, the Ridge Trail, the Slope Trail, and the snowmobile trail.

Mount Megunticook Trail
Distances from park headquarters
- *to* Ocean Lookout: 1 mi. (1 hr.)
- *to* Megunticook summit and Slope Trail junction (via Ridge Trail): 1.4 mi./2.3 km. (1 hr. 20 min.)
- *to* ski lodge (via Slope Trail): 2.9 mi. (2 hr. 10 min.)
- *to* park headquarters (via Slope Trail, snowmobile trail, and park service road): 4.9 mi./7.9 km. (3 hr. 20 min.)

Tableland Trail

This trail starts from the summit of Mount Battie. It crosses the parking area and runs to the northeast and gradually descends, crossing the toll road at 0.3 mi., to the Battie-Megunticook col. At 0.5 mi. pass the Nature Trail on the right, and at 0.6 mi. pass the Carriage Trail on the left. Starting the ascent of the Mount Megunticook mass, the Tableland Trail keeps to the right (east) of two lines of cliffs and, again swinging to the northwest, climbs steeply to Ocean Lookout. The true summit is another 0.4 mi. to the northwest along the Ridge Trail.

Tableland Trail

Distances from Mount Battie summit

> **to** Ocean Lookout: 1.5 mi./2.4 km. (1 hr.)

Maiden Cliff Trail

Maiden Cliff (800 ft./243 m.) rises abruptly above Megunticook Lake. A wooden cross stands near the spot where Elenora French, a young girl, fell to her death in 1864. The trail starts from the northeastern side of ME 52 (at a parking area about 2.9 mi. north of the junction of ME 52 and US 1 in Camden), where the highway approaches a cove of Megunticook Lake. The trail climbs north, at first following a washed-out logging road. At about 0.5 mi. the Ridge Trail to Mount Megunticook diverges right. The Maiden Cliff Trail then climbs more steeply to open ledges and the wooden cross. For a rewarding alternate route to Maiden Cliff, go right on the Ridge Trail. Then in about 0.3 mi. go left (north) on the Scenic Trail. The Scenic Trail reaches Maiden Cliff in another 0.8 mi. after crossing several open ledges with fine views of the lake.

Maiden Cliff Trail

Distances from ME 52

> **to** Ridge Trail junction: *est.* 0.5 mi. (30 min.)
> **to** Maiden Cliff: 1 mi. (50 min.)
> **to** Maiden Cliff (via Ridge and Scenic trails): 1.6 mi./2.6 km. (1 hr. 10 min.)

Scenic Trail

This trail forks left (east) from the Maiden Cliff Trail near Maiden Cliff. It climbs over very open ledge with many views, then descends slightly to a junction with the Ridge Trail 0.8 mi. from ME 52.

Scenic Trail
Distance from Maiden Cliff
> *to* Ridge Trail junction: 0.8 mi./1.3 km. (30 min.)

Ridge Trail

This trail leaves the Maiden Cliff Trail 0.5 mi. from ME 52 and runs along the main ridge of Mount Megunticook, over the true summit, and on to Ocean Lookout. From the Maiden Cliff Trail junction, hike up to the right. In about 0.3 mi. the Scenic Trail to Maiden Cliff diverges left. The Ridge Trail continues to climb, after a brief descent, with occasional lookouts over Megunticook Lake. About 0.5 mi. from the junction with the Scenic Trail, Zeke's Trail comes in from the left (sign). The Ridge Trail crosses over a subsidiary summit (1290 ft.), descends slightly, and then climbs gradually to the true summit, which is wooded. Just beyond the summit, the Slope Trail diverges left (north). The Ridge Trail descends to end at Ocean Lookout.

Ridge Trail
Distances from ME 52
> *to* start (via Maiden Cliff Trail): 0.5 mi. (30 min.)
> *to* Scenic Trail junction: 0.8 mi. (40 min.)
> *to* Zeke's Trail junction: 1.3 mi. (1 hr. 5 min.)
> *to* Megunticook summit and Slope Trail junction: 2.3 mi. (1 hr. 45 min.)
> *to* Ocean Lookout: 2.7 mi./4.3 km. (2 hr.)

Distances from ME 52 via Maiden Cliff and Scenic trails
> *to* Ridge Trail: 1.8 mi. (1 hr. 15 min.)
> *to* Zeke's Trail junction: 2.3 mi. (1 hr. 40 min.)
> *to* Megunticook summit and Slope Trail junction: 3.3 mi. (2 hr. 15 min.)
> *to* Ocean Lookout: 3.7 mi./6 km. (2 hr. 30 min.)

Megunticook Traverse

This traverse is probably the nicest walk in the Camden
Hills area. It offers a series of marvelous views and a lot of
ridge walking. Climb the Mount Battie Trail from Camden.
Then follow the Tableland Trail to Ocean Lookout. Con-
tinue over Mount Megunticook on the Ridge Trail to the
Scenic Trail, which leads to Maiden Cliff. Then descend the
Maiden Cliff Trail to ME 52. This route is equally good in the
opposite direction.

Megunticook Traverse
**Distance from parking area on Megunticook Street (Mount
Battie trailhead)**

to ME 52 (Maiden Cliff trailhead): 5.7 mi./9.2 km. (3 hr.
30 min.)

MOUNT MEGUNTICOOK FROM THE NORTH

Hikers can approach Mount Megunticook and its subsidiary summits from the north via a network of trails that for
the most part branch from the Ski Shelter Trail. These trails
are not as heavily used as those on the southern and western
slopes of the mountain, and the woods have suffered logging
and extensive blowdowns in the past. So be particularly careful not to wander off the routes described. Since *water* supplies in the northern hills are not always dependable, always
carry a canteen.

Ski Shelter Trail

This trail is a state-park fire road. It serves as the chief approach to the trails up Mount Megunticook from the north.
It also is the approach from the north for Bald Rock Mountain and for other trails leading to US 1. The road is in poor
condition in places.

To reach Ski Shelter Trail, take ME 173 from Lincolnville Beach. After 2.3 mi. turn left onto Youngtown Road, and within less than 100 yd., turn left onto the Ski Shelter Trail (which may be closed or impassable). At 1.3 mi. you will reach Heald Picnic Shelter. At this point the Bald Rock Trail goes left past the picnic shelter and leads to the summit of Bald Rock Mountain. About 100 yd. farther along the trail, the Cameron Mountain Trail diverges right, and in another 0.3 mi., the Sky Blue Trail also diverges right. At 2.5 mi. along the trail, Zeke's Trail diverges right and climbs to the Ridge Trail. At 3 mi. the trail reaches an enclosed ski shelter. Groups may use the shelter but they must first register at park headquarters. From the ski shelter, the Slope Trail climbs up to the Ridge Trail near the true summit of Mount Megunticook. The Spring Brook Trail leaves the Snowmobile Trail 0.2 mi. south of the shelter and leads to US 1.

Ski Shelter Trail
Distances from Youngtown Road

to Heald Picnic Shelter, Bald Rock Mountain Trail, and Cameron Mountain Trail: 1.3 mi. (50 min.)

to Sky Blue Trail junction: 1.6 mi. (1 hr.)

to Zeke's Trail junction: 2.5 mi. (1 hr. 30 min.)

to ski lodge (via main trail): 3 mi./4.8 km. (1 hr. 45 min.)

BALD ROCK MOUNTAIN (1100 ft./335 m.)

About 2.5 mi. northeast of Mount Megunticook, this mountain offers fine views from its ledgy summit. The Bald Rock Trail traverses the mountain from US 1 to the Ski Shelter Trail. There is *no dependable water* on the upper part of this route.

From the Ski Shelter Trail, the Bald Rock Trail diverges left (east) at Heald Picnic Shelter, 1.3 mi. from Youngtown

Road. The trail, a well-worn path, climbs to the summit. From there, it descends southeast quite steeply at first and then more gradually. It reaches the west side of US 1 at telephone pole 106, about 4 mi. north of Camden, just north of the Knox-Waldo County line and just south of the Red Barn Shop.

Bald Rock Trail
Distances from Heald Picnic Shelter
   to Bald Rock summit: 0.5 mi./0.8 km. (30 min.)
   to US 1: 1.8 mi./2.9 km. (1 hr. 35 min.)

Cameron Mountain Trail
This interesting trail diverges right (west) from the Ski Shelter Trail about 100 yd. beyond Heald Picnic Shelter. At about 0.1 mi. it turns left, following an old town road. It crosses Black Brook and rises gradually past abandoned farmland, old cellar holes, and apple trees. The trail then follows the boundary of Camden Hills State Park and passes about 0.1 mi. to the south of the summit of Cameron Mountain. Then it descends and in about 300 yd. comes to a junction. The north (right) fork descends and ends at the Youngtown Road in about 0.5 mi. (no sign at road, Central Maine Power pole number 91). The Cameron Mountain Trail turns left (south) and starts to climb. In about 0.7 mi. the Sky Blue Trail diverges left. In another 0.1 mi. the Cameron Mountain Trail ends at Zeke's Trail.

Cameron Mountain Trail
Distances from Ski Shelter Trail (100 yd. beyond Heald Picnic Shelter)
   to Cameron Mountain, south of summit: *est.* 1.1 mi. (35 min.)
   to junction with trail to Youngtown Road: *est.* 1.2 mi. (*est.* 40 min.)

to Sky Blue Trail junction: *est.* 1.9 mi. (1 hr. 25 min.)

to Zeke's Trail junction: 2 mi./3.2 km. (1 hr. 30 min.)

to Megunticook summit (via Zeke's and Ridge trails): 3.5 mi./5.6 km. (2 hr. 25 min.)

Sky Blue Trail

This trail has been cleared and its cairns rebuilt. Although it offers few long views, it makes a very pretty walk in the woods. The Sky Blue Trail leaves Ski Shelter Trail about 0.3 mi. southwest of the start of the Cameron Mountain Trail. It follows a course west parallel to the Cameron Mountain Trail and Zeke's Trail, and about halfway between the two. At about 1.5 mi. it reaches the Cameron Mountain Trail. At this junction, go left to reach Zeke's Trail or right to reach Cameron Mountain.

Sky Blue Trail
Distances from Heald Picnic Shelter

to start (via Ski Shelter Trail): 0.3 mi. (10 min.)

to Cameron Mountain Trail junction: 1.8 mi./2.9 km. (2 hr.)

Zeke's Trail

This trail diverges right (west) from the Ski Shelter Trail about 2.5 mi. from the start of the trail and about 0.5 mi. before the ski lodge. The Cameron Mountain Trail diverges right (north) at 0.8 mi. and leads to a junction with the Sky Blue Trail, to Cameron Mountain, and to Youngtown Rd. At 1 mi. a trail (sign) leads right to Zeke's Lookout which, after a short, steep climb, offers good views of Bald Rock Mountain and Upper Penobscot Bay. Zeke's Trail ends at its junction with the Ridge Trail, about 1 mi. northwest of the summit of Mount Megunticook.

Zeke's Trail
Distances from Heald Picnic Shelter
- *to* start (via Ski Shelter Trail): 1.2 mi. (40 min.)
- *to* Cameron Mountain Trail junction: 2. mi. (1 hr. 10 min.)
- *to* Zeke's Lookout Trail: 2.2 mi. (1 hr. 20 min.)
- *to* Ridge Trail junction: 2.5 mi./4 km. (1 hr. 30 min.)

Slope Trail

This trail goes from the ski shelter to the summit of Mount Megunticook. From the ski shelter go east across the bridge over Spring Brook. This trail was relocated in 1977 because of serious erosion. The trail climbs steeply and reaches the Ridge Trail close to the true summit of Mount Megunticook.

Slope Trail
Distance from ski lodge
- *to* Megunticook summit: 1.5 mi./2.4 km. (1 hr. 15 min.)

Spring Brook Trail

This pleasant trail from the snowmobile trail follows the north side of Spring Brook through lovely open woods to US 1. About 0.2 mi. east of the ski shelter, take the trail to the left. It follows the route of an old woods road, which is wide and generally clear all the way. The trail reaches US 1 at CMP Pole 86, 2.8 mi. north of Camden across from the High Tide Motel.

A 2-mi. snowmobile trail starts near the junction of the Ski Shelter Trail and the Slope Trail. There is a description of it in the section on the Mount Megunticook Trail.

Spring Brook Trail
Distances from ski lodge
- *to* start (via snowmobile trail): *est.* 0.2 mi. (5 min.)
- *to* US 1: 1.5 mi./2.4 km. (45 min.)

Camden Hills North Circuit

This is an interesting and scenic circuit hike. Start at Heald Picnic Shelter and follow the Ski Shelter Trail to Zeke's Trail. Hike up Zeke's Trail 0.8 mi. to the Cameron Mountain Trail; turn right and descend past the junction of the Sky Blue Trail. Continue on the Cameron Mountain Trail, which turns right (east), passes Cameron Mountain, and descends to Black Brook. Climb slightly to Heald Picnic Shelter and the Ski Shelter Trail to return to the start. This route is just as good in the opposite direction.

Camden Hills North Circuit
Distances from Heald Picnic Shelter

to Zeke's Trail (via Ski Shelter Trail): 1.2 mi. (40 min.)

to Cameron Mountain Trail (via Zeke's Trail): 2. mi. (1 hr. 10 min.)

to Heald Picnic Shelter (via Cameron Mountain Trail): 4 mi./6.4 km. (2 hr. 10 min.)

RAGGED MOUNTAIN (1300 ft./396 m.)

This mountain, 4 mi. west of Camden, is the highest of the hills to the southwest of Megunticook River and Lake. Its summit offers views that are comparable to those on the main Megunticook Range. There is a radio tower on the summit.

To approach from Camden, follow US 1 south to John St. on the right (sign *Snow Bowl*). Follow signs to the Snow Bowl.

Park at the Snow Bowl and follow the longest (T-bar) ski lift as far as it goes. Then enter the woods continuing in the same direction on a trail generally following a power line, climbing to the summit.

Ragged Mountain

Distance from Snow Bowl

   to Ragged Mountain summit: *est.* 1.1 mi./1.8 km. (1 hr. 10 min.)

BALD MOUNTAIN (1272 ft./388 m.)

Bald Mountain lies between Ragged Mountain and Megunticook Lake. The approach is via Howe Hill Rd. (Camden), which skirts the northeastern slope of the mountain. Park at a dirt road 0.2 mi. southeast of the Howe Farm (near height-of-land), near power pole 18.

This jeep road climbs steadily, at first southwest, then it swings northwest, leveling off, and becomes a snowmobile trail. It enters the edge of overgrown fields at 0.4 mi. At 0.5 mi. reenter the woods and in 100 yd. turn left off the old road to the trail and climb gradually through many switchbacks to the summit.

Bald Mountain

Distance from Howe Hill Road

   to field area: 0.4 mi.

   to summit: 1.4 mi./2.2 km. (1 hr.)

FRYE MOUNTAIN (1139 ft./347 m.)

Frye Mountain is in Montville. There is a MFS fire tower on its summit. Refer to the USGS Morrill quadrangle, 7.5-minute series.

A dirt road that is good enough for cars passes within 0.3 mi. of the top. From the south and west, take ME 220 north from ME 3 near Liberty for 6 mi. (You will pass the road to Center Montville at about 5 mi.) Turn right (east) onto a dirt road at the sign for "Frye Mountain, Game Management Area, State of Maine." At 0.6 mi. turn right (south). At 0.4

mi. cross a stream. After another 0.6 mi. turn left (east). Drive 1.6 mi. (total 3.2 mi.) to the start of the short trail (right) to the summit just beyond an open gate. You can also reach the mountain by turning south from ME 137 at Fosters Corner in Knox. This turn is 11 mi. west of Belfast and 3.5 mi. east of Knox Center. The trail starts (left) 2.5 mi. down the dirt road.

The trail climbs southeast to the summit.

Frye Mountain
Distance from dirt road
   to Frye summit: 0.3 mi./0.5 km. (15 min.)

MOUNT HARRIS (1233 ft./376 m.)

The highest of the cluster of hills in Dixmont, Mount Harris has a fire tower (locked) on its heavily wooded summit. The view is available only when the ranger is on duty during fire-danger season. The mountain is nearly halfway between Waterville and Bangor. Refer to the USGS Brooks quadrangle, 15-minute series.

The trail begins on ME 7, 1.6 mi. south of Dixmont Corner. A small green sign with the number 6100 is all that marks the start. Park by the side of the road.

The lower portion of the trail is a well-graded jeep road rising gently in an almost straight line to the east. The road turns to the left above the first building it reaches, a hunting camp, but returns to the straight line. After it reaches a brown lean-to (enclosed and locked), the road rises more sharply to an intersection at the crest of the col. The trail to the tower leaves to the left. It rises steeply at first, and then more gently, following a telephone line to the tower on the summit. The warden's cabin and another outbuilding (locked) are nearby.

There is *water* at a public spring at the side of ME 7, 0.1 mi. south of Dixmont Corner.

Mount Harris
Distance from ME 7
  to fire tower: 1.3 mi./2.1 km. (1 hr.)

MOUNT WALDO (1064 ft./324 m.)

This attractive mountain, with its many open ledges, is in Frankfort. It is best known for the granite quarries on its eastern side. Refer to the USGS Bucksport quadrangle, 15-minute series.

The trail approach is via US 1A in Frankfort. Drive west on a blacktop road 0.3 mi. south of the village. Pass under a railroad overpass and climb the hill. At 0.2 mi. turn right and go to a fork. Go left on a dirt road. At 2.1 mi., park. The trail, a jeep road, climbs over mostly open field and ledges to the summit.

Mount Waldo
Distance from parking place
  to Waldo summit: 1 mi./1.6 km. (45 min.)

MONHEGAN ISLAND

This rugged island, with its spectacular sea cliffs and pleasant hiking trails, is 12 mi. off the coast of Maine. In summer, visitors can get to the island either by excursion boat from Boothbay Harbor or by mail boat from Port Clyde. The village of Monhegan clusters around the harbor, while the rest of the island is still in its natural state. The area of the island is about three quarters of a mile by one and a half miles.

There is a hiking trail around the shore of the island, and many trails connect this shore path with the village. The southwestern section of the shore path gets more use and is easier to follow than the northeastern part. The most popular connecting trail is the path that goes from the end of the road in back of the lighthouse to Whitehead, the highest sea cliff on the island. Another popular trail goes through Cathedral Woods, a lovely stand of tall spruce.

Camping is *not* allowed on the island. There are several small hotels and guest houses, and visitors can buy maps of hiking trails at stores on the island.

Southwestern Maine

This section includes the mountains of York and Cumberland counties and those of Oxford County south of and near US 302. The mountains and hills of southwestern Maine are low and woods cover many of them all the way to the top. The summits that are open provide fine views of the surrounding country northwest toward the White Mountains and east and southeast to the coast. Because they are close to summer camps and population centers, many of the mountains in this section are popular hiking areas. Pleasant Mountain (2006 ft.) is the highest. Most of the others are around 1000 ft. or lower.

Camping facilities are available at Bradbury Mountain and Sebago Lake state parks, as well as at many privately operated camping areas.

BRADBURY MOUNTAIN (484 ft./147 m.)

This summit in Pownal is only partly wooded and offers good views of the countryside. Refer to the USGS Freeport quadrangle, 15-minute series, and the North Pownal quadrangle, 7.5-minute series.

To reach Bradbury Mountain, drive west from I-95 on ME 136 in Freeport and immediately turn left on Pownal Rd. Drive 4 mi. to Pownal center and turn right, northeast, on ME 9. Drive 0.8 mi. to Bradbury Mountain State Park, which has parking, picnic tables, playgrounds, and camping areas. A trail leads 0.3 mi. from the northwest corner of the picnic area to the ledgy south summit of Bradbury. Near the top another trail leads right to an outlook toward the north.

Bradbury Mountain
Distance from state park picnic area
to Bradbury Mountain, south summit: 0.3 mi./.5 km.
(15 min.)

RATTLESNAKE MOUNTAIN (1035 ft./315 m.)

This summit in the southwestern part of Casco is a favorite climb for camp groups in the vicinity. Refer to the USGS Gray quadrangle, 15-minute series.

Approaching from the south on US 302, turn right on ME 85 about 0.5 mi. south of Raymond and drive 5.4 mi. to the intersection just north of the outlet of Crescent Lake. (From the north, turn south off ME 11 at Crescent Lake. The intersection is 3 mi. from ME 11.) Turn left (west) and follow Plains Rd. west for 0.6 mi. to Nubble Pond Brook (culvert). Park on the right near the brook and across from a small pond.

The trail, blazed blue in 1986 (no sign), leads north along the western side of the brook and crosses under a power line. At 0.2 mi. it turns sharp right to cross the dam at the foot of Nubble Pond. Then it skirts the rough eastern shore of the pond. Climb the hill and follow the top of the ledges to avoid the jumble of boulders at their feet. The ledges offer good views of the pond and Rattlesnake Mountain. The trail reaches an abandoned campsite on the lake shore at 0.5 mi., and it passes the head of the pond at 0.6 mi., where the trail runs north through abandoned pasture land. Continue on the main trail and watch for a left turn to the northwest. At that point the main trail begins to follow an old logging road. (The road to the right leads 0.6 mi. to ME 85, 0.1 mi. south of Camp Kokatosi.) It passes a *spring* and climbs more steeply to a saddle between the main summit to the north and a subsidiary peak to the south. At the saddle, the trail forks right, climbs gently to the foot of some ledges, and then turns sharp left and climbs to an open ledge near the main summit. This ledge offers good views to the south and west. The actual summit (no trail) is covered with an open growth of oak and pine.

Rattlesnake Mountain
Distances from Plains Road

- *to* right turn over Nubble Pond dam: 0.2 mi. (5 min.)
- *to* north shore of Nubble Pond: 0.6 mi. (20 min.)
- *to* saddle: 1.4 mi. (50 min.)
- *to* ledge near summit: 1.6 mi. (1 hr.)
- *to* Rattlesnake main summit: 1.8 mi./2.9 km. (1 hr. 10 min.)

MOUNT AGAMENTICUS (691 ft./210 m.)

This 691-ft. monadnock rises above the coastal plain of southern York County. Because it was so conspicuous, it was an important landmark for the early European explorers who sailed along the New England coast. According to legend, it was also the burial place of either St. Aspinquid or Passaconaway. There is a fire tower at the top, which was the site of a radar observation post during World War II. There is an unused ski development on the north slope of the mountain. Refer to the USGS York Harbor quadrangle, 7.5-minute series.

The best approach route from the south is the Maine Turnpike. Take the York exit right just before the tollgate; turn left across the turnpike and take the second right on Chase Pond Rd. (Go past Chase Pond on the left.) Turn left on Mountain Rd. and bear left at a small village. From this point it is 1.6 mi. to the Big A summit road. From the north, follow US 1 through Ogunquit. Turn right on Clay Hill Rd.

Cross I-95 at 2.4 mi. from US 1 and at 4.1 mi. turn right on Mountain Rd. At 5.7 mi. reach the summit road.

The blacktop entrance road turns right and goes uphill 0.7 mi. to the summit. The dirt road straight ahead leads around the mountain 1.1 mi. to a road on the right, which leads 0.3 mi. to the parking area at the base of the ski lifts.

The road to the summit, which has two hairpin turns, should be driven with care. At the summit is a parking area and a closed ski lodge. Because of vandalism the road may be closed except when the fire warden is on duty.

The trail (now a jeep road) from the base starts from the northeast corner of the clearing and climbs, steeply at times, around the north and east of the mountain, joining the blacktop road near the top. A path diverges right from the trail near the top and leads through woods to the open summit.

Mount Agamenticus
Distance from ski-area base

to Agamenticus summit: 0.5 mi./0.8 km. (30 min.)

OSSIPEE HILL (1058 ft./322 m.)

Ossipee Hill (also called Ossipee Mountain) is located in Waterboro. There is a MFS fire tower on its summit. The views are especially good to the east over the flat Saco River Valley and on to Portland Harbor and Casco Bay. A forest fire in 1947 burned off much of the mountain. Refer to the USGS Buxton quadrangle, 15-minute series.

From ME 5 at Waterboro Center, take the crossroad southwest and immediately turn sharp right onto a paved road beyond the fire station. This road is good enough for all kinds of cars for 1 mi. The remaining distance to the summit is rough, rocky, and steep; don't try to drive anything but a four-wheel-drive vehicle with high clearance. The road rises gradually west-northwest about 1.8 mi. to a saddle. Then it turns south, veering to the southwest as it approaches the summit.

Ossipee Hill

Distances from ME 5
  to Saddle: 1.8 mi.
  to Ossipee summit: 2.6 mi./4.2 km. (1 hr. 40 min.)

DOUGLAS HILL (1416 ft./430 m.)

This hill, west of Sebago Lake, offers excellent views of the Presidentials, Pleasant Mountain, and the Atlantic Ocean. It is the highest of the Saddleback Hills. Refer to the USGS Sebago Lake quadrangle, 15-minute series.

Turn west from ME 107 onto Douglas Hill Rd. There is no sign, but the intersection is 0.5 mi. north of the junction of ME 107 and Macks Hill Rd., and 1 mi. south of Sebago. After 0.9 mi. take a sharp left turn at the top of a hill and go 0.5 mi. farther to a loop-shaped parking area with a Nature Conservancy sign. The path starts between two stone pillars and is easy to follow to the top, where there is a stone observation tower and a large rock inscribed *Non sibi sed omnibus* ("Not just for myself, but for all").

Douglas Hill

Distance from parking area
  to Douglas summit: 0.3 mi./0.5 km. (15 min.)

MOUNT CUTLER (1232 ft./375 m.)

The open ledges of this summit in Hiram offer good views of the White Mountains to the northwest. Refer to the USGS Cornish and Hiram quadrangles, 7.5-minute series.

At the junction of ME 5 and ME 117 in Hiram, cross the

cement bridge to the west bank of the Saco River. Drive to the left of Hiram Village Store and continue west on Mountain View Rd. to the site of an old railroad station, where there is ample parking. The red-blazed trail starts by following an overgrown road that is across the tracks. In 100 yd. it turns right into a picnic area. (The trail to the left leads to an old gold mine.) The trail up the mountain continues straight ahead from the upper left-hand end of the picnic area. It climbs the first ledge, and soon it turns sharply left. At this turn a faint trail to the right leads 60 yd. to an overlook above the ledges facing the bridge. The main trail soon reaches the long, open ridge of Mount Cutler, where south-facing ledges look down on the Saco River. The trail leads west 0.3 mi. to the east summit and 0.6 mi. farther to the main summit.

Mount Cutler
Distances from railroad station site

   to overlook: 0.4 mi. (20 min.)

   to Mount Cutler, east summit: 0.7 mi. (40 min.)

   to Mount Cutler, main summit: 1.3 mi./2.1 km. (1 hr. 5 min.)

PLEASANT MOUNTAIN (2006 ft./610 m.)

This mountain on the Denmark-Bridgton town line rises abruptly from the comparatively flat surrounding countryside. It is an isolated mountain mass that stretches about 4 mi. on a north–south line. The ledgy, open main summit, where there is an MFS fire tower, was once known as House Peak because there was a hotel there from 1873–1907. At least six other summits along the ridge also have names. The mountain was burned over in about 1860, and the forest and ledges are open enough for many views. The views from the main summit and from Big Bald Peak are outstanding. The southeastern face of Mount Washington, 29 mi. to the northwest, is particularly noticeable. The Pleasant Mountain ski area is on the northern slope of the north peak. Refer to the USGS Fryeburg quadrangle, 15-minute series, and the Pleasant Mountain quadrangle, 7.5-minute series.

Firewarden's Trail (Old Carriage Road)

Although not the most scenic route up Pleasant Mountain, this trail is the most popular one. It climbs to the main summit from the west. From US 302 turn south on the road opposite Cabins in the Pines Motel. This turn is 2.6 mi. west of the access road to the ski area and 7 mi. east of Fryeburg. On the side road, stay right at all road junctions. There is a farmhouse on the left 1.2 mi. from US 302 with free parking and trail signs.

For its first half, the trail is actually a truck road (sometimes open to private cars). It crosses a brook and climbs easily along its north bank. It recrosses the brook at the warden's cabin, where there is a spring and an approved campsite with a shelter. The trail narrows to a rough jeep road (not open to private cars) and swings right (southeast) and climbs steadily to the summit ridge. In the final 0.2 mi., the Bald Peak Trail comes in on the left (sign) and there is a storm shelter to the right.

Firewarden's Trail
Distances from parking area at farmhouse

to warden's cabin, spring, and campsite: 1.3 mi. (50 min.)
to Bald Peak Trail junction: 2.3 mi. (1 hr. 50 min.)
to Pleasant Mountain summit: 2.5 mi./4 km. (2 hr.)

Southwest Ridge Trail

This attractive scenic trail, which was once popular but has not been maintained for many years, is now again being used by hikers and local camp groups and for snowmobiling.

It is therefore becoming less obscure and easier to follow. The trail will be cleared from the southwest summit to the Ledges Trail in the spring of 1988.

The trail leaves the northeast side of Lake Road (gravel) 3.5 mi. from the Moose Pond dam on ME 160 in Denmark and 2.9 mi. from US 302 in East Fryeberg. It begins at a logging yard (1987) opposite a gravel driveway leading to Long Pond and follows a woods road, marked by cairns, generally northeast through mixed hardwoods, becoming steeper through pine forest. At approximately 0.4 mi. the trail turns sharply right (southeast), slabs across the hill, turns left, and reaches the open ledges at 0.6 mi. The trail ascends the mostly open ridge, northeasterly, marked by cairns to the southwest summit (1900 ft.) at 1.6 mi., with almost constant views over Moose Pond and Beaver Pond, as well as back to Long Pond. The trail, keeping to the ridge, descends over a short saddle and ascends to the open middle summit (1904 ft.) at 2.0 mi., drops into a saddle and passes a very small pond, swings east at approximately 2.4 mi., climbs to the ridge, and ends at the Ledges Trail at 2.7 mi.

Southwest Ridge Trail
Distances from Lake Road
- *to* southwest summit: 1.6 mi.
- *to* middle summit: 2.0 mi.
- *to* Ledges Trail: 2.7 mi.
- *to* Pleasant Mountain summit: 2.9 mi./4.7 km. (2 hr. 15 min.)

Ledges Trail (formerly called Moose Trail)
The trail leaves the western side of the paved road along the western side of Moose Pond 3.3 mi. south of US 302, 1.5 mi. south of the Bald Peak Trail, and 0.6 mi. north of the Walker's (narrows) Bridge that separates the two sections of Moose Pond. Park beside the road.

The trail, marked by a red *M* and arrow on a tree, begins on a logging road between power poles 42 and 43 and gradually climbs through overgrown hardwoods. At 0.5 mi. a fork to the right leads to a *spring*.

Following the left fork, the main trail crosses a stream bed (usually dry) and enters an open beech forest. Then, steeper for the next 0.3 mi., it slabs across a wet moss-covered shelf and finally reaches the ledges, with excellent views to the south.

The trail follows the ledges with the southwest summit visible ahead on the left. At 1.6 mi. the Southwest Ridge Trail comes in on the left. It climbs through oak scrub and blueberry bushes to the main summit tower. Views to the west, including Fryeburg and the Saco River basin and ponds, are outstanding.

Descending, the trail enters the woods on a southeasterly bearing from the tower.

Ledges Trail
Distances from paved road

> *to* fork: *est.* 0.5 mi. (25 min.)
> *to* lower end of ledges: 1 mi. (1 hr.)
> *to* Southwest Ridge Trail junction: 1.6 mi. (1 hr. 30 min.)
> *to* Pleasant Mountain summit: 1.8 mi./2.9 km. (1 hr. 40 min.)

Bald Peak Trail

This trail climbs the eastern side of Pleasant Mountain to Big Bald Peak, and then runs south along the ridge to join the Firewarden's Trail just below the main summit.

When combined with the Ledges Trail and a 1.5-mi. walk on the road, the Bald Peak Trail forms an enjoyable circuit. The ski trail described below also allows a circuit. There is *no sure water* on this trail during dry periods.

To reach the trail follow the paved road along the western shore of Moose Pond to a point about 1.8 mi. south of the road's junction with US 302, and about 1.3 mi. south of the Pleasant Mountain ski area. Just south of Pleasant Mountain East and 0.1 mi. south of the entrance to East Pinnacle Condominiums, a logging road on the right (between poles 30 and 31) leads into a yarding area (sign). Park there. The trail (flagged with orange tape) starts west from the back right-hand corner of the clearing, crosses a brook, and climbs steeply. At 0.2 mi. turn left and follow the north bank of the brook. At 0.4 mi. a short spur trail (sign) leads left to the Needle's Eye, a brook cascading through a cleft in the ledge. At 0.7 mi., just before the second of two small brooks, turn left (the North Link Trail turns right). Climb steeply through a stand of hemlocks, then come out of some scrub onto the ledges (cairn) and, turning left 100 yd., reach Big Bald Peak (1940 ft.) at 1.1 mi. There are excellent views in all directions.

At the cairn (and sign), the red-blazed North Ridge Trail comes in on the right from the top of the ski area via the north peak. Descending, note that the trail to the ski area continues straight ahead (north); the Bald Peak Trail bears right (east-northeast).

From Big Bald Peak, the Bald Peak Trail follows the crest of the ridge, first south, and then southwest over two humps toward the main summit. At 2.2 mi. from the start, the trail joins the Firewarden's Trail, which leads left (south) past the storm shelter to Pleasant Mountain summit and the fire tower.

Descending, the Bald Peak Trail diverges right from the Firewarden's Trail (sign) about 0.2 mi. north of the tower.

Another route up the mountain follows the ski trail to the warming hut on north peak. From there, turn left on the

North Ridge Trail and follow it to its junction with the Bald Peak Trail.

Bald Peak Trail

Distances from road
- *to* Needle's Eye Trail: 0.4 mi. (35 min.)
- *to* brook crossing and North Link Trail junction: 0.7 mi. (50 min.)
- *to* Big Bald Peak summit: 1.1 mi. (1 hr. 20 min.)
- *to* Firewarden's Trail junction: 2.2 mi. (1 hr. 50 min.)
- *to* Pleasant Mountain main summit (via Firewarden's Trail): 2.4 mi./3.9 km. (1 hr. 55 min.)

North Link Trail

This new (1987) trail runs from a point 0.7 mi up the Bald Peak Trail to the North Ridge Trail near North Peak. It allows an interesting loop hike over these two peaks.

North Link Trail

Distance from Bald Peak Trail
- *to* North Ridge Trail: *est.* 0.5 mi./0.8 km. (25 min.)

North Ridge Trail

This trail begins at the base of the Pleasant Mountain ski area. From the base lodge (which is open all year), the red-blazed trail follows the chairlift directly up the mountain for 1 mi. to the warming hut at North Peak. The views are extensive. The North Ridge Trail leads south from the warming hut past the chairlift from Pleasant Mountain East. Descend 100 yd. on the upper edge of the southernmost ski trail. At the first turn enter the woods on the right. The North Link Trail enters from the gully on the left. The trail turns due west, stays level for a bit, and then goes slightly downhill. At 1.2 mi. it turns left and leads over a short, steep ledge (the summit of North Peak is now overgrown) and then runs through open pitch pine to a low peak about 0.5 mi. from the warming hut. There, a side trail leads west to a lookout with a view of Big Bald Peak. The main trail bears right and drops down to a col before heading up to Big Bald Peak. Just before the final climb up the cone, the Bald Peak Trail comes in from the left.

North Ridge Trail
Distances from Pleasant Mountain ski area base lodge

- *to* warming hut: 1 mi. (1 hr.)
- *to* North Link Trail junction: 1.1 mi. (1 hr. 5 min.)
- *to* side trail to lookout: 1.5 mi. (1 hr. 25 min.)
- *to* Big Bald Peak summit (via Bald Peak Trail): 2 mi./(3.2 km. (1 hr. 45 min.)

BURNT MEADOW MOUNTAIN
(north peak 1575 ft./479 m.)

Located in Brownfield, this mass consists of three summits of nearly equal height. Deep cols separate the middle peak, Stone Mountain (1624 ft.), from the northern and southern peaks (1575 ft. and 1592 ft., respectively). Fire swept the entire mountain in 1947, and the trails that existed then disappeared. Trail development by snowmobilers and the construction of a ski area, now abandoned, have opened up new routes. Refer to the USGS Kezar Falls quadrangle, 15-minute series, and the Brownfield quadrangle, 7.5-minute series.

One approach is the eastern spur of the northern peak. This trail was reopened in 1984. From the junction of ME 113/5 and ME 160 in East Brownfield, drive west and south on ME 160 through Brownfield and past Burnt Meadow Pond. Park where the prominent eastern spur of the northern peak comes down to the highway. This point is 3 mi. from the junction with ME 113 and 0.4 mi. south of Burnt Meadow Pond. The cairned, blue-blazed trail heads west up the slope, staying on the southern edge of the ridge. At 0.4 mi. it passes over a small hump and drops slightly into a shallow col. Beyond the col, continue west up the crest of the spur, which becomes steeper and more open, with a sharp dropoff on the left, as it rises to the summit. There is *no water* on the trail.

Another approach to the summit leads up the slopes of the Burnt Meadow Mountain ski area, which is visible from ME 113. The ski area is south of the ME 113/60 junction on ME 160 and west of Burnt Meadow Pond. Follow the ski trail to the ridge, turn left, and travel along the ridge (snowmobile trail) for about 0.6 mi. to the summit.

Burnt Meadow Mountain
Distance from ME 160 (via eastern spur)
> *to* northern peak summit: 1.2 mi./1.9 km. (1 hr. 30 min.)

PEARY MOUNTAIN (958 ft./292 m.)

The open ledges of this little mountain in Brownfield afford good views of the White Mountains and the mountains of western Maine. Refer to the USGS Brownfield quadrangle, 7.5Dminute series.

At the junction of ME 160 and ME 113 in East Brownfield proceed north on ME 113 for 2.2 mi. to Farnsworth Rd. Turn west on Farnsworth Rd. 1.4 mi. to the bridge crossing the Little Saco River. The trail (snowmobile trail), not marked, begins at the east side of the stream and heads south on the level and then at a gradual grade to a col at 0.8 mi. at a small clearing, with a fireplace on the right. Turn left (southeast) off the trail at this point through open woods and ledges 0.2 mi to the south summit. There are good views in all directions. The main summit is 0.4 mi. northeast across open ledges and scrub without a trail. Views are to the east and north.

Peary Mountain
Distances from trailhead
to col: 0.8 mi. (35 min.)
to south summit: 1 mi./1.6 km. (45 min.)
to main summit: 1.4 mi./2.3 km. (1 hr.)

STARKS MOUNTAIN (1037 ft./315 m.)

The most traveled and scenic route up this low mountain near Fryeburg is along the ski trail. Refer to the USGS Fryeburg quadrangle, 15-minute and 7.5-minute series.

Turn southeast from US 302 on a road 1 mi. southwest of the junction with ME 113. Cross the railroad tracks and follow a dirt road left 0.8 mi. to an open area at the base of the ski trail. Park here. Turn right and follow the ski slope up the incline to the end of the ski trail. Then hike through a wooded area on a jeep trail and over open ledges to the radio tower on the summit. There are splendid views from the trail on the way up as well as from the top. Many varieties of moss grow on the ledges.

Starks Mountain
Distance from parking area
to Starks summit: 0.5 mi./0.8 km. (30 min.)

JOCKEY CAP (600 ft./182 m.)

This ledge near Fryeburg, ME, rises perpendicularly about 200 ft. above the valley and offers an excellent view in all directions. At the top, there is a bronze profile of the surrounding summits, a monument to Robert E. Peary. Refer to the USGS Fryeburg quadrangle, 15-minute and 7.5-minute series.

A trail leaves the north side of US 302, 1 mi. east of Fryeburg, through a gateway between a store and the Jockey Cap

Cabins. It soon reaches Molly Lockett's cave, named for the last of the Pequawket Indians who is said to have used it for a shelter. The trail then divides. The left branch continues ahead, circling to the west; the right branch turns abruptly right and climbs steeply, hugging the east side of the ledge. Be alert descending, since there are many side paths that do not lead back to the cabins (Round trip by either route: 25 min.)

Jockey Cap

Distance from US 302
   to summit: 0.2 mi./3 km. (15 min.)

Oxford Hills

This section describes the part of Oxford County that lies between US 302 on the south and the Androscoggin River on the north. The summits in the eastern part of the Oxford Hills are scattered. They include, among others, Streaked Mountain (1770 ft.) near South Paris, Speckled Mountain (2207 ft.) in the secluded Shagg Pond area, Mount Zircon (2240 ft.) south of Rumford, Mount Abram (1960 ft.), with its ski slope, near Locke Mills, and Mount Tire'm (1104 ft.), a good viewpoint in Waterford.

Farther west the hills build up into the continuous mountainous areas of the Evans Notch-Chatham region, which is along the Maine-New Hampshire border. Most of these mountains lie within the White Mountain National Forest, where the network of trails is more complete and signs and maintenance are usually better. This guide describes those summits that lie in Maine, plus West Royce, just over the line in New Hampshire. For a description of the other New Hampshire summits, see the *AMC White Mountain Guide*. Most of the western Oxford hills appear on the Carter-Mahoosuc map in this guide.

The minerals of the Oxford Hills are interesting, especially the Mount Mica Mine near Paris Hill and the Bumpus Mine between Bethel and Lynchville.

There are four small White Mountain National Forest campgrounds in the region covered here. One is Crocker Pond, which you can reach from US 2 at West Bethel or from ME 5 south of Bethel. Hastings Campground is on the Evans Notch Rd. just south of its junction with the Wild River Rd. The Cold River and Basin campgrounds are 0.3 mi. west of the Maine-New Hampshire border and just south of Evans Notch.

STREAKED MOUNTAIN (1770 ft./539 m.)

Streaked Mountain in Hebron and Buckfield, is a conspicuous rounded summit with open ledges that command fine views in all directions. It is easy to reach, and there is a MFS fire tower on the summit. Refer to the USGS Buckfield quadrangle, 15-minute series, and the West Sumner quadrangle, 7.5-minute series.

Turn southeast from ME 117 on a paved road about 5.3 mi. northeast of ME 26 in South Paris and 5.3 mi. southwest of Buckfield. Drive 0.5 mi. past the power line, which leads straight up the mountain. The path starts to the right of the brook, soon enters the woods, and climbs steeply onto the ledges. After that it is an open climb to the top, as the trail slabs along the ledges to the left and joins the power line. *Descending*, leave the power line at the second pole, and slab left down the ledges. Be careful not to go too far south and miss the point where the trail enters the woods.

From the Buckfield side, the climb to the summit is longer but more gradual. Turn south off ME 117 on Sodom Rd., about a mile west of the center of Buckfield and 3.5 mi. east of the Buckfield/Paris line. Keep straight on paved and gravel road 2.3 mi. Park out of the way of logging operations at "Times Square" painted in yellow on a small hemlock tree with a geodetic marker at its foot. The trail begins on a woods road to the right, crossing Bicknell Brook several times. Go right of the triangular piece where the road from Kings Hill comes in from the left. (See the snowmobile signs to Streaked Mountain.) The road widens through logging operations, then reenters woods. Bear left up into small hemlocks at the next fork, then through hardwoods. Turn left at the intersection with Whitman School Rd. (unmarked here). After passing a house on the left, the road swings around right, passes a cabin, and goes west and southwest up ledges to the summit.

Streaked Mountain
Distance from road on South Paris side
  to Streaked Mountain summit: 0.5 mi./0.8 km. (30 min.)
Distance from "Times Square" on Buckfield side
  to Streaked Mountain summit: 4 mi./6.4 km. (2 hr.)

SINGLEPOLE RIDGE (1420 ft./433 m.)

Across the valley southwest of Streaked Mountain, this open ridge offers a broad view to the west and southwest. Brett Hill Rd. climbs south off ME 117, 3.1 mi. west of the Buckfield/Paris line for 0.4 mi. and turns west. The trail begins straight ahead (south) on a gravel road. Take the left fork at 0.4 mi. where the trail levels out. At 1.1 mi. take the right fork up ledge or bear right at the next fork soon thereafter. The open ledge summit at 1.3 mi. continues to an outlook at 1.4 mi. Back down 0.1 mi. a road leads north by a quarry and down to rejoin the trail.

Singlepole Ridge
Distance from Brett Hill Road turn
  to summit: 1.3 mi./2.1 km. (40 min.)

CROCKER HILL (1374 ft./419 km.)

Crocker Hill, locally called Brown Mountain, in Paris, site of George L. Vose's 1868 panorama of the White Mountains, also offers views of the surrounding countryside and other mountains. Refer to the USGS West Sumner quadrangle, 7.5-minute series.

Leave Paris Hill between two houses on a rise at the east end of Lincoln St. and continue east (Mt. Mica Rd.) for 0.8 mi. Take the dirt road left 0.8 mi. to a left turn and park. The Old Crocker Hill carriage road leaves straight ahead. The first road left leads to the old stamping mill. The main trail is a little farther on. Take the left fork where the old carriage road divides. The trail ascends gradually then veers sharply right just above the mill. A few yards after the switchback, on the left, is the old mine shaft. Farther on, after a switchback left, the trail leaves the road and proceeds right up over ledges.

At the first summit clearing continue east to another clearing for an overlook of other hills and villages. An alternate return trail leads right (south) from the path between the two clearings. This trail proceeds down through the woods and comes out at the fork in the carriage road.

Details about local climbs and mineral dumps can be obtained at either the white or the red house on the dirt road (AMC members).

Crocker Hill
Distance from parking place
   to Crocker Summit: 0.5 mi./0.8 km. (30 min.)

BEAR MOUNTAIN (1208 ft./367 m.)

Access to Bear Mountain, in Hartford, is via the Old County Rd. This road used to serve a fire tower (now dismantled) and logging operations. It is no longer good enough for passenger cars. Refer to the USGS Buckfield quadrangle in both the 15-minute and the 7.5-minute series.

From ME 4 at North Turner, turn west on ME 219. At 0.4 mi. turn right across the outlet of Bear Pond. Then take an immediate (0.1 mi.) left along the northern shore of the pond. Follow the blacktop road 2.3 mi. to a crossroad, turn right, and drive 0.1 mi. to the last house on the left. Ask the owner for permission to park in the farmyard. Follow the road past a brook immediately beyond the farm and, still following the road, gradually climb the ridge. As the road levels out, a trail to the right leads to the western summit of Bear Mountain. (Stay to the right at all intersecting logging roads.) There is a good view to the southwest.

The main road continues straight ahead toward the height-of-land. After passing a road on the left, it swings around to the right, south. Note the view to the south across Bear Pond. Usually, trucks and jeeps can handle the road to the summit.

Bear Mountain
Distances from farmyard
to side trail to western summit: *est.* 0.8 mi. (35 min.)
to main summit: 2 mi./3.2 km. (1 hr. 25 min.)

BLACK MOUNTAIN (2133 ft./650 m.)

A broad, flat mass, this mountain lies in Sumner and Peru, east of adjacent Speckled Mountain. There are about five more or less definite summits, running roughly east and west. A trail with no signs climbs to the easternmost summit (2080 ft.) from the Sumner side. Refer to the USGS Buckfield quadrangle, 15-minute series, and the Worthley Pond quadrangle, 7.5-minute series.

Turn north off ME 219, 3.3 mi. west of Hartford/Sumner Elementary School. Go left on Labrador Pond Rd. at 1.4 mi. At 2.4 mi. take the right fork onto Black Mountain Rd. (Redding Rd., the left fork, reaches Shagg Pond in 5 mi.) Drive another 1.5 mi. to the last house, bear left 0.4 mi. on a rough dirt road, and park near a wood road on the right. Cross the brook, fork left at the first logging yard, and take the right trail up the mountain (approximately 20° mag.). The road levels out in 0.5 mi. and crosses the brook. About 4 min. beyond the brook, take the left (north) fork at a cairn and in about another 200 yd. turn right (northeast) onto the trail (cairn). The trail, partly eroded but well cleared in 1986, climbs steadily northeast to ledges and the eastern summit. The view to the east and south is only partly open. Woods cover the main summit, 0.5 mi. to the west-northwest, and there is no trail.

Black Mountain
Distance from parking place
>   to Black Mountain, eastern summit: 1.3 mi./2.1 km.
>   (1 hr. 20 min.)

BALD MOUNTAIN (1692 ft./516 m.)

This mountain is in the northeastern corner of Woodstock near Shagg Pond. Together with neighboring Speckled Mountain, just to the east, it offers interesting hiking in a little-known, secluded area. It is easiest to reach by approaching Shagg Pond through Sumner from ME 219. Refer to the USGS Bryant Pond and Buckfield quadrangles, 15-minute series, and the Mount Zircon quadrangle, 7.5-minute series.

From the public landing at Shagg Pond, continue along the road for 0.5 mi. to a parking area at the top of the hill. (You can also reach the parking area by driving southeast from Abbotts Mill.) Park and take the road on the right leading to Little Concord Pond, which comes in sight in 0.4 mi. The trail up Bald Mountain leads right just before the road reaches the pond. The trail starts at the top of a 20-ft. ledge (cairn). To reach it, climb the crack of the ledge to the right. At the top, locate the cairn and from there hike up the ridge to the summit. From the ledges south of the summit there is a fine view of the Shagg Pond area. The next item describes how to reach Speckled Mountain from the Bald Mountain ledges.

Bald Mountain
Distances from parking area
   to Little Concord Pond: 0.4 mi.
   to Bald Mountain summit: 1 mi./1.6 km. (1 hr.)

SPECKLED MOUNTAIN (2183 ft./665 m.)

Speckled Mountain is to the east of Bald Mountain in Peru. The route to it from the summit of Bald Mountain drops into a col and follows the ridge to the Speckled summit. This mountain's outstanding feature is its rugged southern face—a line of nearly sheer cliffs. The views from the summit are extensive in all directions. Refer to the USGS Bryant Pond and Buckfield quadrangles, 15-minute series, and the Mount Zircon quadrangle, 7.5-minute series.

Route from Bald Mountain
From the ledge viewpoint on Bald Mountain follow the open ledge southeast to find a red-blazed trail north to the col, cross a snowmobile trail, then climb generally east to the ridge and summit of Speckled Mountain. The trail is obscure in some areas.

Route from Bald Mountain
Distance from Bald Mountain ledges
   to Speckled Mountain summit: 1.3 mi./2.1 km. (1 hr. 10 min.)

Speckled Mountain Pasture Trail
The Speckled Mountain Pasture Trail offers a direct approach to the mountain in addition to the traverse from Bald Mountain. Views are open to the north.

From ME 108 in West Peru, drive southwest past a school for about 4.8 mi. The trail starts as a jeep road to the left (south) at the top of a rise. In dry weather, a car with high clearance and four-wheel drive can keep going for about 0.2 mi. from the road to a small gravel pit on the left (a good parking area), or possibly for 0.4 mi. to a small turn-off. Jeeps can go all the way to the stone wall mentioned below.

From the main road, go 1 mi. to an old wood yard and a fork in the road. Take the right fork (the left fork is a snow-mobile trail, which crosses the brook) and follow the road, passing an old camp on the right, for another mile to a large and obvious stone wall. Turn left and follow the line of the wall. After the wall ends in about 0.3 mi., just after crossing a logging road, its line becomes a yellow/red-blazed prop-erty line of the Oxford Paper Company and leads directly to-ward the ridge of Speckled Mountain. About 200 ft. from the ridge, the blazed property line turns west. From this point, you can follow the blazes, cairns, and yellow flagging to the summit.

Speckled Mountain Pasture Trail
Distance from paved road
   to Speckled Mountain summit (via ridge): 3 mi./4.8 km. (2 hr.)

MOUNT ZIRCON (2240 ft./683 m.)

This mountain is in the towns of Milton and Peru. The view is well worth the climb. To reach Mount Zircon, take the highway between Rumford and Abbotts Mill on the south bank of the Androscoggin. Refer to the USGS Bryant Pond quadrangle, 15-minute series, and the Mount Zircon quadrangle, 7.5-minute series.

The Mount Zircon Spring Water Company asks hikers to inform them before climbing, either at the office or by tele-phone (207-369-9943). A private road (rebuilt in 1987) with a locked gate leaves the highway just west of the Mount Zircon

Spring Water Company bottling plant. Take the left fork at 1.0 mi. The road becomes an overgrown path 0.2 mi. after passing the spring house on the left at 1.5 mi. The trail, marked with orange arrows and blazes, leaves the eastern side of the path about 2 mi. south of the highway. It is steep, but mostly wide and clear to the rocky summit. Hikers can get *water* just south of the foot of the trail near the site of the former warden's cabin.

Mount Zircon
Distances from main highway
> *to* start of trail (via truck road): 2 mi. (1 hr. 10 min.)
> *to* Zircon summit: 2.8 mi./4.5 km. (1 hr. 55 min.)

MOUNT ABRAM (1960 ft./597 m.)

Mount Abram, in Greenwood, offers interesting views to the north and west from high pastures and ledges. There is a ski area on the northeastern slope of the mountain, but it does not affect the route described here. A chairlift runs to the summit, however. Refer to the USGS Bryant Pond and Bethel quadrangles, 15-minute series, and the Bryant Pond and Greenwood quadrangles, 7.5-minute series.

Take a paved road that goes east from ME 35 about 3 mi. south of Bethel and about 0.3 mi. north of the Albany-Greenwood town line. About 1 mi. from the turn take the left fork to B.L. Harrington's farm high on the western slope of the mountain. A dirt road bears right just before the farm and continues for 0.4 mi. up to the renovated old Harrington homestead. From the northern end of this building walk north then to the right across an open field. The trail starts up the slope in about 0.1 mi. crossing a small brook at the edge of the woods. At 0.3 mi. take the right fork uphill in an easterly direction. (The left fork is a gently undulating snow-mobile trail, through woods, around the mountain. It crosses a field to a large red house, reaching Howe Hill Rd. 0.6 mi. from the junction.) Continue up the trail, cross the clearing and then up steeply, reaching a hedgerow with snow-making pipes at 0.7 mi. Clamber across, noting the location for return, and turn right up a wide ski trail to the summit and Ski Patrol hut. The best views are to the west, reached by an open path to a field a bit below the summit. The ski trail can be rejoined from the field's lower right corner.

Alternatively, you can leave ME 26 on a road leading south in Greenwood. At about 1.4 mi. the road bears left (west), and soon after that a road leads left to the base of the ski area. From there, you can follow ski trails to the summit.

Mount Abram
Distance from old Harrington homestead
   to Abram summit: 1.1 mi./1.8 km. (1 hr.)

MOUNT TIRE'M (1104 ft./336 m.)

Mount Tire'm in the town of Waterford yields a good view, with little effort, of the Long Lake region. Refer to the USGS Norway quadrangle, 15-minute series.

The Old Squire Brown Trail
The trail starts 100 yd. beyond (northwest of) the Waterford Center Community Building, where you can park. A sign on the left, "The Old Squire Brown Trail," marks the start. Visitors are requested to stay on the trail, because it is on private property. After passing two stone walls, the trail curves left and crosses a gully. About 75 yd. beyond, the path forks. Follow the right fork. Then the trail emerges from the woods with widening views of the hills and lakes of Waterford and Norway. From the summit, you can see the Presidential Range.

The Old Squire Brown Trail
Distance from Waterford Center Community Building
 to Tire'm summit: 0.7 mi./1.1 km. (40 min.)

SABBATTUS MOUNTAIN (1253 ft./382 m.)

The chief feature of this summit in Center Lovell is the immense, nearly vertical cliff that forms its southwestern face. From the top of the cliff impressive views of the countryside spread from Pleasant Mountain to the Baldfaces. Refer to the USGS Fryeburg quadrangle, 15-minute series, and the Center Lovell quadrangle, 7.5-minute series.

You can reach the trail by following ME 5 north from Lovell to Center Lovell. Turn right, east, 0.7 mi. past the Center Lovell General Store and continue to a fork 1.6 mi. from ME 5. Bear right at the fork and drive 0.3 mi. on the dirt road, past a house, to a small parking area on the left. The trail starts opposite the parking area. It runs along the left side of a stone wall and through a logged area. It then climbs easily past an old fire-tower site to the open summit ledges. A faint trail to the east leads in 0.3 mi. to a large boulder.

Sabbattus Mountain
Distance from parking area
 to Sabbattus summit: 0.8 mi./1.3 km. (30 min.)

EVANS NOTCH-CHATHAM REGION

The Cold River runs south from Evans Notch and flows into an extensive valley 3 mi. to the south. The valley floor is not over 600 ft. above sea level. It is divided between Stow, Maine, and Chatham, New Hampshire; the line runs almost directly up the valley. The principal summits in Maine are East Royce (3116 ft.), Ames (2686 ft.), Speckled (2906 ft.) and, to the north of Evans Notch, Caribou (2828 ft.).

The AMC Cold River Camp is in North Chatham. Two WMNF campgrounds, Basin and Cold River, are at the north end of the valley, on the west side of NH/ME 113 about 0.3 mi. west of the ME/NH border. The WMNF Hastings Campground entrance is 0.2 mi. south of the junction of NH/ME 113 and Wild River Rd. Wild River Campground (WMNF) is reached by Wild River Rd. It is about 5.7 mi. southwest of the junction of Wild River Rd. and NH/ME 113. The Kimball Ponds, South Chatham, and Fryeburg offer opportunities for fishing.

To obtain more current information about the condition of trails in the Evans Notch-North Chatham area, contact the WMNF Evans Notch Ranger District, Bridge St., Bethel ME 04217 (207-824-2134).

The 7.5-minute USGS maps are a very valuable addition to the map with this guide. Trails are named on the 7.5-minute quadrangles. See especially those for Wild River, in New Hampshire, and for Speckled Mountain, East Stoneham, Bethel, Center Lovell, and Gilead, in Maine. In the older 15-minute series, see the Bethel and Fryeburg quadrangles for Maine, and the Gorham and North Conway quadrangles for New Hampshire.

Evans Notch Road (NH/ME 113)

This scenic auto road, NH/ME 113, continues the Valley Rd. of North Chatham northward past the Brickett Place, under the impressive cliffs of East Royce, and through Evans Notch to Hastings. It crosses Evans Brook twice and ends 3.4 mi. further at US 2, just east of the bridge over Wild River in Gilead.

Evans Notch Road
Distances from the Brickett Place
   to Royce Trail (west): 75 ft.
   to service road to Speckled Mountain (east): 0.3 mi.

to Laughing Lion trailhead: 2.1 mi.

to East Royce (west) and Spruce Hill (east) trailheads: 3.1 mi.

to Haystack Notch (east) trailhead: 4.6 mi.

to Mud Brook (east) trailhead: 5.6 mi.

to Caribou (east) trailhead: 6.3 mi.

to Wheeler Brook Trail (Little Lary Brook Road) (east): 7 mi.

to Hastings (west) trailhead: 7.5 mi.

to Roost (east) trailheads: *est.* 7.1 mi. and 7.8 mi.

to US 2/Gilead: 10.9 mi.

MOUNT ROYCE (east summit 3116 ft. and west summit 3202 ft./950 m. and 976 m.)

This mountain north of North Chatham has two distinct summits. While the summit of West Royce is in New Hampshire, this section includes the trail description from the junction of the trails to the two summits. For descriptions of other trails to New Hampshire summits from the Evans Notch-Chatham region, see Section 10 of the 1987 edition of the *AMC White Mountain Guide*.

Royce Trail (AMC)

This trail starts on the western side of NH/ME 113 about 75 ft. above the entrance to the Brickett Place (about 0.3 mi. north of the entrance to the WMNF Cold River Campground). Follow the narrow logging road for about 0.3 mi. Cross Cold River, and bear right on the trail, which is blazed in blue. At 1.4 mi., the trail crosses and recrosses the river; then, crossing the southern branch of Mad River, it rises more steeply and soon passes Mad River Falls. A side trail leads left 70 ft. to a viewpoint. About 0.8 mi. above the falls, the logging road becomes a trail—rather rough with large boulders—and rises steeply below the imposing ledges for which this mountain is famous. At 1 mi. beyond the falls, the Laughing Lion Trail enters on the right. At a height-of-land, 0.2 mi. farther, after a very steep climb, a connecting trail to the East Royce Trail leads right 150 ft. to open ledges that offer excellent views of the Chatham Valley. The connecting trail continues 200 yd. to join the East Royce Trail.

From there, the Royce Trail levels off, turns left (west), descends slightly, and in 0.1 mi. crosses a brook. After that it descends, then climbs to the height-of-land between the peaks, where the Burnt Mill Brook Trail to Wild River Rd. (see the *White Mountain Guide*) bears slightly right, while the Royce Trail turns abruptly left (west) and climbs the steep wall of the col. It then continues by easy grades over ledges and through stunted spruce to the summit, where it meets the Basin Rim Trail (see the *White Mountain Guide*).

Royce Trail
Distances from NH/ME 113 (Evans Notch Road)
   to Mad River Falls: 1.6 mi. (1 hr.)
   to Laughing Lion Trail junction: 2.6 mi. (2 hr.)
   to Royce Connector Trail junction: 2.8 mi. (2 hr. 20 min.)
   to West Royce summit: 4.0 mi./6.4 km. (3 hr. 30 min.)

Laughing Lion Trail (CTA)

This trail leaves the west side of NH/ME 113 just north of a roadside picnic area, about 2.1 mi. north of the Brickett Place. It descends in a northerly direction to Cold River, then climbs steeply, mostly southwest and west, with occasional fine views down the valley. The trail continues north, generally steep, leveling off just before it ends at the Royce Trail, south of the col between East and West Royce.

Laughing Lion Trail
Distances from NH/ME 113 (Evans Notch Road)
   to Royce Trail junction: 1 mi. (1 hr.)

to East Royce summit (via Royce Trail): 1.8 mi./2.90 km. (2 hr.)

Royce Connector Trail (AMC)

This short trail connects the Royce Trail and the East Royce Trail. (Distance from Royce Trail junction to East Royce Trail junction: 0.2 mi.)

East Royce Trail (AMC)

This trail, blazed in blue, leaves the west side of NH/ME 113 (off-road parking) just north of the height-of-land, and 3.1 mi. north of the Brickett Place. It immediately crosses Evans Brook and rises steeply, crossing several other brooks in the first half-mile. At a final brook crossing at 1 mi. (*last water*) the Royce Connector Trail to West Royce enters from the left. The East Royce Trail emerges on open ledges at about 1.1 mi., reaches an open subsidiary summit at 1.3 mi., and the true summit, also bare, 0.1 mi. farther. A spur trail can be followed over several more ledges to a large open ledge with a beautiful outlook to the north and west.

East Royce Trail
Distance from NH/ME 113 (Evans Notch Road)
to East Royce summit: 1.4 mi./2.3 km. (1 hr. 50 min.)

Wheeler Brook Trail (WMNF)

This trail leaves the south side of US 2 about 2.4 mi. east of the junction of NH/ME 113 and US 2. It follows the west side of Wheeler Brook, crosses the brook several times, and, keeping generally to an old logging road, rises to its highest point, along the northwest slope of Peabody Mountain (2462 ft./750 m.; wooded, no trail). The trail descends generally southwest and ends at Little Lary Brook Rd. From here, it is 1.3 mi. to the junction with NH/ME

113, 7 mi. north of the Brickett Place and 3.9 mi. south of the US 2 intersection.

Wheeler Brook Trail

Distances from US 2
 to Little Lary Brook Road: 3.4 mi. (2 hr. 40 min.)
 to NH/ME 113 (via Little Lary Brook Road): 4.7 mi./7.6 km. (3 hr. 20 min.)

THE ROOST (1374 ft./419 m.)

This small hill, near Hastings, has fine views of the Wild River Valley, the Evans Brook Valley, and many mountains.

Roost Trail (WMNF)

This trail leaves the east side of NH/ME 113 from the north end of the lower (north) bridge over Evans Brook at Hastings. It climbs a steep bank for 100 ft., then bears right (east) and rises gradually along a wooded ridge, crosses a brook (*water unreliable*) at 0.3 mi., rises somewhat more steeply at its upper end, and emerges on a small rock ledge. A side trail descends east through woods to spacious open ledges where the views are excellent. The main trail continues, descends generally southeast at a moderate grade, crosses a small brook, and swings back west on an old road to return to Evans Notch Rd. just south of the upper (south) bridge over Evans Brook at Hastings.

Roost Trail
Distances from north trailhead, NH/ME 113
 to the Roost: 0.5 mi. (25 min.)
 to south trailhead, NH/ME 113: 1.3 mi./2.1 km. (50 min.)

MOUNT CARIBOU (2828 ft./862 m.)

This mountain, called Calabo in the 1853 Walling map of Oxford County, is in the town of Mason, ME. The bare, ledgy summit affords excellent views. The Caribou and Mud Brook trails make a pleasant loop.

Caribou Trail (WMNF)

The trail leaves the east side of NH/ME 113 about 6.3 mi. north of the Brickett Place. There is parking space for several cars at the trailhead. The trail immediately crosses Morrison Brook and follows it for about 2.3 mi., crossing and recrossing several times. One crossing, at 1.6 mi., is at the head of 25-ft. Kees Falls. The trail levels off at the height-of-land as it crosses the col between Gammon Mountain and Mount Caribou. Here the Mud Brook Trail leaves right for the summit of Mount Caribou, passing Caribou Shelter and Caribou Spring (*water unreliable*) in 0.3 mi. The Caribou Trail continues ahead at the junction, descends more rapidly, and turns northeast toward the valley of Bog Brook, east of Peabody Mountain. The trail ends at Bog Rd., which leads to US 2, 1.3 mi. west of West Bethel. In the reverse direction, park near the gate, 2.9 mi. south of US 2. Bear left on the logging road just before Bog Rd. swings right over a bridge. The trail leaves on the right in 0.2 mi., following yellow blazes and arrow signs.

Caribou Trail
Distances from NH/ME 113

to Mud Brook Trail junction: 2.7 mi. (2 hr.)

to Mount Caribou summit: 3.2 mi. (2 hr. 30 min.)

to Bog Road: 5.2 mi./8.4 km. (3 hr. 25 min.)

Mud Brook Trail (WMNF)

This trail leaves NH/ME 113 5.6 mi. north of the Brickett Place, 2 mi. south of the bridge at Hastings, and just north of the Mud Brook bridge. It runs generally east along the north side of Mud Brook, rising gradually for 1.8 mi., then crossing a branch brook and swinging more steeply left (north). The trail crosses several smaller brooks and, 1 mi. from the beginning of the steep ascent, comes out on a small bare knob with excellent views east. There is a short descent into a small ravine, where *water (unreliable)* may be found. The trail then emerges above the timberline and crosses ledges for about 0.3 mi. to the summit of Mount Caribou. It descends north, passes Caribou Spring (*water unreliable*) left, Caribou Shelter right 200 ft. farther, and meets the Caribou Trail in the col.

Mud Brook Trail
Distances from NH/ME 113

to Mount Caribou summit: 3.1 mi. (2 hr. 20 min.)
to Caribou Trail junction: 3.6 mi./5.8 km. (2 hr. 35 min.)

Haystack Notch Trail (WMNF)

The shortest route from Hastings to Mason, this trail starts on the east side of NH/ME 113, 4.6 mi. north of the Brickett Place. It runs generally east, easy going with little climbing, through Haystack Notch and down the valley of the west branch of the Pleasant River to meet the Miles Notch Trail at an old road heading northeast to a paved road that leads generally north-northwest to West Bethel on US 2, across from the post office. In the reverse direction, use care to follow the trail and not several side paths.

Haystack Notch Trail
Distances from NH/ME 113

to Miles Notch Trail junction: 5.2 mi./8.4 km. (3 hr.)

to West Bethel (via old dirt road and paved road): 11.6 mi.

SPECKLED MOUNTAIN (2906 ft./886 m.)

This mountain lies east of Evans Notch, in Batchelder's Grant and Stoneham, ME. It is one of at least three mountains in Maine that have been known by this name. The summit's open ledges have excellent views in all directions. There is a *spring* about 0.1 mi. northeast of the summit, off the Red Rock Trail.

Bickford Brook Trail (WMNF)

This trail extends from the Brickett Place on NH/ME 113 to the top of Speckled Mountain. The trail enters the woods near the garage. The WMNF service road to Speckled Mountain enters on the left at 0.3 mi. In 0.6 mi. the Blueberry Ridge Trail leaves right (east) toward Bickford Slides. Another path leaves right 0.2 mi. farther for the upper end of the Slides, forming a loop. A third path to the Upper Slides leaves on the right at 0.2 mi. above the second (upper loop) path. The Bickford Brook Trail crosses a branch of the brook, then bears slightly left and rises more steeply. Farther up on the ridge the Spruce Hill Trail enters left. The trail then passes west and north of the summit of Ames Mountain and into the col between Ames and Speckled mountains, where the Blueberry Ridge Trail reenters on the right. The trail then continues upward 0.6 mi. more to the summit.

Bickford Brook Trail
Distances from the Brickett Place, NH/ME 113

to Blueberry Ridge Trail, lower junction: 0.6 mi. (30 min.)

to Spruce Hill Trail junction: 2.8 mi. (2 hr. 15 min.)

to Blueberry Ridge Trail, upper junction: 3.5 mi. (2 hr. 45 min.)

to Speckled Mountain summit: 4.1 mi./6.6 km. (3 hr. 15 min.)

Spruce Hill Trail (WMNF)

In combination with the Bickford Brook Trail, this trail is the shortest route to Speckled Mountain. It leaves the east side of NH/ME 113 3.1 mi. north of the Brickett Place, opposite the East Royce Trail (off-road parking). It ascends generally southeast through woods (with excellent views of Evans Notch) to the summit of Spruce Hill, descends to a subsidiary col, then climbs to connect with the Bickford Brook Trail. Descending, use care to note the point where the Spruce Hill Trail leaves the Bickford Brook Trail.

Spruce Hill Trail

Distances from NH/ME 113

to Bickford Brook Trail junction: 1.8 mi. (1 hr. 15 min.)

to Speckled Mountain summit (via Bickford Brook Trail): *est*. 3.1 mi./5 km. (2 hr. 15 min.)

Red Rock Trail (WMNF)

This trail, with fine views of the mountains in this section of Maine, leaves west from the Miles Notch Trail about 0.1 mi. north of an old sign marking height-of-land in Miles Notch. It bears northwest, then soon west, and ascends Red Rock Mountain. It follows the ridge to Butters Mountain with several changes in elevation. Just beyond, in the col, the Great Brook Trail diverges southeast descending to Stoneham. The trail then turns south, soon crosses the summit of Durgin Mountain, and bears southwest to the summit of Speckled Mountain. There is a *spring* near the trail about 0.1 mi. northeast of the summit.

Red Rock Trail
Distances from Miles Notch Trail junction
- *to* Great Brook Trail junction: 3.3 mi.
- *to* Speckled Mountain summit: 5.5 mi./8.9 km. (3 hr. 15 min.)

Miles Notch Trail (WMNF)

Access to the trailhead is from ME 5 in North Lovell, ME. Go north-northwest on Stoneham Rd. toward Evergreen Valley for 1.9 mi. Turn right (north) on Hut Rd. at the bottom of the hill just before a bridge (Great Brook). The trailhead is 1.5 mi. from this corner.

The Miles Notch Trail leads at first east, then generally north, and at about 0.5 mi. turns left, following yellow blazes. It climbs over a ridge and descends to nearly the starting elevation, then turns left again. The trail crosses a branch of Beaver Brook, becomes steep, and passes through Miles Notch down to where, at 3.7 mi., the Red Rock Trail leaves left (west) for Speckled Mountain. From here it descends along Miles Brook, crossing the brook and a field to the junction with the Haystack Notch Trail in Mason. A wood road may be followed, northeast, out to Flat Rd. and to West Bethel on US 2 opposite the post office.

Miles Notch Trail
Distances from trailhead
- *to* Red Rock Trail junction: 3.7 mi. (2 hr. 45 min.)
- *to* Haystack Notch Trail, old road junction: 6.1 mi./9.8 km. (3 hr. 30 min.)

Great Brook Trail (WMNF)

For access refer to the Miles Notch Trail. The trail sign is in a clearing just beyond the Miles Notch Trail. Around the corner is a gate, which is open in summer, and the road can be driven another 0.8 mi. to a locked gate. There are potholes in Red Rock Brook here, and just beyond, a bridge over Great Brook. The trail leaves the old road, follows Great Brook, mostly northwest, becoming steeper in the last 0.5 mi., reaches the ridge, and joins the Red Rock Trail in the col between Butters and Durgin mountains.

Great Brook Trail

Distances from trailhead

- *to* Red Rock Trail junction: *est.* 3.8 mi.
- *to* Speckled Mountain summit (via Red Rock Trail): 6 mi./9.7 km. (4 hr. 10 min.)

Cold Brook Trail

Access to the Cold Brook Trail is from ME 5 in North Lovell. Follow a road northwest (sign "Evergreen Valley") for 2 mi. Take the first right (sign "EVTOA") after a bridge (Great Brook) for 0.3 mi. At the WMNF (hiker) sign the dirt road straight ahead is the trail, and usually may be driven for 0.5 mi.

At 1.6 mi. pass a house "Sugar Hill," the Duncan McIntosh house, and 0.3 mi. farther cross Cold Brook. At 2.5 mi. the Link Trail, from Evergreen Valley, comes in on the left. The trail emerges on open ledges 1.5 mi. south of the summit with outstanding views for the next mile. The trail ends at the Red Rock Trail just east of the summit.

Cold Brook Trail

Distances from trailhead (paved road)

- *to* Sugar Hill: 1.6 mi. (55 min.)
- *to* Link Trail: 2.5 mi. (1 hr. 20 min.)
- *to* Speckled Mountain summit: 4.7 mi./7.6 km. (3 hr. 20 min.)

Link Trail (WMNF)

Park in the large lot below the "Inn" at Evergreen Valley Resort in East Stoneham, ME.

Follow the paved road uphill past the Inn and the condominiums on the left. Continue climbing steeply straight ahead on a dirt road. At 0.5 mi. turn right to the Chalet. Turn left and pass the small structure on the right (sign). This part of the trail, blazed blue, 1986, leads generally north to meet the Cold Brook Trail at an elevation of about 1200 ft.

Link Trail
Distances from Inn at Evergreen Valley

   to right turn to Chalet: 0.5 mi.
   to Cold Brook Trail junction: 1.4 mi./2.3 km. (1 hr.)
   to Speckled Mountain summit: 3.6 mi./5.8 km. (3 hr.)

BLUEBERRY MOUNTAIN (1820 ft./555 m.)

This mountain is a long, flat, outlying spur running southwest from Speckled Mountain. The top is mostly one big ledge, with sparse and stunted trees. There are numerous open spaces with excellent views, especially the southwest ledges on the summit. There is *water* in many places at the top except in dry seasons.

Stone House Trail (CTA)

Approach this trail and the White Cairn Trail from Shell Pond Rd., which leaves NH/ME 113 on the east side, 1.3 mi. north of the AMC Cold River Camp. A padlocked steel gate on Shell Pond Rd. 1.1 mi. in from NH/ME 113 makes it necessary to park cars at that point.

The trail leaves on the left 0.5 mi. beyond the gate, east of an open shed, follows a logging road, and approaches Rattlesnake Brook. Off-trail, downstream from an old logging road bridge, is Rattlesnake Flume, a gorge worth visiting. At a point 0.2 mi. upstream from the flume, the logging road bears uphill left, and the trail continues straight ahead. Just beyond, a side trail descends right about 150 yd. to Rattlesnake Pool, at the foot of a small cascade. In about 0.3 mi. the trail bears left on a still older logging road and at 1 mi. begins to climb, straight and steep, generally northwest, to the top of the ridge, where it ends at the Blueberry Ridge Trail, only a few steps from the top of Blueberry Mountain.

Stone House Trail
Distances from Shell Pond Road
> **to** Rattlesnake Flume: *est.* 0.2 mi. (5 min.)
> **to** Blueberry Mountain summit: 1.3 mi./2.1 km. (1 hr. 30 min.)

White Cairn Trail (CTA)

This trail provides access to the open ledge on Blueberry Mountain and, with the Stone House Trail, makes an easy half-day circuit. The trail leaves Shell Pond Rd. at a small clearing 0.2 mi. beyond the locked gate. It follows old logging roads north and west to an upland meadow, then climbs steeply up the right (east) margin of the cliffs visible from the road to a broad view of the Baldfaces and Royces. Following the crest of the cliffs to the west, the trail turns north, traversing open ledges and scrub growth along a line of cairns, to end at a junction with the Blueberry Ridge Trail, 0.2 mi. west of the upper terminus of the Stone House Trail. A short side trail crosses the upper ledges to the right (east) to a second outlook.

White Cairn Trail
Distances from Shell Pond Road
> **to** cliffs: *est.* 1 mi. (1 hr.)

to Blueberry Ridge Trail junction: *est*. 1.5 mi./2.4 km.
   (1 hr. 30 min.)

Blueberry Ridge Trail (CTA)

This trail leaves the Bickford Brook Trail at a sign 0.6 mi.
beyond the trailhead at the Brickett Place on NH/ME 113. It
descends to cross Bickford Brook, then ascends steeply
southeast to an open area just over the crest of Blueberry
Ridge, where the White Cairn Trail enters from the right.
The Stone House Trail comes in 0.2 mi. farther on the right a
short distance beyond the top of Blueberry Mountain. A
half-mile overlook loop with excellent views to the south
leaves the Blueberry Ridge Trail shortly after the White
Cairn junction and rejoins it shortly before the Stone House
junction. From the junction with the Stone House Trail,
marked by signs and a large cairn, the Blueberry Ridge Trail
to Speckled Mountain bears left and descends to a *spring
(water unreliable)*, a short distance from the trail on the left
(north). The trail turns sharply right here, continues over
ledges marked by cairns, through occasional patches of
woods, and over several humps.

Above the top of the Rattlesnake Brook ravine the trail
ends at the Bickford Brook Trail in a shallow col about 0.6
mi. below the summit of Speckled Mountain. The Bickford
Brook Trail leads somewhat more steeply through woods
and over ledges to the rocky top.

Blueberry Ridge Trail
Distances from the Brickett Place, NH/ME 113

to start of Blueberry Ridge Trail (via Bickford Brook
   Trail): 0.6 mi. (30 min.)
to Blueberry Mountain, Stone House Trail junction: 1.5
   mi. (1 hr. 30 min.)
to Bickford Brook Trail junction: 3.7 mi. (2 hr. 40 min.)

to Speckled Mountain summit (via Bickford Brook
   Trail): 4.3 mi./6.9 km. (3 hr. 20 min.)

ALBANY MOUNTAIN (1910 ft./582 m.)

Views from the open summit ledges are excellent in all directions. The area is just off the east side of the Carter-Mahoosuc map. Refer to the USGS Bethel quadrangle, 15-minute series, and the East Stoneham quadrangle, 7.5-minute series.

Albany Notch Trail (WMNF)

From US 2 at West Bethel, opposite the post office, go south on the unmarked road, which becomes FR 7, then take FR 18, following signs for Crocker Pond Campground. About 5.5 mi. from US 2 and 0.5 mi. before the campground, the trail leaves right (southwest). Park off the road. The trail is wide and almost level for 1 mi. At 0.6 mi. just before a small brook crossing, the Albany Mountain Trail leaves left (south). The Albany Notch Trail ascends to the height-of-land. Beyond there, at 1.7 mi., another trail goes left (east) and connects with the Albany Mountain Trail. The Albany Notch Trail continues south to old woods roads and ME 5.

Albany Notch Trail

Distance from FR 18
   to ME 5: *est.* 3.8 mi./6.1 km. (1 hr. 55 min.)

Albany Mountain Trail (WMNF)

This trail ascends Albany Mountain on its north slope, from the Albany Notch Trail 0.6 mi. from FR 18. About 0.5 mi. below the summit, a trail branches right (west), leading 0.5 mi. to the Albany Notch Trail on the south side of the notch. The Albany Mountain Trail continues ahead and shortly enters the open summit area. From this point the trail is well cairned and leads directly to the summit. (There are many side paths made by blueberry pickers.)

Albany Mountain Trail
Distance from Albany Notch Trail

to Albany Mountain summit: *est.* 1.4 mi./2.3 km. (1 hr. 10 min.)

TO KEZAR LAKE

Shell Pond Trail (WMNF)

Drive 1.3 mi. north of Cold River Camp on NH 113 and turn right on Shell Pond Rd. Cross a bridge over the Cold River, bear right and continue 1.1 mi. to a locked steel gate where cars must be parked. Follow the road about 0.5 mi. to the Stone House. The Shell Pond Trail starts just beyond the house (sign), goes southeast across a level field, bears left, then right, and crosses Rattlesnake Brook in about 0.4 mi. It enters the woods east of the brook and passes north of Shell Pond. It climbs gradually, crossing a brook, and ends at Deer Hill Rd. (FR 9), 1.3 mi. from the Stone House.

Shell Pond Trail
Distances from gate on Shell Pond Road

to Stone House: *est.* 0.5 mi. (15 min.)
to Deer Hill Road: *est.* 1.8 mi./2.9 km. (1 hr.)

Horseshoe Pond Trail (CTA)

This trail, blazed yellow, starts from Deer Hill Rd. (FR 9) 4.7 mi. from NH 113 at a parking area on a curve where the pond is visible. It descends past the Styles grave, enclosed by a stone wall, enters a logging road, turning right. In a few steps a path leaves left for the northwest shore of Horseshoe Pond. The main trail follows the road 300 yd., then leaves right at a cairn, ascending through an area, clearcut in 1982, to the Pine-Lord loop path north of Lord Hill.

Horseshoe Pond Trail
Distance from Deer Hill Road
   to northwest shore of Horseshoe Pond: 0.3 mi./0.5 km. (10 min.)
   to Pine-Lord loop path: *est.* 1.1 mi./1.8 km. (50 min.)

DEER HILL (1367 ft./417 m.)
LITTLE DEER HILL (1080 ft./329 m.)

Deer Hill, often called Big Deer, is located in Stow, ME, across the Cold River, east of the AMC Cold River Camp. The views from the east and south ledges are excellent. Little Deer, a lower hill west of Deer Hill that rises only about 600 ft. above the valley, has fine views of the valley and the Baldfaces from its summit ledges.

Paths to Big Deer Hill and Little Deer Hill (CTA)

The Leach Link Trail leaves Shell Pond Rd. just east of the bridge over Cold River, and runs 1.1 mi. to the dam at the AMC Cold River Camp, where one can also enter the trail. From here the Leach Link Trail continues along the river, while the path to Little Deer Hill runs level for a short distance, then rises slowly, crosses a logging road, and climbs at a moderate grade through the woods. It crosses two open ledges with views of the valley, then ascends through a short woods section before reaching the open summit of Little Deer 0.6 mi. from the dam. As an alternative, one can continue along the Leach Link Trail and ascend Little Deer via the recently reopened Ledge Trail, which passes interesting ledges and a cave, but is very steep and rough, dangerous in icy conditions, and not recommended for descent.

At the summit of Little Deer one has a choice of several routes. One can descend on the steep path that runs south from the summit and, turning right at the base of the hill, return to the starting point via the Leach Link Trail. Another path leads east from the northeast corner of the summit ledge and descends into the col. The trail then ascends gradually, generally east, to the Big Deer summit at 1.4 mi. from Cold River Camp. A few steps east of the summit there is a viewpoint, and 0.3 mi. south the trail crosses another outlook, then descends through woods. A branch trail leaves left (southeast) and runs to Deer Hill Rd. 1.4 mi. from NH 113, and a side path runs left from this branch trail to Deer Hill Spring ("Bubbling Spring"), an interesting shallow pool with air bubbles rising through a small light-colored sand area. Just beyond this junction the trail swings right (west) and for a short distance passes through scrub in an old clear-cut area. It descends through woods, crosses an old road, then a small brook in a shallow gully, shortly bears left, then sharp left at a junction, where the south path to Little Deer Hill turns right. From this junction the trail runs nearly level out to the Leach Link Trail on the east side of the Cold River.

Deer Hill and Little Deer Hill
Distances from dam at AMC Cold River Camp
to Little Deer Hill summit: 0.6 mi. (30 min.)
to Big Deer Hill summit: 1.4 mi./2.3 km (1 hr. 15 min.)

PINE HILL (1240 ft./378 m.)
LORD HILL (1257 ft./383 m.)
HARNDON HILL (1395 ft./425 m.)

These three hills lie east of North Chatham. Although they are not high, their open ledges and pastures offer interesting views.

Paths to Pine Hill and Lord Hill (CTA)

The loop path to these hills was formerly called the Conant Trail. From NH 113 take Deer Hill Rd. (FR 9) 1.4 mi., then turn right and park. The path runs east (left at crossroads) across Colton Brook on a bridge—Colton Dam is located several hundred yards to the right from here—and soon divides. From here the path makes a loop (total distance approximately 5 mi.). To the right, the trail follows a logging road 0.6 mi. to an old cellar hole, then turns left on a logging road, then immediately left again. The trail turns left again and ascends Pine Hill, rather steeply at times, passing a fine ledge part of the way up, and reaches the summit, which has a good view north. The trail descends northeast, turns right into the woods and runs east, then turns north and passes through the cutover area, and crosses Bradley Brook in the col. It then climbs over an old road, passes an outlook over Horseshoe Pond, and reaches ledges near the summit of Lord Hill. It turns right and descends into the cutover area, then turns left at the junction right with the Horseshoe Pond Trail. The trail slabs the south side of Harndon Hill, past a cellar hole, to Harndon Hill Rd., then shortly enters a logging road, which leads back to the loop junction.

Pine Hill and Lord Hill Loop
Distances from parking area

> *to* circle junction: 0.4 mi.
> *to* Pine Hill summit: 1.9 mi.
> *to* Lord Hill ledges: 3.1 mi.
> *to* Horseshoe Pond trail junction: 3.3 mi.
> *to* circle junction: 4.9 mi./7.9 km. (3 hr.)

MINOR POINTS OF INTEREST IN
NORTH CHATHAM

Bickford Slides

Between Blueberry Mountain and the west ridge of Speckled Mountain, Bickford Brook twice passes a series of flumes, falls, and boulders of unusual beauty. There are three routes to the slides from the Bickford Brook Trail. (1) The Blueberry Ridge Trail leaves on the right 0.6 mi. from the Brickett Place, leading in 0.1 mi. to the upper end of the lower slide; (2) a path leaves on the right at 0.8 mi., leading in 0.1 mi. to the base of the upper slide and crosses the brook; and (3) a path leaves on the right at about 1 mi. for the top end of the upper slide, crosses the brook, and descends on the high bank of the gorge. Path #2 joins path #3 after crossing below the upper slide, and the trail continues down to the Blueberry Ridge Trail, making a loop of 0.8 mi. (Round-trip distance from the Brickett Place, visiting both slides: *est.* 2.3 mi., 1 hr. 35 min.)

On the way to Speckled Mountain by the Bickford Brook Trail a detour to visit the upper slide adds about 0.3 mi. Descending Blueberry Mountain, the Blueberry Ridge Trail crosses Bickford Brook at the top of the lower slide.

Cold River

A path, Leach Link, turns left (northwest) from the dam across the river from the AMC Cold River Camp, leads along the east bank of Cold River, across the outlet brook from Shell Pond, and ends at Shell Pond Rd. (Distance: 1.1 mi.)

Deer Hill Spring

Deer Hill Spring is an interesting shallow pool with air bubbles rising through a small light-colored sand area.

Turn east on the road that leaves NH/ME 113 at 0.7 mi. south of the AMC Cold River Camp entrance and just south of bridge over Chandler Brook. Cross the Cold River and continue on Deer Hill Rd. Park at a turnout in about 1.4 mi. The trail leaves left (north) and climbs easily north and northeast for about 0.6 mi. Bear right at a cairn and descend southeast and east 0.1 mi. to the spring, which is also called Bubbling Spring. (Distance from parking area: 0.7 mi.)

A short cutoff from this trail to Big Deer leaves left (north) about 75 ft. before the trail turns right to descend to the spring. The cutoff ascends west and northwest and ends at the trail leading to Big Deer (south side), about 100 ft. above an abandoned mica mine. Turn right for the summit of Big Deer. Turn left to descend to the woods road on the east side of Cold River. (Length of cutoff: 0.2 mi.)

Grafton Notch and Mahoosuc Range Areas

This section covers the area bounded on the south and west by the Androscoggin River; on the north by Umbagog, Richardson, and Mooselookmeguntic lakes of the Rangeley Lakes chain; and on the east by ME 17. Grafton Notch, in the heart of this area, lies between Old Speck (4180 ft.) on the west and Baldpate Mountain (3812 ft.) on the east. It is traversed by ME 26.

The Mahoosuc Range, which appears on the Carter-Mahoosuc map that comes with this guide, extends southwest from Old Speck across the Maine-New Hampshire line to Mount Hayes near Gorham, New Hampshire. As the crow flies, the range is about 17 mi. long, but it is nearly 30 mi. long by trail. Mount Goose Eye (3870 ft.) and Mahoosuc Notch are among the many interesting features of the Mahoosuc Range. Both lie on the Maine side of the border, but the usual access is via the Mahoosuc Trail, which involves overnight camping, or via trails from the Success Pond Rd., which leads east from Berlin, New Hampshire, to ME 26 north of Grafton Notch.

Rumford Whitecap (2197 ft.) is the most popular of the low range of mountains lying between Andover and Rumford.

To provide detailed descriptions of alternative approaches from the west to the trails in the Mahoosuc Range, this guide incorporates relevant trail descriptions from the Mahoosuc Range Area of the 1987 edition of the *AMC White Mountain Guide*. In addition to the map in this guide, refer to the USGS Old Speck and Gorham, NH/ME quadrangles, 15-minute series, or map 7 in the MATC *Guide to the Appalachian Trail in Maine*.

GRAFTON NOTCH STATE PARK

Grafton Notch State Park contains 3132 acres extending on both sides of ME 26, west and north, from the Newry-Grafton town line to about 1.5 mi. north of the Appalachian Trail crossing. It includes the summit and northeastern slopes of Old Speck and the lowest western and southwestern slopes of Baldpate, including Table Rock.

The area is now a major hiking center. In addition to the mountain trails, there are short, graded trails and paths that lead from some parking areas to points of interest nearby.

Scenic Areas and Short Walks

Step Falls

At the lower (southern) end of Grafton Notch, a short trail from the east side of the road leads 0.5 mi. to Step Falls, a series of cascades, with a total drop of 200 ft. The falls are on Wight Brook, which drains the southeastern slope of Baldpate Mountain. The area is a Nature Conservancy reservation and there is parking on the east side of ME 26 where the trail (sign) starts.

Screw Auger Falls and the Jail

Farther north, in the Pools, a parking area and picnic tables overlook Screw Auger Falls. The "Jail" is just above the picnic area (about 0.4 mi. west of the falls). It is a large pothole. It is not visible from the road, and nothing marks its location; but you can find it easily by entering the woods to the south (left) of the highway about 100 yd. east of the first highway bridge above Screw Auger Falls. To reach the Jail from below, enter the woods about 150–200 yd. further east of the bridge and go south to the brook. Follow the brook upstream to a falls. The Jail is on the right (north) bank.

Mother Walker Falls and Moose Cave

Mother Walker Falls are 1.2 mi. north of Screw Auger Falls. There is a parking area on the north side of ME 26. Moose Cave, a narrow and deep flume, is about 0.2 mi. farther north and 0.6 mi. south of the Old Speck Trail (Appalachian Trail). It is about 0.1 mi. from the parking area via a series of trails, walks, and steps. There is a grand view of Table Rock from the highway at this point.

Grafton Notch Parking Area

Near the height-of-land, 2.7 mi. northwest of Screw Auger Falls, there is a Maine Department of Parks and Recreation parking area (sign, "Hiking Trails") on the left (west) side of ME 26. All trails on Old Speck and Baldpate Mountain leave from this point. The Appalachian Trail crosses ME 26 at this point.

Spruce Meadow Picnic Area

The Spruce Meadow Picnic Area is approximately 0.6 mi. farther on ME 26 and offers outstanding views down the Notch. It also provides excellent facilities for picnicking.

OLD SPECK (4180 ft./1274 m.)

Old Speck, called that to distinguish it from the "Speckled Mountains" in Stoneham and Peru, dominates the western side of Grafton Notch. Long thought to be the second highest peak in the state after Hamlin Peak on Katahdin, Old Speck has now yielded that honor to Sugarloaf Mountain and ranks third. There is an open observation tower on the wooded summit. Refer to the Carter-Mahoosuc map with this guide or the USGS Old Speck quadrangle, 15-minute series.

Old Speck Trail

The Old Speck Trail, part of the Appalachian Trail and so blazed in white, leaves ME 26 near the height-of-land, about 2.7 mi. northwest of Screw Auger Falls, where the road is level and there is a state park parking area with the sign "Hiking Trails" on the west side of the road. The trail climbs the scenic north ridge of Old Speck. From the north side of the parking lot follow the left trail (the right trail goes to Baldpate Mountain). In 0.1 mi. the Eyebrow Trail leaves on the right to circle an 800-ft. cliff shaped like an eyebrow. The Old Speck Trail crosses a brook and soon begins to climb, following a series of switchbacks to approach the falls on Cascade Brook. Above the falls the trail, now heading more north, crosses the brook for the last time (*last water*). Beyond the brook there are views along the top of the Eyebrow. The Old Speck Trail passes the upper terminus of the Eyebrow Trail, which is to the right, about 0.1 mi. beyond the brook crossing. The main trail bears left, climbs gradually to the north ridge, where it bears more left, and follows the ridge, which has views southwest. At about 3.1 mi. the Link Trail leaves left and descends 0.3 mi. to a brook, the old fire warden's cabin site, and the lower terminus of the East Spur Trail. The Old Speck Trail turns more south and climbs to its end at the Mahoosuc Trail, 0.3 mi. west of the summit. Follow the Mahoosuc Trail (AT) 1.2 mi. right for Speck Pond Shelter. The summit, to the left (east), is flat and wooded, and the only views are from the observation tower.

Old Speck Trail
Distances from parking area, ME 26

> *to* first brook crossing: 0.3 mi.
> *to* last brook crossing: 1.1 mi.
> *to* Eyebrow Trail junction, upper terminus: 1.2 mi.
> *to* Link Trail junction: 3.1 mi.
> *to* Mahoosuc Trail junction: 3.5 mi.

to Old Speck summit (via Mahoosuc Trail): 3.8 mi./6.1 km. (3 hr. 30 min.)

Link Trail and East Spur Trail

These trails, longer and rougher than the more direct Old Speck Trail, provide a scenic alternate route to the summit. The East Spur offers expansive views from its ledgy crest, particularly to the south and east, and greater variety than the Old Speck Trail. *Do not* take the East Spur route in wet or icy conditions.

The Link Trail (blue-blazed) leaves the Old Speck Trail to the left (east) at 3.1 mi. and descends for 0.3 mi. through scrub and conifers to the site of the fire warden's cabin on the abandoned Fire Warden's Trail. From the cabin site, the East Spur Trail leaves to the left (east) and immediately crosses a brook (*last sure water*). Following blue blazes, it runs east through often thick trees and shrubs to reach the open crest of the spur. Turning sharp right, it climbs steeply and steadily over rough terrain south and southwest through short patches of scrub. About halfway up, the trail passes the Tri-Boulder Cave (the largest boulder is white and can be seen from above).

Link Trail and East Spur Trail
Distances from parking area, ME 26

to start of Link Trail (via Old Speck Trail): 3.1 mi.

to East Spur Trail junction: 3.4 mi.

to Old Speck summit (via East Spur Trail): 4.4 mi./7.1 km. (4 hr.)

Eyebrow Trail

The Eyebrow Trail traverses the top of the prominent cliff that dominates the northern end of Grafton Notch. This trail, with the Old Speck Trail, makes a loop over the entire Eyebrow's summit and cliff and is good for descending. The views of the notch and surrounding mountains are outstanding from the Eyebrow summit, 1100 ft. above the floor of the notch. The trail features rock outlooks, views of sheer faces, and a magnificent beech and hardwood forest on its lower part. Carry *water* in dry weather.

From the trailhead at the state parking area, follow the Appalachian Trail (Old Speck Trail) south. At 1.2 mi., 0.1 mi. beyond the last crossing of Cascade Brook, the Eyebrow Trail (orange-blazed) leaves to the right. Continue northeast over open ledges along the Eyebrow. There are outstanding views from the top of the nearly vertical cliff (1.3 mi.). Continue north and east, descending steadily through softwoods, to a small brook that cascades down over a steep ledge at 1.6 mi. *Caution.* In this section, be careful of wet moss and other slippery surfaces. The trail continues east down a steep slope, which flattens out and heads southeast, traversing some magnificent beech and hardwood ridges under the Eyebrow Cliff. The trail then heads south, curving around a large boulder on the right, and meets the Appalachian Trail at 2.1 mi. The trailhead is only 200 yd. beyond.

Eyebrow Trail
Distances from parking area, ME 26
> *to* start (via Appalachian Trail): 1.2 mi.
> *to* top of Eyebrow: 1.3 mi.
> *to* Appalachian Trail junction: 2.1 mi.
> *to* state parking area (via Appalachian Trail): 2.2 mi./3.5 km. (1 hr. 40 min.)

MAHOOSUC RANGE AREA

This section includes the region along the Maine-New Hampshire border from Lake Umbagog southward to the big loop of the Androscoggin River from Gorham to Bethel. The area is drained principally by this river and its branches.

The Mahoosuc Trail extends the entire length of the Mahoosuc Range from Gorham to Old Speck, and there are many side trails. All of these trails in this section are east of NH 16, north of US 2, and west of ME 26.

Grafton Notch State Park includes the highway corridor of ME 26 and the summit of Old Speck. The remainder of the ridge crest, followed by the Appalachian Trail from the NH/ME boundary to Dunn Notch passes through "Public Reserved Land."

In 1976 the State of Maine negotiated an exchange of land with the Brown Paper Company, now the James River Corp., which had owned most of the Mahoosuc Range summits. The state gave up rights in public lots and lands in various townships in the western part of the state for a block of land along the Mahoosuc Range extending west and south from the boundary of Grafton Notch State Park.

State laws restrict wood and charcoal fires to designated sites (shelters and Trident Col).

SUCCESS POND ROAD

From Berlin

Success Pond Road runs from Berlin to Grafton Notch, about 20 mi. The entrance to the road may be reached by going north on NH 16 through Berlin, then crossing the Androscoggin River, on the bridge at the traffic lights north of the city proper. At 0.2 mi. from NH 16 turn right (south) on Hutchins St., which at 0.4 mi. turns left, crosses a railroad track, then turns right again. At about 1 mi. turn left on a gravel road (sign, 1986, "OHRV parking 1/2 mi."). The road continues through a yarding area. This road is usually not open in winter.

From Grafton Notch

Success Pond Rd. leaves the west side of Grafton Notch

Highway (ME 26) 1.7 mi. north of Spruce Meadow Picnic
Area (no sign). It passes a small sand pit on the right and
continues in a west-southwest direction to Berlin, about 20
mi., passing on the left the Speck Pond Trail at 7 mi., the
spur road to the Notch Trail at 9 mi., the Goose Eye Trail
and Carlo Col Trail at 11.5 mi., and the Success Trail at
14.5 mi.

MOUNT SUCCESS (3590 ft./1094 m.)

Mount Success, in Success, New Hampshire, (reached also
from Shelburne on the south via the Austin Brook and
Mahoosuc trails) is accessible from Success Pond Rd. 5.5
mi. from Berlin and 14.5 mi. from ME 26.

Success Trail
This trail follows a logging road, forks right at 0.1 mi.,
and goes straight through a clearing, entering woods at 0.4
mi. (sign). Climb steadily for a mile and pass, on the right, a
short loop trail to a viewpoint. Reach the crest of a ridge
then descend to a brook (unreliabale). Climb a shallow ravine to the Mahoosuc Trail. Turn right (south) 0.6 mi. to the
summit of Mount Success.

Success Trail
Distances from Success Pond Road
to Mahoosuc Trail junction: 2.4 mi. (2 hr.)
to Mount Success summit (via Mahoosuc Trail): 3
mi./4.8 km. (2 hr. 30 min.)

MOUNT CARLO (3562 ft./1086 m.)

Mount Carlo, in Riley, Maine, may be climbed from a
common trailhead with the Goose Eye Trail on Success Pond
Rd. 8.5 mi. from Berlin and 11.5 mi. from ME 26.

Carlo Col Trail

This trail bears left from the southeast side of the road 100 yd. to a fork (left is the Goose Eye Trail). Take a sharp right 50 yd. to join a broad logging road for 0.8 mi., southeast, with little elevation gain. The trail turns left at a yarding area and immediately crosses the main brook, continues near it for about 0.3 mi., then turns obliquely left away from the brook and follows a branch road with a steeper rise. It crosses back to the south, over the north and south branches of the main brook, and bends east up the rather steep south bank of the south branch to its head at Carlo Col Shelter (*last water* for several miles). Continuing up the dry ravine, the trail ends at the Mahoosuc Trail about 0.3 mi. beyond the shelter, in a small box canyon known as Carlo Col. Turn left (northeast) 0.4 mi. to the Mount Carlo summit.

Carlo Col Trail
Distances from Success Pond Road
- *to* Mahoosuc Trail junction: 2.6 mi. (2 hr.)
- *to* Mount Carlo summit: 3 mi./4.8 km. (2 hr. 30 min.)

MOUNT GOOSE EYE (3860 ft./1177 m.)

Mount Goose Eye, in Riley, Maine, shares a common trailhead with Mount Carlo (see above) and makes possible a very interesting loop hike.

Goose Eye Trail

This trail bears left from the southeast side of the road 100 yd. to a fork (right is Carlo Col Trail). Go left (east), then swing left to northeast, crossing brooks at about 0.3 and 0.5 mi. from the road. It follows logging roads, crosses others, makes a wide right turn, and begins the ascent. At 1.4 mi. reach the yellow-blazed ME/NH state line. The grade increases to the top of a subsidiary ridge, where the trail bears left and crosses to the shoulder of the main peak, emerging from the woods on a short, steep, rocky ridge just below (north of) the bare west summit, the main peak of Goose Eye. *Caution.* Just as the trail leaves the woods, it climbs about 30 ft. up a steep ledge, where one must use care if wet or icy, and then continues over bare ledge to the summit.

About 200 yd. east of the summit the trail ends at the Mahoosuc Trail. Bear right (south) for Mount Carlo, or continue east to the east and north peaks of Goose Eye at 0.3 and 1.3 mi.

Goose Eye Trail
Distance from Success Pond Road
> to Mount Goose Eye, main summit: 3.1 mi./5 km. (2 hr. 40 min.)

Notch Trail
This trail ascends to the southwest end of Mahoosuc Notch from a spur road that leaves Success Pond Rd. 11 mi. from Berlin and 9 mi. from ME 26.

The spur road crosses two bridges and the trail begins at 0.6 mi. (sign), then follows a logging road into the woods. (The road may be passable to this point.) The trail ascends gradually on logging roads, passing an area of beaver activity, and reaches the Mahoosuc Trail (AT) at the height-of-land. The "Notch" is northeast (left) from this junction.

Notch Trail
Distance from Success Pond Road
> to Mahoosuc Trail junction: *est.* 2.8 mi./4.5 km. (1 hr. 50 min.)

Speck Pond Trail
This trail ascends to Speck Pond from Success Pond Rd. From Berlin fork right at 11.6 mi. to the trailhead at 12.5 mi. and 7.5 mi. from ME 26. The trail enters woods and follows

the north side of a brook 1.5 mi., then turns left. Climb generally east, steeply at times, to the junction, right, with the May Cutoff, a 0.2 mi. link, south, to the AT on Mahoosuc Arm. The Speck Pond Trail reaches a viewpoint to the pond and Old Speck, then descends steeply to the pond, campsite, and the AT.

Speck Pond Trail
Distance from Success Pond Road
to Speck Pond Campsite: *est.* 3.3 mi./5.3 km. (2 hr. 40 min.)

May Cutoff
This trail is a link from the Speck Pond Trail south to the AT on Mahoosuc Arm with little change in elevation.

May Cutoff
Distance from Speck Pond Trail
to Mahoosuc Trail/AT: 0.2 mi./3 km. (10 min.)

MAHOOSUC TRAIL

This AMC trail extends the entire length of the range from Gorham, New Hampshire, to the summit of Old Speck. Beyond its junction with the Centennial Trail, the Mahoosuc Trail is a section of the Appalachian Trail. In addition to the tentsite at Trident Col there are four shelters—Gentian Pond, Carlo Col, Full Goose, and Speck Pond (with tent platforms and a caretaker). Camping is carefully regulated to protect fragile soils, vegetation, and water purity. This is a rugged trail, with many ups and downs, some rocky. Mahoosuc Notch is regarded by many who have hiked the entire length of the Appalachian Trail as the most difficult mile. It can be hazardous in wet or icy conditions and can remain impassable through the end of May. The times shown are calculated for one or two people; a group will take longer. *Hikers are cautioned not to rely on finding water except where indicated.*

Mahoosuc Trail, Part I. Gorham to Mount Hayes

Since this section of the Mahoosuc Trail is not part of the Appalachian Trail, its blazes are blue rather than white. To reach the trail, cross the Androscoggin River by the footbridge under the Boston & Maine Railroad bridge 1.3 mi. north of the Gorham post office on NH 16. On the east bank follow the road to the right (southeast) along the river for 0.6 mi., then cross the canal through the open upper level of the powerhouse (left of entrance). Beyond, keep straight ahead about 100 yd. to the woods at the east end of the dam, where the trail sign will be found. The trail is blue-blazed. Turn left and follow an old road north along the side of the canal for 125 yd. and then turn right uphill. At 0.2 mi. from this turn the trail crosses beneath a power line; on entering the clearing, bear right for 30 ft. and then turn left up across it. Just after entering the woods the trail bears right and reaches but does not cross a brook, follows it closely for 100 yd., and ascends at only a slight grade for about 0.3 mi. to where a side trail to Mascot Pond leads right 0.2 mi. to the pond, just below the cliffs that are visible from Gorham. The Mahoosuc Trail ascends a brook valley, which it crosses four times. About 2.5 mi. from the Boston & Maine bridge, it passes Popsy Spring on the left and soon emerges on the southwest side of the flat, ledgy summit of Mount Hayes (2566 ft.). At the top of the steep climb, an unmarked path leads a few yards right to the best viewpoint south over the valley. A cairn marks the true summit of Mount Hayes.

Mahoosuc Trail, Gorham to Mount Hayes
Distance from NH 16

to Mount Hayes summit: 3.1 mi./5. km. (2 hr. 20 min.)

Mahoosuc Trail, Part II. Mount Hayes to Gentian Pond

The trail passes over the flat summit of Mount Hayes, and in 0.2 mi. passes the upper terminus (right) of the Centennial Trail, on open ledges with good views north. From here the Mahoosuc Trail is part of the Appalachian Trail, marked with white blazes. It descends north to the col between Mount Hayes and Cascade Mountain. (There is sometimes *water* in this col, either on the trail or a few yards to the east.) The trail then climbs up Cascade Mountain by a southwest ridge, emerging on a bare summit ledge (2606 ft.). It turns back sharply into the woods, descending gradually northeast and east to the east end of the mountain. It enters a fine forest and descends rapidly beside cliffs and ledges to Trident Col. A side path leads left about 200 yd. to Trident Col tent site, with space for four tents. *Water* is available about 50 yd. below (west of) the site.

The bare ledges of the rocky cone to the east of Trident Col repay a scramble to the top. About 0.3 mi. beyond the col the trail enters an old logging road, follows it for 100 yd., then branches left, descends to the southeast, and slabs the ridge past the foot of this peak, of a second similar peak, and of the peak just west of Page Pond, which together form the Trident. The trail crosses three or four brooks, at least one of which should have *water*, then it ascends to Page Pond.

The trail passes the south end of the pond, crosses a beaver dam, and climbs gradually, then steeply, to the summit of Wocket Ledge, a spur from Bald Cap Dome. The fine view from some ledges 50 ft. to the northwest, reached by a side trail, should not be missed. The Mahoosuc Trail descends east, crosses the upper west branch of Peabody Brook, then climbs around the nose of a small ridge and descends gradually to the head of Dream Lake. The trail bears left here, then right around the north end of the lake and crosses the inlet brook. Just beyond, the Peabody Brook Trail leaves right.

From the Peabody Brook Trail junction, the Mahoosuc Trail follows a logging road left 100 yd. It soon recrosses the inlet brook, traverses a slight divide into the watershed of Austin Brook, climbs through some swampy places, and descends to Moss Pond. It continues past the west shore of the pond and follows an old logging road down the outlet brook. About 0.3 mi. below Moss Pond the trail turns abruptly right downhill from the logging road to Gentian Pond, skirts the southwest shore of the pond, crosses a small brook first, then soon drops to cross the outlet brook. A few yards beyond are the Gentian Pond Shelter (capacity 20) and tent sites, and the Austin Brook Trail diverges right and leads to North Road in Shelburne.

Mahoosuc Trail, Mount Hayes to Gentian Pond
Distances from Mount Hayes summit

   to Centennial Trail junction: 0.2 mi.
   to Cascade Mountain summit: 2.1 mi.
   to Trident Col tent site: 3.5 mi.
   to Page Pond: 4.3 mi.
   to Wocket Ledge: 5 mi.
   to Dream Lake, inlet brook crossing: 6.1 mi.
   to Gentian Pond Shelter: 8.3 mi./13.4 km. (5 hr. 40 min.)

Mahoosuc Trail, Part III. Gentian Pond to Carlo Col

From Gentian Pond Shelter the trail climbs about 0.5 mi. to the top of the steep ridge whose ledges overlook the pond from the east, then descends more gradually. About 0.5 mi. farther it passes through a col, climbs over two steep humps, with *water* in the col beyond the second hump, and then begins to ascend the southwest side of

Mount Success. The grade is steep and the footing is rough for about the next 0.5 mi. The trail climbs over open ledges with an outlook to the southwest, passes through a belt of high scrub, and finally comes out on the summit of Mount Success.

The trail turns sharp left here and descends through scrub then forest to the sag between Mount Success and an un-named peak, marked "3345" on the Carter-Mahoosuc map, where the Success Trail diverges left. The main trail climbs slightly, slabs the east side of "3345," and then descends in a general northeast direction to a rough col. The trail then rises steadily, passes the Maine-New Hampshire border signs, and climbs up and down two cols that resemble box ravines. The second (east) col, 0.5 mi. from the Maine-New Hampshire border, is known as Carlo Col. The Carlo Col Trail to Success Pond Rd. diverges left here, and the Carlo Col Shelter is located at the head of a brook about 0.3 mi. down the Carlo Col Trail.

Mahoosuc Trail, Gentian Pond to Carlo Col
Distances from Gentian Pond Shelter
to Mount Success summit: 2.9 mi.
to Success Trail junction: 3.5 mi.
to Carlo Col Trail junction: 5.4 mi./8.7 km. (5 hr. 20 min.)

Mahoosuc Trail, Part IV. Carlo Col to Mahoosuc Notch

From Carlo Col the trail climbs steadily to the bare southwest summit of Mount Carlo with an excellent view. It then passes to the south of the wooded northeast summit, descends northeast, through a mountain meadow where there is sometimes *water*, to the col. The trail turns more north and climbs the steep side of Mount Goose Eye.

Caution. Hikers should use care on the ledges. The trail emerges on an open ridge about 200 yd. east of the main (west) peak, which is reached by the Goose Eye Trail. The Mahoosuc Trail then turns sharply to the right (east) and follows the bare ridge crest about 200 yd. to the scrub. It continues in the same direction through the col and climbs steeply through woods and open areas to the bare summit of the east peak of Mount Goose Eye, where it turns sharply north down the bare ridge, and enters the scrub at the east side of the open space. Beyond the col the trail runs in the open nearly to the foot of the north peak, except for two interesting box ravines, where there is often *water.* At the foot of the north peak the trail passes through a patch of woods, then climbs directly to the summit. Here it turns east along the ridge crest and swings northeast down the steep slope, winding through several patches of scrub. At the foot of the steep slope it enters the woods, slabs the west face of the ridge, and descends to the col. Full Goose Shelter is located on a shelf here. There is a *spring* 100 ft. behind (east of) the shelter. The trail then turns sharply left and ascends, coming into the open about 0.3 mi. below the summit of the south peak of Fulling Mill Mountain. At this peak the trail turns sharply left, runs a few hundred yards through a meadow, and descends northwest through woods, first gradually then steeply, to the head of Mahoosuc Notch. Here the Notch Trail to Success Pond Rd. diverges sharply left (southwest).

Mahoosuc Trail, Carlo Col to Mahoosuc Notch
Distances from Carlo Col Trail junction

to Mount Carlo, southwest summit: 0.4 mi.

to Goose Eye Trail junction: 1.8 mi.

to Mount Goose Eye, east peak: 2.1 mi.

to Mount Goose Eye, north peak: 3.3 mi.

to Full Goose Shelter: 4. mi.

to Fulling Mill Mountain: 4.8 mi.

to head of Mahoosuc Notch, Notch Trail junction: 5.8 mi./9.5 km. (4 hr. 10 min.)

Mahoosuc Trail, Part V. Mahoosuc Notch to Grafton Notch

From the head of Mahoosuc Notch the trail turns sharply right (northeast) and descends the length of the narrow notch along a rough footway, passing through a number of boulder caverns, some with narrow openings, where progress will be slow and where ice remains into the summer. The trail is blazed on the rocks with white paint. Be extremely careful in the notch on account of slippery rocks and dangerous holes. Heavy backpacks will impede progress considerably. *Caution.* Mahoosuc Notch may be impassable through early June because of snow; snowshoes may not help.

At the lower end of the notch the trail leaves the brook, bears left, ascends gradually, and, after slabbing the eastern end of Mahoosuc Mountain for about 0.5 mi., follows the old logging road leading up the valley of Notch 2, then crosses to the north side of a brook.

The trail then climbs, winds along rocks and ledges, and climbs through fine forest, in general slabbing the ridge of Mahoosuc Arm at a very steep angle. A little more than halfway up it passes the head of a little flume, in which there is sometimes *water*. Near the top of Mahoosuc Arm the trail travels along ledges and deer runs to the bare summit. The May Cutoff to the Speck Pond Trail leaves left here. The Mahoosuc Trail follows the open, winding ridge for about 0.5 mi., southeast, northeast, and north, then drops steeply about 0.3 mi. to Speck Pond, about 3500 ft., said to be the highest pond in Maine. It is bordered with thick woods. The trail crosses the outlet brook and continues around the east side of the pond about 0.3 mi. to Speck Pond Campsite (in summer, there is a caretaker and a fee for overnight

camping). The Speck Pond Trail descends west from here to
Success Pond Rd.

The trail then climbs about 0.3 mi. to the southeast end of
the next hump on the ridge, passes over it, and slabs the east
face of a small second hump. In the gully beyond, a few yards
east of the trail, there is a *spring*. The trail climbs to the open
shoulder of Old Speck. The path is obvious up this open ridge,
and hikers need only stay on the crest. Near the top of the
shoulder the trail bears right, reenters the woods, and follows
the wooded crest about 0.5 mi. to the summit of Old Speck. At
a point 0.3 mi. before reaching the summit, the Old Speck
Trail (AT) descends left for 3.5 mi. to Grafton Notch. To the
right the Mahoosuc Trail ends at the summit tower.

*Mahoosuc Trail, Mahoosuc Notch to Grafton Notch
Distances from head of Mahoosuc Notch, Notch Trail
junction*

    to foot of Mahoosuc Notch: 0.9 mi.

    to Mahoosuc Arm summit: 2.4 mi.

    to Speck Pond Shelter: 3.3 mi.

    to Old Speck Trail junction: 4.1 mi.

    to Old Speck summit: 4.4 mi./7.1 km. (5 hr. 30 min.)

FROM SHELBURNE

North Road

Trails leading from Shelburne into the Mahoosuc area all
start at North Rd., which turns north off US 2 about 3.5 mi.
east of Gorham, crosses the Androscoggin River on the Lead
Mine Bridge at a small dam and power plant, and continues
east along the north side of the Androscoggin Valley into
Maine, rejoining US 2 about 1 mi. north of Bethel. Cross
roads connect with US 2 via bridges at Shelburne and Gilead. There is little traffic on North Rd., so it is pleasant for

driving or walking. Along with 275 yd. on US 2, North Rd. links the Appalachian Trail between the Rattle River and Centennial trails. From the Rattle River Trail, turn west on US 2 and north on North Rd. for about 0.7 mi. to Hogan Rd., a dirt road on the left, to reach the Centennial Trail.

North Road Link, Appalachian Trail
Distances from Rattle River Trail
to North Road: 0.2 mi.
to Hogan Road: 0.9 mi./1.4 km. (25 min.)

Centennial Trail

The Centennial Trail is a part of the Appalachian Trail. The AMC constructed the Centennial Trail in 1976, its centennial year.

Follow North Rd. 0.7 mi. north from its western end on US 2 and turn left onto a dirt road (Hogan Rd.). Follow it 0.3 mi. to a parking area on the left. Parking is also permitted at the junction of North and Hogan roads. Please avoid blocking the road.

The trail, blazed in white, leaves north from Hogan Rd. and turns left into the woods, heading generally northwest. After 135 ft. it bears left up a steep bank, levels off, and reaches stone steps in 0.1 mi. The trail climbs rather steeply, then more gradually, with a limited view of the Androscoggin River. It turns left onto a woods road and crosses a brook at about 1.2 mi. (*last reliable water*). The trail then crosses a logging road and at 1.6 mi. turns sharply right—the ledge to the left has fine views of the Moriahs and Mount Washington. The trail soon descends into a small valley, then rises to open ledges with a fine view of the Mahoosuc Range and the Androscoggin Valley to the right. At 3.3 mi. the trail reaches an easterly summit of Mount Hayes, where there is an excellent view from open ledges of the Carter-Moriah Range and Northern Presidentials. The trail descends slightly, then ascends across a series of

open ledges to end at the Mahoosuc Trail at 3.7 mi. Mount
Hayes is 0.2 mi. to the left with fine views. The Appalachian
Trail at this point follows the Mahoosuc Trail toward Cascade
Mountain, 1.9 mi. to the right.

Centennial Trail

Distance from Hogan Road
   to Mahoosuc Trail junction: 3.7 mi./6 km. (2 hr. 35 min.)

Peabody Brook Trail

This trail ascends to the AT at Dream Lake. There is no
overnight parking at the base of this trail. The trail, blazed in
blue, leaves the north side of North Rd. in Shelburne, 1.3 mi.
from US 2. It passes between two cottages and forks right as
a logging road, almost level until after crossing Peabody
Brook at 0.2 mi. The trail, still a logging road, heads generally north along the brook and bears left at 0.8 mi., where a
newer logging road bears right. About 100 yd. beyond, the
road becomes a trail and soon begins to climb moderately.
At 1.2 mi. a path leaves left and descends about 0.5 mi. to
Giant Falls. The trail rises more steeply, and at 1.5 mi. there
is a good view (left) of Mount Washington and Mount Ad-
ams through open trees. The trail climbs a short ladder just
beyond. About 0.5 mi. farther, it crosses the east branch of
the brook, then recrosses in 0.3 mi. From here the trail is
nearly level and enters a rather broad open area, making a
sharp left turn in about 0.4 mi. Soon Dream Lake becomes
visible on the left. The Dryad Fall Trail leaves right, 0.2 mi.
beyond the sharp turn. The Peabody Brook Trail ends at the
Mahoosuc Trail, 120 yd. from this junction.

Peabody Brook Trail

Distances from North Road
   to Giant Falls path junction: 1.2 mi.
   to Dryad Fall Trail junction: 3 mi.
   to Mahoosuc Trail junction: 3.1 mi./5 km. (2 hr. 20 min.)

Austin Brook Trail

This trail ascends to the Mahoosuc Trail at Gentian Pond from the North Rd. 0.6 mi. west of Meadows Rd., which leaves US 2 at Shelburne Village.

The trail begins just west of Austin Brook. There is limited parking on the south side of the road. The trail, heading north through a gate on private land, passes between the garage (left) and a camp called "The Wigwam" about 0.3 mi. from the road. The trail turns sharply left and continues 0.5 mi. to cross Austin Brook; turn left on a logging road. Continue past a stream crossing. Beyond the crossing, the Dryad Fall Trail leaves left. About 0.3 mi. farther, take the left fork of the road. The Austin Brook Trail continues along the logging road, which soon turns sharp right. From this point follow arrows at branch roads, bearing right.

In about 0.8 mi. the trail crosses the brook that drains Gentian Pond, crosses a clearing, enters a logging road, soon bears left away from it, and begins the rather steep climb of about 0.5 mi. to the Mahoosuc Trail at Gentian Pond Shelter.

Austin Brook Trail
Distance from North Road
to Gentian Pond: 3.3 mi./5.3 km. (2 hr. 30 min.)

Dryad Fall Trail

Dryad Fall, one of the highest cascades in these mountains, is particularly interesting for a few days after a rainstorm, since its several cascades fall at least 300 ft. over steep ledges.

The trail is blazed in orange. The trail leaves left from the Austin Brook Trail about 2 mi. from North Rd. and gradually climbs old logging roads through woods for about 0.5 mi. It then drops down to Dryad Brook, which it follows nearly to the base of the falls. From here the trail climbs steeply northeast of the falls. After rising several hundred feet with good views of the falls, the trail bears right and joins a logging road. It ascends to the left on this road, which soon meets another logging road. It follows this road left, crossing Dryad Brook above the falls and climbing left. The trail then heads generally west for 0.8 mi., until it slabs off obliquely right. From here almost to Dream Lake it goes through woods, generally west, rising at a moderate grade.

At the crest of the ridge the trail again meets a logging road, then descends to end at the Peabody Brook Trail. Turn right and follow the trail for about 100 yd. to the Mahoosuc Trail.

Descending, watch carefully for where the trail turns down steeply (right) off the logging road above the falls.

Dryad Fall Trail
Distances from Austin Brook Trail

    to Dryad Fall: *est.* 0.8 mi.
    to Dream Lake: *est.* 1.5 mi./2.4 km. (1 hr. 25 min.)

Lary Flume

This is a wild chasm in the south slope of the Mahoosuc Range that resembles the Ice Gulch and Devils Hopyard, with many boulder caves and one fissure cave.

There is no trail, but experienced climbers have followed up the brook, which may be reached by going east where the Austin Brook Trail begins its last 0.5 mi. of ascent to Gentian Pond.

Table Rock Trail

The Table Rock Trail, which climbs 900 ft., offers a short, fairly steep, but spectacular climb to the prominent rock ledge on Baldpate Mountain, which is on the eastern side of Grafton Notch. From this ledge, the trail continues to rejoin the Appalachian Trail. There is an extensive slab-cave system, possibly the largest in the state, on this trail.

The trail leaves the Appalachian Trail to the right (south) 0.1 mi. from the trailhead on ME 26 (described below). For 0.3 mi. from this junction the trail rises gently along the side of a hill above a marsh until it reaches a drop-off. From there it climbs steadily through mature hardwoods and reaches a rocky, caribou-moss-covered area called the boulder patch at 0.6 mi. After several switchbacks along rocky ledges, the trail enters a deep ravine between two rock faces. At the top of the ravine bear right. The trail climbs less steeply to a prominent outlook at 0.8 mi. At 0.9 mi. it reaches the base of the ledges that form Table Rock, where the slab-caves begin. *Caution.* Be careful if you explore the caves. Some are quite deep, and a fall could cause serious injury.

On the trail, continue south around the bottom of Table Rock. (On the ledges above, note the weather-formed rock that looks like a shark's fin.) At 1 mi., after swinging behind Table Rock, you will meet a blue-blazed trail. Table Rock is 20 yd. to the left.

To the right, the blue-blazed Upper Table Rock Trail continues, with only a slight change in elevation, about 0.5 mi. to the Appalachian Trail. Turn right (east) to reach Baldpate; go left (west) to return to the trailhead on ME 26.

Table Rock Trail
Distances from state parking area, ME 26

 to start (via Baldpate Mountain Trail): 0.1 mi.

 to Table Rock and junction with upper trail: 1 mi.

 to state parking area, ME 26 (via Baldpate Mountain Trail): 2.4 mi./3.9 km. (1 hr. 45 min.)

BALDPATE MOUNTAIN (east summit 3812 ft. and west summit 3680 ft./1162 m. and 1122 m.)

Baldpate Mountain, once known as Saddleback and Bear River Whitecap, rises to the east of Grafton Notch. There are two main summits: the fine open East Peak and the West Peak. The Appalachian Trail traverses both. Refer to the USGS Old Speck Mountain quadrangle, 15-minute series, or map 7 in the MATC *Guide to the Appalachian Trail in Maine.*

Baldpate Mountain via the Appalachian Trail

The Appalachian Trail, which traverses the range, is maintained by the MATC and blazed in white. The following describes approaches from both the west and east.

From Grafton Notch

The trail leaves the north side of the state-park parking lot on ME 26 (take the trail to the right). It soon crosses ME 26. Then it runs briefly through woods and beside a marsh until, at 0.1 mi., it crosses a brook on a log footbridge. Almost immediately after crossing the bridge, the trail passes the start of the Table Rock Trail, which leaves right. At 0.4 and 0.6 mi. trails lead left to Grafton Notch Shelter (MATC, accommodates six). After that, the trail rises gradually on an old woods road. At 0.9 mi. it passes another blue-blazed trail on the right that leads to Table Rock. The main trail climbs steadily and then more steeply to the western knob of Baldpate, with good views to the northwest. The trail then slabs the northern side of the knob to a ridge extending toward West Peak, soon descending to a brook. Then it climbs steeply over rough terrain to the West Peak, which is covered with scrub, but offers vistas in almost all directions. The trail, turning in a more northerly direction, drops only about 240 ft. before climbing to East Peak nearly a mile beyond. From there it continues to Andover-East B Hill Rd.

From Andover-East B Hill Road

The trail leaves the left (south) side of East B Hill Rd. about 8 mi. west of Andover Village. It descends from the road, crosses a small brook, then turns south along the edge of a progressively deeper gorge cut by this brook, which it follows for 0.5 mi. before turning west into the mouth of Dunn Notch. At 0.8 mi. the trail crosses the west branch of the Ellis River (a large stream at this point) at the top of a double waterfall that plunges 60 ft. into Dunn Notch. You can reach the bottom of the falls via an old logging road across the stream. (Upstream, there are a small rocky gorge and the beautiful upper falls.) The Appalachian Trail crosses the old road and climbs steeply up the eastern rim of the notch. It then climbs moderately to the south.

At 1.3 mi. the trail turns left and climbs gradually through open hardwoods along the edge of the north arm of Surplus Mountain. At 3 mi. it slabs right (southwest) around the nose of Surplus and climbs gently along a broad ridge and passes near the summit. In another mile, it descends steeply over rough ground to the Frye Notch Lean-to near the head of Frye Brook. At 1.2 mi. from the lean-to, the trail reaches and climbs the crest of a ridge to the open summit of Baldpate's East Peak. The trail then drops down, climbs West Peak, and descends into Grafton Notch via the trail from the west described above.

Baldpate Mountain via the Appalachian Trail
Distances from parking area, ME 26

to lower side trail to Table Rock: 0.1 mi. (5 min.)
to upper side trail to Table Rock: 0.9 mi. (45 min.)
to Baldpate, West Peak: 2.9 mi. (2 hr. 30 min.)
to Baldpate, East Peak: 3.8 mi. (3 hr. 10 min.)

to Andover-East B Hill Road: 10.1 mi./16.3 km. (6 hr. 40 min.)

Distances from Andover-East B Hill Road

   to waterfall: 0.8 mi. (55 min.)

   to Frye Notch Lean-to: 4.6 mi., (3 hr.)

   to Baldpate, East Peak: 6.3 mi.(4 hr. 30 min.)

   to Baldpate, West Peak: 7.2 mi. (5 hr. 15 min.)

   to state parking area, ME 26: 10.1 mi./16.3 km. (7 hr.)

PUZZLE MOUNTAIN (3133 ft./955 m.)

Puzzle Mountain in Newry is a flat-topped rocky mass, oc-
cupying a large area. The true summit is wooded but the bare
peak to the southwest is only a few feet lower. Hikers using
the route should have a compass. *Water* may be available to
within 0.3 mi. or less of the summit. Refer to the USGS Old
Speck Mountain quadrangle, 15-minute series.

From the junction of ME 26 and US 2 at Newry, turn
northwest on ME 26 for 3.6 mi. to a well-cleared logging
road on the right. This road, the start of the trail, is 0.2 mi.
beyond Great Brook. Bearing 115°, the road parallels the
brook for 0.3 mi. and then joins the brook. At 0.6 mi. take
the right fork (with the brook), and at 0.9 mi. cross the
brook on a good bridge. At 1 mi. the road crosses a small
feeder brook and reaches a clearing 50 yd. farther. At 1.1
mi., with the summit of Puzzle in view at 30°, leave the road,
turn left, descend to the brook, and cross it on a log bridge
into a clearing. From the clearing, begin the climb up on an
overgrown logging road bearing 30° and following a stream
bed (dry in summer). At 0.3 mi. from the second crossing of
the brook, follow the right fork while continuing the gentle
ascent. After a few yards, a fork—right—returns to the
brook. Stay on the left fork and follow it uphill, still at 30°.
As the road and the stream bed peter out, the trail takes a
swing to the north and 20 ft. later forks again to the north

and northwest. The northwest fork is ax-blazed for 100 yd. through underbrush, and at 0.5 mi. from the second crossing there is an oil drum just left of the trail. Turn directly right into open hardwood forest and follow the ax-blazed trail, always going uphill, at about 30°; 0.4 mi. later, a steeper climb begins through softwoods and ledges. The ledges are cairned, and there are fine views of the Mahoosucs to the rear. At 0.6 mi. from the oil barrel the trail descends into a small, thickly wooded ravine with a brook at the bottom. After crossing the brook, the trail ascends more steeply with a stream to the left and climbs more ledges to the summit. Blazes and cairns have been placed nearly to the true summit, but the best views are from open ledges southeast of the summit.

Puzzle Mountain
Distances from ME 26

to first fork in road: 0.6 mi.

to Puzzle Mountain summit: 2.5 mi./4 km. (3 hr.)

RUMFORD WHITECAP (2197 ft./670 m.)

This mountain is a long, bare-topped ridge in the northwest part of Rumford. It runs east and west and yields excellent views with relatively little effort. Refer to the USGS Rumford quadrangle, 15-minute series, and the East Andover quadrangle, 7.5-minute series.

The trail climbs up from the west. From US 2 0.5 mi. west of Rumford Point, go north on ME 5 toward Andover. About 3 mi. from US 2 turn right (east) on side road that crosses the Ellis River. In 0.3 mi. turn left (north); and then in 1.6 mi., turn right (east) on Farmer's Hill Rd. toward Roxbury Notch. At 0.8 mi. the trail leaves the right side of the road on a logging road (not passable for cars) and climbs steeply. Just after a badly eroded section of the road at about

0.5 mi., turn left onto the trail. It shortly crosses a brook (dry in dry weather) and leads generally east through the woods to open ledges at the western end of the ridge.

The final 1 mi. is a delightful walk along the open ridge to the summit. From the summit, the antenna on Black Mountain and the Satellite Station at Andover are visible. The trail through the woods and along the ridge is marked by ribbons and cairns with few paint blazes. *Descending*, since there are many cairns and paths leading in different directions, take great care to find and follow the correct trail west into the woods. Ribbons mark the critical points.

Rumford Whitecap
Distances from Farmer's Hill Road
  to left turn off logging road: 0.5 mi.
  to ledges: 1 mi.
  to Rumford Whitecap summit: 2 mi./3.2 km. (1 hr. 40 min.)

Old Blue Mountain (3600 ft./1097 m.)

The Appalachian Trail crosses Old Blue Mountain, which is south of Elephant Mountain and east of the road from Andover to the South Arm of Lower Richardson Lake. The summit of Old Blue is covered with dense evergreen trees 2 to 3 ft. high, allowing excellent views in all directions. Refer to the USGS Old Speck Mountain, Rangeley, and Rumford quadrangles, 15-minute series, and the East Andover quadrangle, 7.5-minute series, or map 7 in the MATC *Guide to the Appalachian Trail in Maine*.

To reach the Appalachian Trail, follow the road to the South Arm for 8.5 mi. north of Andover to Black Brook Notch. From the South Arm Rd., the Appalachian Trail climbs very steeply up the east wall of Black Brook Notch. At 0.6 mi. the trail reaches the top of the notch, then it gradually climbs to the base of Old Blue, which it reaches at

2.3 mi. Here the trail begins the final 0.5-mi. ascent to the summit.

From the summit, the Appalachian Trail descends north 800 ft. into the high valley between Old Blue and Elephant Mountain. In this valley the Appalachian Trail runs through a virgin red spruce forest for more than a mile.

For detailed information about the Appalachian Trail north of Old Blue, see the 1988 edition of the MATC *Guide to the Appalachian Trail in Maine.*

Old Blue Mountain
Distances from South Arm Road
to top of Black Brook Notch: 0.6 mi.
to base of Old Blue: 2.3 mi.
to Old Blue summit: 2.8 mi./4.5 km.(2 hr. 40 min.)

BEMIS MOUNTAIN (3592 ft./1095 m.)

Bemis Mountain is an open ridge with outstanding views. It rises south of Mooselookmeguntic Lake. The ridge, which runs northeast–southwest, has four peaks descending in elevation to the northeast. The highest peak is wooded. The three lower peaks all have excellent views. The Appalachian Trail crosses the Bemis Ridge. Refer to the USGS Oquossoc and Rangeley quadrangles, 15-minute series, or map 7 in the MATC *Guide to the Appalachian Trail in Maine.*

Access to the Appalachian Trail is from a logging road that follows the bed of the old Rumford and Rangeley Lakes Railroad, which ran between Rumford and Oquossoc in the 1930s. From a prominent crossroads on ME 17, 32 mi. north of its junction with US 2 in Mexico and 3.7 mi. south of its junction with ME 4 in Oquossoc, take the gravel road west for 1 mi. to another crossroads. From there, take the gravel road (railroad route) south along the shore of Mooselookmeguntic Lake and cross the inlet to the lake. The Appalachian Trail crossing is 7.1 mi. from ME 17 (no sign).

From the railroad bed, the Appalachian Trail climbs west through the woods for 0.5 mi. before emerging onto open ledges. The trail goes on across the ridge crossing three peaks —First Peak (2604 ft.), 1.1 mi.; Second Peak (2923 ft.), 2 mi.; Third Peak (3138 ft.), 3.9 mi. At 4 mi. the trail begins the ascent to the two wooded knobs of Fourth Peak (3592 ft.), which is reached at 5.1 mi.

For an interesting loop hike, continue on the Appalachian Trail to the Elephant Mountain Lean-to (6.8 mi.), and return to the railroad bed via the Bemis Valley Trail. The Bemis Valley Trail crosses the railroad bed 1 mi. south of the Appalachian Trail crossing. For a detailed description of the Appalachian Trail beyond Fourth Peak and the Bemis Valley Trail, see the 1988 edition of the MATC *Guide to the Appalachian Trail in Maine*.

Bemis Mountain

Distances from railroad bed

to Fourth Peak: 5.1 mi./8.2 km. (3 hr. 30 min.)

to Elephant Mountain Lean-to: 6.8 mi.

to railroad bed (via Bemis Valley Trail): 11.3 mi.

to start of trail (via railroad bed): 12.3 mi./19.8 km. (7 hr.)

Weld Region

Weld Village lies on the eastern shore of Lake Webb (678 ft.) and is almost encircled by mountains. Tumbledown Mountain (3068 ft.), with its tremendous cliffs, three peaks, and high pond is the most interesting mountain in the area and one of the state's outstanding summits. Little Jackson (3434 ft.), Jackson (3535 ft.), and Blueberry (2942 ft.) mountains are also in the Tumbledown Range, which forms the northern and northwestern walls of the valley. Mount Blue (3187 ft.) lies to the east. The ledgy summits of Bald Mountain (2386 ft.) and Saddleback Wind Mountain (2572 ft.) close the valley on the southeast. Brush (2430 ft.) and West (2782 ft.) mountains are to the west.

Mount Blue State Park (1273 acres) has two sections. The area along the western shore of Lake Webb offers picnicking, swimming, and camping facilities. The section east of the lake and Weld includes the Center Hill parking overlook and picnic area and Mount Blue itself. Information on accommodations and trail conditions may be obtained at the supervisor's headquarters 1.5 mi. from Weld on the road toward Center Hill and Mount Blue.

TUMBLEDOWN MOUNTAIN (3068 ft./935 m.)

Although not the highest peak of the Tumbledown Range, Tumbledown Mountain, at the southwestern end, is in many ways the most interesting. The enormous cliff on the southern side of the mountain attracts many rock climbers. Of the three summits, 3068-ft. West Peak is slightly higher than the others. Another feature of the mountain is Tumbledown Pond (called Beaver or Crater by some), located on the eastern slope of the mountain and surrounded on three sides by higher elevations. The views from the summit ridges are good, except where higher mountains in the range block them to the north and northeast. There are four trails to the pond. In addition to the map in this guide, you can refer to the USGS Dixfield, Rumford, and Rangeley quadrangles, 15-minute series, and the Roxbury quadrangle, 7.5-minute series.

The Loop Trail

The Loop Trail leaves Byron Notch Rd. 5.8 mi. west of Weld Corner, heading north on the east side of the brook. There is sometimes a sign at the start of the trail, but vandals steal it periodically. There is a clearing diagonally opposite the trail's entrance into the woods. The trail (blue blazes) rises gradually, crossing a brook twice, and at 1.0 mi. passes the huge Tumbledown Boulder. From there it rises steeply, coming out on open ledges (Great Ledges) from which there are splendid views of the 700-ft. cliffs of Tumbledown Mountain. On the ledges, at a large cairn, the Loop Trail to the saddle turns right.

The trail crosses a brook and then climbs steeply in a gully. Near the top of the gully, a side trail leads right to a fissure cave ("Fat Man's Misery"). Above this is an opening in the boulders with iron rungs. At 0.6 mi. from the Great Ledges cairn, reach the saddle with a *spring (unreliable in dry weather)*. From here the trails lead east and west.

There are no trails on the North Peak of Tumbledown, but you can reach it by bushwhacking through the valley between the East and North peaks or by going east around Tumbledown Pond and up the upper reaches of Parker's Ridge.

The Loop Trail
Distances from Byron Notch Road
to Tumbledown Boulder: 1 mi.
to cairn (Great Ledges): 1.3 mi.

to saddle (Tumbledown Ridge Trail): 1.9 mi./3.1 km. (1 hr. 45 min.)

Brook Trail

This is a direct route to Tumbledown Pond from Byron Notch Rd. It leaves the road 1.8 mi. west of the start of the Parker's Ridge Trail and 4.4 mi. west of Weld Corner. The trail diverges north just before where the road crosses a large double steel culvert over Tumbledown Brook at prospect "X" 1102. The trail is marked "Brook Trail" on a rock at the start and is blue-blazed throughout its length. For the first mile it is a logging road passable for jeeps. At 1 mi. the trail diverges to the right into a low spot, then climbs steeply, generally following the brook to the pond.

Brook Trail
Distances from Byron Notch Road
to right turn off logging road: 1 mi.
to Tumbledown Pond: 1.5 mi./2.4 km. (1 hr. 30 min.)

Parker's Ridge Trail

This is the oldest and easiest of the trails up Tumbledown. Take the road to the right (northwest) from Byron Notch Rd. about 2.7 mi. west of Weld Corner and about 0.3 mi. west of a cemetery. Follow the road northwest about 0.9 mi. to a clearing and shelter. Park here. From this area the Little Jackson Trail leaves on a logging road, northwest.

The Parker's Ridge Trail, blazed blue, enters the woods left (west), crosses a brook, and turns northwest, joining a logging road. For 1 mi., the trail rises gently through second growth, then steeply for a short distance over three ledges. After that, the trail rises steadily. Then it crosses the open ledges of Parker's Ridge with views of Tumbledown's three peaks ahead and descends west to Tumbledown Pond.

Parker's Ridge Trail

Distances from parking area
- *to* Parker's Ridge: 1.9 mi.(2 hr.)
- *to* Pond (outlet): 2.2 mi./3.5 km. (2 hr. 10 min.)

Tumbledown Ridge Trail

From the pond outlet junction with the Brook Trail and Parker's Ridge Trail the Tumbledown Ridge Trail ascends west over mostly open ledge to East Peak and to the junction with the Loop Trail. A short spur extends to the summit of West Peak offering views into the Swift River valley and to Old Blue and Elephant mountains to the west.

Tumbledown Ridge Trail

Distances from pond outlet
- *to* East Peak: 0.4 mi.
- *to* Loop Trail junction: 0.6 mi.
- *to* West Peak: 0.7 mi./1.1 km. (45 min.)

Pond Link Trail

From the Parker's Ridge Trail 0.1 mi. east of the pond the Pond Link Trail, blazed blue, heads north skirting the east end of the pond for about 100 yd. then turns east to ascend to the height-of-land between Parker's Ridge and Little Jackson at 0.3 mi. from the pond. The trail continues generally east to a junction with the Little Jackson Trail. This makes an interesting loop trip.

Pond Link Trail

Distances from the pond
- *to* start of Pond Link Trail: 0.1 mi.
- *to* height-of-land: 0.3 mi.
- *to* Little Jackson Trail: *est*. 1 mi./1.6 km. (40 min.)

LITTLE JACKSON MOUNTAIN (3434 ft./1047 m.)
JACKSON MOUNTAIN (3535 ft./1077 m.)
(TUMBLEDOWN RANGE)

For the road approach see the Parker's Ridge Trail section. If you want to supplement the map in this guide, refer to the USGS Rangeley and Rumford quadrangles, 15-minute series, and the Roxbury quadrangle, 7.5-minute series.

The trail leaves the shelter area northwest on a logging road. There are no trail signs along the way, but the trail is fairly well worn. Keep left on the logging roads and stay close to the edge of the valley that leads toward the Jacksons. About 0.5 mi. from the shelter, the route heads north toward the col between Little Jackson on the west and Jackson on the east. At about 1.5 mi. the trail turns right, northeast, and the blue-blazed Pond Link Trail leads straight ahead, northwest. At about 2.3 mi. the trail crosses a brook and continues onto open ledges 0.3 mi. beyond. At the ledges, the trail turns left and, ascending across open ledges with fine outlooks, climbs to the summit of Little Jackson.

Descending from the open areas on Little Jackson, the trail bears well to the right and is somewhat hard to see, so it is easy to get confused in the puckerbrush.

Few hikers visit the summit of Jackson, a large rambling mountain partially covered with spruce. It is possible to climb up from the col between Jackson and Little Jackson. The distance from the col to the summit is about 1 mi.

Little Jackson Mountain
Distances from parking area

to Pond Link Trail junction: *est*. 1.5 mi.

to col: 2.5 mi. (2 hr.)

to Jackson summit (via bushwhack from col): *est*. 3.5 mi.

to Little Jackson summit (via trail): 3.3 mi./5.3 km. (2 hr. 30 min.)

BLUEBERRY MOUNTAIN (2942 ft./897 m.)

See the USGS Phillips quadrangle, 15-minute series, if you want to supplement the map in this guide.

The trail leaves ME 142 1.5 mi. from Weld Corner toward Phillips. Blueberry Mountain Bible Camp maintains a road that runs 1.8 mi. to a clearing above the buildings. A gate near the base may be locked, blocking cars, but to date, personnel at the camp have been cooperative about letting people use their road as a foot trail. From the left (west) side of the clearing, follow a logging road to a trail with blue blazes. Trail maintenance has been sporadic. It rises steeply, first through conifers and then over ledges, to the summit. There are interesting geological formations at the top, which is bare and offers excellent views in all directions. There is *no water* on the trail.

Blueberry Mountain Trail
Distances from ME 142
   to clearing (via bible camp road): 1.8 mi.
   to Blueberry summit: 3.1 mi./5 km. (2 hr. 40 min.)

MOUNT BLUE (3187 ft./971 m.)

From Mount Washington, this peak is one of the most perfect cones on the skyline. The former fire tower on the summit has no cab. In addition to the map in this guide, you can refer to the USGS Dixfield quadrangle, 15-minute series, and the Mount Blue quadrangle, 7.5-minute series.

In Weld Village, take the road that leads uphill east from the four corners and bear left at the fork at 0.5 mi. Take the right fork at a little over 3 mi. and continue to the parking place at about 6 mi. The trail crosses a field northeast of the woods, where it is joined by an old telephone line. The path is broad and well worn and passes the old fire warden's cabin, where there is a fine *spring*. From this point the trail becomes somewhat steep until it reaches the summit, where in addition to the tower, there is a board shelter once used by the fire warden, but there is *no water*. The summit is wooded, but views are excellent from ledge outcroppings around it.

Mount Blue
Distances from parking place
   to fire warden's cabin: 0.6 mi.
   to Mount Blue summit: 1.7 mi./2.7 km. (1 hr. 40 min.)

BALD MOUNTAIN (2386 ft./727 m.)

The trail up Bald Mountain leaves the southern side of ME 156 about 8.5 mi. west of Wilton and about 5.5 mi. east of Weld at a small parking area, where there is a sign on a post marking the start of the trail. In addition to the map in this guide, you can refer to the USGS Dixfield quadrangle, 15-minute series, and the Mount Blue quadrangle, 7.5-minute series.

Cross the brook immediately (*last sure water*) and enter the woods. The trail climbs steadily through the woods, marked by paint blazes. On the open ledges it is marked by paint and cairns to the summit, where there are fine views in every direction. A faint trail may be followed 2 mi. farther to the summit of Saddleback Wind Mountain, which is slightly higher but attracts fewer visitors.

Bald Mountain
Distances from ME 156
   to ledges: 0.9 mi. (45 min.)
   to Bald Mountain summit: 1.5 mi./2.4 km. (1 hr. 15 min.)

SADDLEBACK WIND (2572 ft./784 km.)

The Anderson Brook Trail up Saddleback Wind in Carthage makes an excellent loop when combined with the Bald Mountain Trail. However, the route is bushy and hard to follow, so you should carry a map and compass. If you want to supplement the map in this guide, see the USGS Dixfield quadrangle, 15-minute series, and the Mount Blue quadrangle, 7.5-minute series.

The trail starts on the south side of ME 156 about 6.2 mi. from Wilton (and 7.7 mi. from Weld). There is no mark or sign, but the trail starts by a log bridge over a stream. Park by the bridge, being careful not to block the logging road. After crossing the bridge, turn right (northwest) across a field and follow the logging road about 0.5 mi. to the top of a small rise. The road ends in another 200 ft. A small blaze and ribbons on a tree mark an overgrown road that leads left up an obvious ridge. The trail is sparsely marked by ribbons and hard to pick out. Follow the ridge for 0.8 mi. to open and steep ledges. After a 200-ft. climb, the trail reaches a beautiful open ridge, which leads for 0.8 mi. through interesting convolutions in the rock, to the summit.

To reach Bald Mountain, drop into the col between Saddleback Wind and a secondary peak, and then drop into the major col between the two mountains. The route is extremely hard to follow and densely wooded; carry a compass. From the bottom of the second col, the climb up Bald Mountain is over open rock.

Anderson Brook Trail
Distance from ME 156
    to Saddleback Wind summit: 2.5 mi./4 km. (2 hr.)

SUGARLOAF MOUNTAIN (1521 ft./464 m.)

Sugarloaf Mountain in Dixfield is conspicuous because of its two prominent summits. It offers fine vistas from its open northern summit. Refer to the USGS Dixfield quadrangle, 7.5- and 15-minute series.

For the shortest route to the summit go north from the corner of Main (US 2) and Weld Streets in Dixfield. Take ME 142 for 1.7 mi. to a hard-to-see path on the right. (CMP Pole J19 is across the highway from the start.) Turn right to the house on the right. The trail diverges left directly behind the house. It immediately rises and becomes a broad, steep path up a hogback.

You can take one of two trails. An extremely steep, direct trail turns to the left (northwest) through hardwoods and open ledges to the summit. A trail that is easier but nearly as steep turns to the right. Follow it 30 ft. southwest. Then turn left into a stand of poplars obscuring the trail. Continue northeast to the col, where there is a small frog pond (dry in the fall). From there, hike north between two boulders about 200 ft. to a gravelly path through the ledges. Then go northwest to the summit through woods or along the tops of the steep ledges to the west. The southern summit is a bushwhack southeast from the frog pond. It has some interesting ledges.

Sugarloaf Mountain
Distance from ME 142

> *to* Sugarloaf summit (via either trail): 0.8 mi./1.3 km. (45 min.)

BULL ROCK (920 ft./280 m.)

Perched on the side of Sugarloaf Mountain in Dixfield, Bull Rock offers a delightful preview of the views from Sugarloaf. Hang glider pilots now fly from Bull Rock and land in the field by the road.

Start from Dixfield as for the trail to Sugarloaf and proceed 1.5 mi. north on ME 142 to CMP Pole J12 on the left. The trail leaves the highway on the right near a tiny brook. It passes behind a house on the right and rises quickly on a sharp hogback. After 10 to 15 min., the ledges of Bull Rock are visible to the right.

Bull Rock

Distance from ME 142

   to Bull Rock ledges: 0.4 mi./0.6 km. (20 min.)

Rangeley and Stratton Area

This section includes the mountains north of Rangeley Lakes; the area westward to Lake Aziscohos and the New Hampshire border; the isolated mountains north toward the Canadian border reached by a network of private logging roads and ME 27; and the important and outstanding cluster of 4000-ft. mountains, including Saddleback, Abraham, Sugarloaf, Crocker, and Bigelow, reached through the towns of Rangeley, Stratton, Kingfield, and Phillips. This last group includes eight of the state's 4000-ft. peaks. Sugarloaf, at 4237 ft., is Maine's second highest mountain (aside from the subsidiary summits of Katahdin), although Abraham (4049), Saddleback (4116), and especially Bigelow (4150) are more interesting for hiking.

There are two large ski areas in this region on Sugarloaf and Saddleback Mountains.

Accommodations are ample along ME 16/27 between Rangeley, Stratton, and Kingfield. The Rangeley Lake State Park on the southern shore opened in 1967, with full camping, boating, and swimming facilities. You can drive to the park via ME 17 or 4. There are additional public facilities at Mount Blue State Park in Weld, just south of this section.

The town of Eustis maintains Cathedral Pines camping area and trailer park, with laundry and recreation building, on ME 27, 3 mi. north of the ME 16/27 junction at Stratton and 2.3 mi. south of Eustis.

The MFS maintains the following camping areas (fires permitted): on the northern side of ME 16 about 5 mi. east of Rangeley and near Dallas; on the western shore of Flagstaff Lake at the end of the "Old Flagstaff Rd." 2 mi. east of a junction with ME 27 (near Flagstaff Memorial Church) 0.8 mi. north of Cathedral Pines campground; on the western side of ME 27 about 3 mi. south of Chain of Ponds; at Upper

Farm on the eastern shore of Chain of Ponds just off Me 27; and on the eastern shore of Chain of Ponds at its northern end, off ME 27.

MOUNT AZISCOHOS (3215 ft./980 m.)

South of Lake Aziscohos, this mountain offers excellent views of the Rangeley Lakes region. Fifteen lakes are visible from the summit. The trails lead to the eastern, and slightly lower, of the two peaks, where an abandoned MFS fire tower is down. Refer to the USGS Oquossoc and Errol quadrangles, 15-minute series.

There are two routes up the mountain. Opinions differ as to what they should be named; therefore, the descriptions are simply "from the northwest" and "from the north." *Caution.* Both trails as of 1987 are badly overgrown and blocked by many blowdowns. This guide includes the following old data, with the hope that the trails may be reopened.

From the Northwest

Sometimes called the Tower Man's Trail or South Trail, this route begins on the southern side of ME 16, at a small parking area 100 yd. east of the bridge over the Magalloway River at Aziscohos Dam. The trail follows an old dirt logging road, crosses the remains of a bridge at 0.8 mi., and continues gradually uphill. Cross the small stream at 1.1 mi. and take the left (south) fork. At 1.7 mi. the road reaches the clearing at the site of the former MFS fire warden's cabin, where there is an enclosed *spring*. Hike on the left side of the clearing and enter the open softwood forest. The trail continues on steeper but relatively easy grades, and at 2.4 mi. the trail from the north comes in on the left. Turn right and continue to the summit at 2.5 mi.

Mount Aziscohos, from the Northwest
Distances from ME 16
   to cabin site: 1.7 mi.
   to junction with trail from the north: 2.4 mi.
   to Aziscohos summit: 2.5 mi./4 km.) (2 hr. 30 min.)

From the North
The route from the north begins on ME 16, 1 mi. east of the bridge over the Magalloway River at Aziscohos Dam. At first it leads gradually uphill on an old tote road through open hardwood and mixed forest, then it turns sharply left at 0.5 mi. As of 1987, orange tape marks the trail. At 1 mi. the trail enters conifers and it crosses a brook at 1.1 mi. After that, it continues more steeply through open conifers and reaches the route coming in from the northwest at 2 mi. To the left, it is 0.1 mi. to the summit.

Mount Aziscohos, from the North
Distances from ME 16
   to brook crossing: 1.1 mi.
   to junction with trail from the northwest: 2 mi.
   to Aziscohos summit: 2.1 mi./3.4 km.(2 hr. 10 min.)

BALD MOUNTAIN (2443 ft./745 m.)
This small mountain is in a prime location between Mooselookmeguntic and Rangeley lakes. The views, however, are marginal, because despite the mountain's name, the woods have grown up around the bedrock summit. The summit's abandoned tower is in bad repair and may be dangerous to climb. A ski area on the northern slope has been out of business for many years and the ski trails are overgrown. Refer to the USGS Oquossoc quadrangle, 15-minute series.

To reach the hiking trail, go west from Oquossoc on ME 4 to the terminus of that highway at Haines Landing. Turn left (south) before the landing and follow a road paralleling the lake shore for about 1 mi. to the foot of the trail on the left. A short distance from the start of the trail, take the right fork and climb east and southeast to the summit. The trail is well used and easy to see in the hardwood forest at the base of the mountain, but it becomes braided at the higher elevations, where it requires care to stay on the main trail.

Bald Mountain

Distance from road
  to Bald Mountain summit: 1 mi./1.6 km. (1 hr.)

WEST KENNEBAGO MOUNTAIN
(3705 ft./1129 m.)

This isolated mountain is north of the Rangeley Lakes and west of Kennebago Lake. There is a fire tower on the south peak, which also offers fine views of the area, and is the highest of the several summits of the north-south ridge that forms the mountain. Refer to the USGS Cupsuptic quadrangle, 15-minute series. (Note: the trail now begins north of the one shown on the 1931 USGS map).

Access to the fire warden's trail is via the Brown Company (now the James River Corp.) system of private roads. Turn north from ME 16 on a company road 4.9 mi. west of the ME 4/16 junction in Oquossoc and 0.3 mi. west of the MFS buildings at Cupsuptic. Drive 3.2 mi. from ME 16 to a junction with a well-maintained, wide gravel road. Turn right (east) and in 5.3 mi. the road reaches the fire tower trail, which is marked by an MFS sign.

The trail starts as a road but soon becomes a path and climbs rather steeply. At 0.9 mi. the trail levels out among conifers and bears left. Then it begins to climb again, crosses a small stream, and turns sharp right. At 1.4 mi. the trail reaches the warden's camp (3186 ft.), a picturesque log cabin built in 1911. There is a *spring* behind the camp 300 ft. to the left. The trail leaves the camp from the upper right (northwest) corner of the clearing. At 1.7 mi. it reaches the ridge, where the trail turns left (south) following the ridge to the fire tower.

West Kennebago Mountain
Distances from road

   to warden's camp: 1.4 mi.

   to West Kennebago, southern summit: 2.1 mi./3.4 km. (2 hr.)

EAST KENNEBAGO MOUNTAIN
(3791 ft./1155 m.)

East of Kennebago Lake, this is a long, wooded ridge running east-west in T2 R4 T2 R5. (T and R stand for township and range; Maine uses this system to designate its unincorporated towns.)

This is in part a bushwhack trip. Refer to the USGS Kennebago Lake quadrangle 15-minute series, and the Kennebago Lake, Quill Hill, and Tim Mountain quadrangles, 7.5-minute series. East Kennebago also appears on the Rangeley-Stratton map in this guide.

From ME 16 about 9 mi. southwest of Stratton turn right (west), then turn right again. Set the altimeter at 1300 ft. here. At about 1 mi. take the right fork to a gate on the right. Park here if the gate is locked. Go through the gate and take an immediate left (sign: "Eustis Ridge, Stratton"). Follow this road about 2 mi. to nearly 2000 ft. elevation and watch for a cairn on the left. Turn left and follow this upper road. *Caution.* Note this junction carefully to avoid a wrong turn on the descent. The road climbs generally north then northeast, becoming more overgrown. Pass two branch roads on the left. Cross a yellow-blazed boundary line and approach a brook at about 2950 ft. A tree on the left should have two red markers on it. Set the compass heading at 342°. Follow up this stream, soon bearing left away from the brook to the saddle northeast of the summit. Turn left (southwest), heading 228°, and climb almost a half-mile to the flat summit. The register bottle is just south of the summit plateau and marked by two red ribbons around a tree. (This trail information was current Sept. 1981.)

East Kennebago Mountain

Distance from gate

  to East Kennebago summit: *est.* 5 mi./8.1 km. (3 hr. 45 min.)

SNOW MOUNTAIN (3960 ft./1207 m.)

Snow Mountain is southwest of Chain of Ponds. There is an abandoned MFS fire tower on the summit. The mountain offers extensive views in all directions, including an extended sweep into Canada over Lake Megantic. From the summit, you can see many miles of Benedict Arnold's route to Quebec in 1775, which followed the headwaters of the Dead River past Chain of Ponds and into Quebec Province. Refer to the USGS Chain Lakes quadrangle, 15-minute series, and the Chain of Ponds and Jim Pond quadrangles, 7.5-minute series.

The approach is via a dirt road leading left (west) from ME 27, 0.3 mi. north of the Alder Stream/Jim Pond town line and 7.5 mi. north of Eustis. Park at a gravel pit 2.8 mi. from ME 27. (As of 1987, the road is passable 0.8 mi. farther.) At 0.3 mi. pass a road on the left to Round Pond. Cross and recross a stream. At 2.1 mi. turn left at a yarding area and cross a stream. At 3.6 mi. turn sharply left and cross a brook. At 4 mi. the road to the left leads to Snow Mountain Pond. The former fire warden's cabin there is now private property. Turn right to the fire warden's trail (sign) and climb steeply north, passing a *spring*. At 5.2 mi. the trail from Big Island Pond comes in on the left. Turn right and climb northeast to the summit.

Descending, don't miss the point where the fire warden's trail turns left and the trail from Big Island Pond goes right.

Snow Mountain
Distances from parking area
to Snow Mountain Pond: 4 mi. (2 hr.)
to Snow summit: 5.4 mi./8.7 km. (3 hr. 10 min.)

EUSTIS RIDGE (1623 ft./495 m.)

Eustis Ridge is a fine outlook over Flagstaff Lake, the Bigelow Range, and other peaks to the south. It is right on the road, and there is a state picnic area. Refer to the USGS Stratton and Kennebago Lake quadrangles, 15-minute series, and Tim Mountain quadrangle, 7.5-minute series if you want to supplement the map in this guide.

From Stratton, drive north on ME 27 to Cathedral Pines. About 3.5 mi. from Stratton, turn left on a paved road (signs) and drive west 2 mi. to the picnic area.

SADDLEBACK MOUNTAIN AND THE HORN
(summit 4116 ft. and The Horn 4023 ft./1255 m. and 1226 m.)

Saddleback Mountain, southeast of Rangeley, is one of Maine's outstanding mountains. It is a long range extending east and west. Pronounced saddles separate its several peaks. Two of the peaks are over 4000 ft.—Saddleback summit and The Horn. The bare summits of both offer far-flung views in all directions. Saddleback, with its widespread areas above tree line, is also unusually exposed. *Caution.* High winds or restricted visibility can be dangerous. You can refer to the USGS Phillips and Rangeley quadrangles, 15-minute series, as well as the map in this guide, or map 6 in the MATC's *Guide to the Appalachian Trail in Maine*.

There are several points of interest on the southwestern side of the mountain. Piazza Rock is an enormous overhanging flat boulder with a growth of mature trees, and nearby, the Caves offer ample opportunities for exploration. Both are on the Appalachian Trail, 1.4 mi. north of ME 4. Eddy Pond, one of several small ponds on Saddleback, is particularly attractive.

The Saddleback Mountain Ski Area is on the northwestern slope of the mountain. In 1987 the NPS and the Ski Area were involved in a major dispute over the extent of protection to be provided to the AT on Saddleback.

Appalachian Trail

To approach Saddleback from the west, follow ME 4 for 32 mi. north from the ME 4/US 2 junction in Farmington or for 9.9 mi. south from the ME 4/16 junction in Rangeley. The Appalachian Trail crosses ME 4 in a steep winding section of the road. Park on the wide gravel shoulder on the eastern side of the highway.

From ME 4, the Appalachian Trail descends and crosses the Sandy River at 0.1 mi. The trail climbs out of the valley, crossing a gravel logging road at 1.1 mi. At 1.4 mi. the trail passes the Piazza Rock Lean-to (built in 1935 by the Civilian Conservation Corps; reconditioned by the MATC; accommodates six; MFS Campsite). A side trail leads left 500 ft. to the top of Piazza Rock. Not far beyond, on the Appalachian Trail, a side path leads left 100 yd. to the Caves, a series of boulder caves with narrow passages. The Appalachian Trail then climbs steeply, passes along Ethel Pond's western shore, and turns sharp left away from the end of the pond. The trail then continues to rise, passes Mud Pond, and descends slightly to Eddy Pond (last sure *water*). Watch for a point near the eastern shore of Eddy Pond about 3.2 mi. from ME 4 where the trail, after turning left on a road for a few feet, turns sharp right from the road onto a trail. It rises steeply through conifers, emerging in 0.8 mi. on a scrub-covered slope.

This open crest is particularly interesting, but the cairns are small, the path is not well worn, and the trail is fully exposed. It should not be traveled in bad weather. After nearly 0.8 mi. over rocky slopes and heath, the trail descends slightly into a sag, where a blue-blazed side path (may be hard to see) leads right (south) about 0.1 mi. through scrub to a *spring* (not dependable). The main trail climbs 0.1 mi. further to the summit.

The Appalachian Trail continues over open slopes, descends steeply into the col between Saddleback and The Horn, and reaches the summit of The Horn 1.6 mi. from the main summit.

For the continuation of the Appalachian Trail beyond the Horn, see the 1988 edition of the MATC *Guide to the Appalachian Trail in Maine.*

Appalachian Trail, Saddleback Mountain
Distances from ME 4

to junction with logging road: 1.1 mi.
to Piazza Rock Lean-to: 1.4 mi.
to Piazza Rock (via side trail): 1.5 mi.
to Saddleback summit: 5.1 mi./8.2 km. (2 hr. 30 min.)
to The Horn summit: 6.7 mi./10.8 km. (3 hr. 30 min.)

MOUNT ABRAHAM (4049 ft./1234 m.)

Mount Abraham (or Abram) lies northwest of Kingfield and south of Sugarloaf and Spaulding Mountains. It is an impressive ridge about 4.5 mi. long that runs on a northwest-

southeast axis and consists of about eight peaks ranging
from 3400 to over 4000 ft. The highest peak, with an abandoned MFS fire tower, lies north of the middle of the ridge.
The extensive areas above timberline on Abraham give it an
unusually alpine appearance for its height. Although the
trailless ridge south of the tower has been traversed, that
route is not advisable since the distances are deceptive and
the scrub is very dense between peaks. Two trails ascend to
the abandoned fire tower. The Fire Warden's Trail approaches the mountain from Kingfield. It has not been maintained for many years and is not safe for spring climbing due
to very high water at the Rapid Stream crossing. The Mount
Abraham Side Trail, cut in 1987, approaches from the Appalachian Trail north of Mount Abraham and west of Spaulding Mountain. Refer to the USGS Kingfield and Phillips
quadrangles, 15-minute series, or map 6 in the MATC *Guide
to the Appalachian Trail in Maine* if you want to supplement
the map in this guide.

Fire Warden's Trail

To reach the trail follow ME 27 north from Kingfield.
Turn left (west) on the paved road (West Kingfield St.) at Jordan's Lumber Company store, 0.2 mi. north of the bridge
over the Carrabassett River. At 3 mi. from ME 27 the road
becomes gravel. Go straight through a crossroad at 3.5 mi.
to 3.7 mi., where the road forks. Go right. From this point
the road is a logging road. At 6 mi. a road turns left to a
washout (impassable for all vehicles) on the east side of
Rapid Stream just before it reaches the stream itself.

The logging road bridge across Rapid Stream has washed
out. It is dangerous to cross Rapid Stream at high water.
Cross the stream and follow the road for about 0.5 mi. to a
crossroad. The trail continues straight into the woods.

The trail follows the south bank of Norton Brook, crosses
the brook, and continues along the north bank, gradually

climbing. In another 0.3 mi. it turns northwest. The next 2 mi. of the trail, to the abandoned warden's cabin, skirts the northeast flank of the mountain, crossing four major brooks. Grades are easy. There is a good *spring* to the right of the cabin.

From the old cabin (2127 ft.), the trail turns left straight up the slope and climbs steeply through the woods for a mile, then comes out on an old slide with good views. At about 0.1 above the cabin, a side trail leads left to a brook (last sure *water*). The remainder of the trail is completely exposed, except for a few short stretches of scrub. In this section an abandoned telephone line and the few cairns should be followed carefully in bad weather. The trail rises steadily across a boulder field to the fire tower.

Fire Warden's Trail
Distances from Rapid Stream
to crossroad near Norton Brook: 0.5 mi.
to fire warden's cabin: 3 mi.
to Abraham summit: 4.5 mi./7.2 km. (3 hr. 45 min.)

Mount Abraham Side Trail

For the approach to this trail see the description of the Appalachian Trail route to Spaulding Mountain in this guide.

From the junction of the Appalachian Trail and the blue-blazed side trail to the Spaulding Mountain summit continue south on the Appalachian Trail, descending the cone of Spaulding Mountain to the site of the future Spaulding Mountain lean-to with (in 1987) two tent sites, a *spring*, and a privy. A temporary side trail marked by orange tape leads 0.6 mi. north to the old Spaulding Mountain lean-to, which is still functional.

Continue south on the Appalachian Trail to the junction of the Mount Abraham Side Trail. The Appalachian Trail continues southwest, climbing Lone Mountain. Refer to map

6 in the 1988 edition of the MATC *Guide to the Appalachian Trail in Maine*. The Mount Abraham Side Trail leads 1.7 mi. southeast following a very old tote road, climbing gradually then steeply up the south ridge of Mount Abraham, which is characterized by a very dense forest. The trail emerges from the trees and ascends a rock field to the tower.

Mount Abraham Side Trail
Distances from Caribou Valley Road

- *to* junction of Appalachian Trail and Spaulding summit trail: 3.9 mi.
- *to* site of new Spaulding Mountain campsite: *est.* 4.5 mi.
- *to* junction of Appalachian Trail and Mount Abraham Side Trail: *est.* 4.9 mi.
- *to* Mount Abraham summit: 6.6 mi./10.6 km. (5 hr. 25 min.)

CROCKER MOUNTAIN (north peak 4168 ft. and south peak 4000 ft./1270 m. and 1219 m.)

The northern extension of the Crocker-Redington Pond Range, this mountain is 3.5 mi. west of Sugarloaf and separated from it by the Caribou Valley (south branch of the Carrabassett). The summit of the north peak, despite its height, has few views and is heavily wooded to the top. The south peak, 1 mi. to the south, has a definite summit with fine views and rises 380 ft. above the col between it and the north peak. Hikers may approach the mountain via the Appalachian Trail from ME 27 or the Caribou Valley Rd.

Approach via Appalachian Trail from ME 27

For the approach from the north and ME 27, follow the highway 2.6 mi. northwest from the Sugarloaf access road. Park off the highway at this point. (Sign, Appalachian Trail crossing.) Leaving the south side of the highway, the Appalachian Trail climbs steadily through woods for nearly 1.5 mi. before reaching the northernmost knoll of the north peak. A spruce section begins at about 1 mi. and continues to about 2 mi., where the trail slabs the western side of the ridge through birches. It continues up the western side of the ridge, reenters conifers at about 3.5 mi., and passes a small stream (usually reliable—last *water*). After that, the trail rises more steeply to the crest and reaches the summit of the north peak at 4.9 mi. The descent into the col begins immediately. The trail leads to the low point of the col and soon begins to climb toward the rocky summit of the south peak. To reach the summit, take the 150 ft., blue-blazed path (sign) to the right (west), where the Appalachian Trail makes a sharp left turn for the descent to the Caribou Valley.

Crocker Mountain via Appalachian Trail
Distances from ME 27

to Crocker, north ridge: 1.5 mi.

to stream in conifers: *est.* 3.5 mi.

to north peak summit: 4.9 mi./7.9 km. (4 hr.)

to south peak summit (via blue-blazed summit trail): 5.9 mi./9.5 km. (4 hr. 30 min.)

to Caribou Valley Road: 8 mi/12.9 km. (5 hr. 30 min.)

Approach via Caribou Valley Road

This road leads south from ME 27 1 mi. northwest of the entrance to Sugarloaf. The Appalachian Trail crosses the road 4.5 mi. south of ME 27; 50 yd. beyond this crossing, an old metal gate is usually open.

The Appalachian Trail leaves the road to the right (west) and climbs steadily but not too steeply through birch woods. Nearly a mile from the road, a blue-blazed trail leads right 0.2 mi. to the Crocker Cirque Campsite (built by the MATC in 1975; it has a two-tent platform, fireplace, and latrine). On the side trail to this campsite is the last sure *water*. Beyond the turn-off to the campsite the Appalachian Trail begins the steep climb to the shoulder of the south peak. The trail leads up the shoulder through woods for the next mile to the crest of the south peak. Then it turns sharply right, and at the same point, the 150-ft. side trail (sign) to the actual summit of the south peak leaves to the left. The Appalachian Trail then descends into the col, from which it climbs steadily to the summit of the north peak.

Crocker Mountain via Caribou Valley Road
Distances from Caribou Valley Road
to side trail to campsite: 0.9 mi.(35 min.)
to south peak summit: 2.1 mi. (2 hr.)
to north peak summit: 3.1 mi./5 km. (2 hr. 45 min.)
to ME 27: 8 mi./12.9 km. (5 hr.)

SUGARLOAF MOUNTAIN (4237 ft./1291 m.)
SPAULDING MOUNTAIN (3988 ft./1216 m.)

Sugarloaf Mountain

Sugarloaf Mountain is the second-highest mountain in Maine. Many other peaks are more popular with hikers. Sugarloaf is known and frequented chiefly for skiing. The ski area is on the northern slope, and since it is in one of the heaviest snow belts in the northeastern United States, spring skiing is frequently good after other areas further to the south have closed for the season. For the hiker the view from the symmetrical, bare cone is well worth the climb of almost 2500 ft. The number of peaks visible is perhaps unequaled in the state except from Katahdin. Spaulding Mountain (3988 ft.) is about 2.5 mi. to the south of Sugarloaf and is connected with it by a high ridge.

A rough road (not good enough for cars but easy to follow on foot in bad weather) has been built to the summit. It starts behind the maintenance-vehicle storage building at the base, near the ski area parking lot, and climbs at first west, then south, and finally east to the summit. This road, or the network of ski trails on the mountain, provides an approach from the north. The road is about 4 mi. long; the ski trails are shorter but steeper.

You can also approach Sugarloaf from the south. The Appalachian Trail leaves the Caribou Valley Road 4.5 mi. south of ME 27. After leaving the road to the east, the trail soon crosses the South Branch of the Carrabassett (dangerous in high water), follows up the stream for a time, and then begins to climb, at first gently and then more steeply. After that, it crosses ledges and skirts the top of a cirque on the western side of Sugarloaf. The last *water* is a stream 1.8 mi. from the road. At 1.9 mi. the Appalachian Trail turns right toward Spaulding Mountain, while the blue-blazed Sugarloaf Side Trail leaves to the left and reaches the summit in 0.6 mi.

Sugarloaf Side Trail
Distances from Caribou Valley Road
> *to* junction Sugarloaf Side Trail (via Appalachian Trail):
>   1.9 mi. (1 hr. 45 min.)
> *to* Sugarloaf summit: 2.5 mi./4 km. (2 hr. 15 min.)

Spaulding Mountain
From its junction with the Sugarloaf Side Trail, the Appalachian Trail (south) traverses the crest of the ridge between Sugarloaf and Spaulding, with views and steep cliffs on the left. At 1.5 mi. the trail begins the ascent of Spaulding, first steeply, then gradually. Near the top, a blue-blazed trail leads left 500 ft. to the summit.

For a description of the Appalachian Trail south of Spaulding, see the Mount Abraham Side Trail description in this guide or the 1988 edition of the MATC *Guide to the Ap-palachian Trail in Maine.*

Spaulding Mountain
Distance from Caribou Valley Road
  to Spaulding summit (via Appalachian Trail): 4 mi. (6.4
  km.), 3 hr. 25 min.

THE BIGELOW RANGE

LITTLE BIGELOW (3040 ft./927 m.)
AVERY PEAK (4088 ft./1246 m.)
WEST PEAK (4150 ft./1265 m.)
SOUTH HORN (3831 ft./1168 m.)
NORTH HORN (3810 ft./1161 m.)
CRANBERRY PEAK (3213 ft./979 m)

The Bigelow Range runs east-west for some 12 mi. It is sec-ond only to the Katahdin region in interest and opportuni-ties for superb ridge walking. The central features are the twin "cones," Avery Peak and West Peak, which project above the ridge. The equally symmetrical twin "horns," far-ther west and only slightly lower, are North Horn and South Horn. Still farther west is Cranberry Peak with its bare ledges. To the east of Avery Peak, but separated from it by a deep notch, lies Little Bigelow Mountain.

The Bigelow Mountain Preserve, established by the people of Maine in referendum (June 1976), includes the Bigelow Range and the land surrounding it. The 33,000-acre preserve is administered by the Maine Department of Conservation and the Maine Department of Inland Fisheries and Wildlife. As of 1988 virtually all of the land for the preserve has been acquired by the state.

Prior to the New England hurricane of 1938, the western portion of the range was an almost unbroken, uncut softwood forest. That and subsequent storms greatly damaged the forest, and only small uncut sections remain. Water is scarce in some areas of this range.

From Avery Peak, there is a magnificent outlook over the rugged wilderness of peaks, ponds, streams, and extensive Flagstaff Lake—perhaps the best view in the state except for the one from Katahdin.

Flagstaff Lake, a man-made reservoir (Maine's fourth-largest body of water) lies just north of the Bigelow Range. Like the range, the lake stretches east to west.

West of the Horns lies the Horns Pond, a beautiful mountain tarn. Cranberry Pond, Arnolds Well, and other landmarks are further west.

In addition to the map in this guide refer to the USGS Stratton and Little Bigelow quadrangles, 15-minute series.

The Fire Warden's Trail is the shortest approach to the main peaks of the Bigelow Range; but the Horns Pond Trail is longer, less steep, and more interesting. It leads to the Horns Pond, where it joins the Appalachian Trail to follow the ridge between the Horns, over South Horn and West Peak, and on to Avery Peak. As a third approach to the west of the first two trails, the Appalachian Trail runs from ME 27 to the ridge west of the Horns Pond. These trails approach from the south (ME 16/27). A fourth and longer approach, the Bigelow Range Trail from Stratton east to the Appalachian Trail, east of Cranberry Pond, involves more ridge travel up and down the many peaks of the range. It extends the range's full length, from the western end to Avery Peak. A road runs along the southern shore of Flagstaff Lake from the Long Falls Dam Rd. toward Stratton. It offers a fifth approach to the highest peaks via the Safford Brook Trail.

Fire Warden's Trail

A rough dirt road, Stratton Brook Rd. (usually passable) runs east from ME 27 about 3.2 mi. northwest of the Sugarloaf Ski Area access road and 4.5 mi. southeast of Stratton. Drive in, cross the Appalachian Trail at 1 mi., and continue straight ahead, turning left at 1.6 mi. in a logging yarding area. The road beyond the yarding area is very rough. The bridge over the Stratton Brook is washed out. There is very limited parking here. From this point cross Stratton Brook and continue on the road. At 0.2 mi. reach a fork (site of former parking area); go left. (The right fork descends to a partially destroyed bridge.) From this point the trail leads north for 0.2 mi., then runs east on the level for about 0.5 mi. After that, it climbs steeply over ledges to a shelf. The grade is easy for the next 1.5 mi., during which the trail crosses several brooks. At 1.6 mi. from the parking area, the Horns Pond Trail leaves left (northwest). At 3 mi. from the Statton Brook, the trail runs under the West Peak of Bigelow and the grade becomes increasingly steep. The trail gains nearly 1700 ft. in the next 1.5 mi. as it climbs north-northeast to the Bigelow col, where it meets the Appalachian Trail at 3.5 mi. The Avery Memorial Lean-to (accommodates six, MFS campsite) is located here. The caretaker uses the old fire warden's cabin, which is kept locked.

From the col, go right (east) via the Appalachian Trail 0.4 mi. to reach Avery Peak and its abandoned fire tower. To reach West Peak, go left (west) on the Appalachian Trail about 0.4 mi.

Descending, the trail diverges from the Appalachian Trail in Bigelow Col at the Avery Lean-to and goes down to the southwest.

Fire Warden's Trail
Distances from Stratton Brook

to Horns Pond Trail junction: 1.6 mi.

to Bigelow Col and Appalachian Trail junction: 3.5 mi. (3 hr. 40 min.)

to Avery Peak: 3.9 mi./6.3 km. (4 hr.)

to West Peak: 3.9 mi./6.3 km. (4 hr.)

Horns Pond Trail

This trail starts at the same point as the Fire Warden's Trail (see above). The Horns Pond Trail diverges left (northwest) from the Fire Warden's Trail 1.6 mi. from the Stratton Brook. The Horns Pond Trail heads northwest, climbing gradually. At 3 mi., the trail skirts the southern edge of a former bog area with an excellent view of the South Horn. The trail continues to rise gradually, then it gets steeper. At 4.1 mi. the Horns Pond Trail intersects the white-blazed Appalachian Trail. Bear right on the Appalachian Trail for 0.2 mi. to the two Horns Pond lean-tos (caretaker, accommodate six each, MFS campsite). A 50-yd. blue-blazed trail behind the East Lean-to leads to the Horns Pond.

Horns Pond Trail
Distances from Stratton Brook

to start (via Fire Warden's Trail): 1.6 mi.

to Appalachian Trail: 4.1 mi.

to Horns Pond Lean-tos: 4.3 mi./6.9 km. (3 hr.)

Appalachian Trail (from the South)

This trail (partly maintained by the Maine Chapter of the AMC) leaves ME 27 2.6 mi. northwest of the Sugarloaf Mountain access road. In the first mile, the trail descends slowly and crosses Stratton Brook Rd. at 0.9 mi. (This road, and the so-called Jones Pond Rd. soon after it, form alternate starting points for the hike.) After the Jones Pond Rd., the trail descends immediately to cross Stratton Brook on a foot bridge. In the next mile, the trail passes through spruce woods and then joins an old tote road. Turn left on the tote road, which soon crosses a stream. At 1.9 mi. turn right off the road and cross a tote road 2.5 mi. from ME 27. The trail passes an abandoned beaver pond and then climbs gradually but steadily as it approaches the basin of Cranberry Pond, where it passes a *spring* (last sure *water* before the Horns Pond).

At 3.4 mi. the Appalachian Trail turns sharp right (north). The Bigelow Range Trail (sign) continues straight ahead (west). The Appalachian Trail climbs steeply through a boulder field. At 4 mi. it reaches the crest of the ridge. There it turns right (east) and follows the ridge, crossing a minor summit. At 5 mi., where the trail takes a sharp left, there is a lookout 50 ft. to the right over the Horns Pond to the Horns. The trail descends steeply. At 5.1 mi. the Horns Pond Trail comes in on the right. The Appalachian Trail continues along the south shore of the Horns Pond, passing the two Horns Pond lean-tos at 5.3 mi.

From the Horns Pond, the Appalachian Trail continues east, climbing South Horn. At 5.8 mi. the blue-blazed North Horn Trail leads 0.2 mi. left to the North Horn. A little farther on, the Appalachian Trail crosses the South Horn. Then it continues along the crest of the Bigelow Range, reaching West Peak at 8 mi. The trail then descends to the Avery Memorial Lean-to at 8.4 mi, where the Fire Warden's Trail comes in on the right directly in front of the lean-to. The Appalachian Trail continues east, climbing to the summit of Avery Peak at 8.8 mi.

From Avery Peak, the Appalachian Trail descends east to its junction with the Safford Brook Trail. For a description of the Appalachian Trail east of the Safford Brook Trail, see the 1988 edition (map 5) of the MATC *Guide to the Appalachian Trail in Maine.*

Appalachian Trail (from the South)
Distances from ME 27

   to Stratton Brook Road: 0.9 mi.

to Stratton Brook: 1 mi.

to Bigelow Range Trail junction: 3.4 mi.

to Horns Pond Trail junction: 5.1 mi.

to Horns Pond lean-tos: 5.3 mi./8.5 km. (3 hr. 40 min.)

to South Horn summit: 5.9 mi.

to West Peak summit: 8 mi.

to Avery Lean-to and Fire Warden's Trail junction: 8.4 mi./13.5 km.), (5 hr. 55 min.)

to Avery Peak: 8.8 mi./14.2 km. (6 hr. 15 min.)

Bigelow Range Trail

This blue-blazed trail starts at the western end of the range, on ME 27/16 0.5 mi. southeast of Stratton and about 100 yd. northwest of the Eustis-Coplin town line. From the highway, follow a dirt road east. At 0.5 mi. from ME 27/16 the road ends at a clearing. The trail passes through woods for 0.3 mi. Then the trail climbs gradually about 0.2 mi. on a wide logging road. The trail reaches the first barren ledges at 1.9 mi. and bears right. Arnolds Well (a deep cleft in the rocks; *no drinking water*) is 20 ft. to the right. The trail turns up the ledges. There is a good view from the top of the first ledges. The trail leads through scrub and logged areas along the northern edge of the ridge with fine views. After reaching open ledges, it makes a short, steep ascent to Cranberry Peak at 3.2 mi.

After a short, steep descent the trail descends more gradually. Then it follows the north shore of Cranberry Pond, to end at a junction with the Appalachian Trail at 4.9 mi.

Bigelow Range Trail
Distances from ME 27

to clearing: 0.5 mi.

to first ledges: 1.9 mi.

to Cranberry Peak: 3.2 mi. (2 hr. 40 min.)

to Appalachian Trail junction: 4.9 mi./7.9 km. (3 hr. 50 min.)

Bigelow Range from the North (Safford Brook Trail and Appalachian Trail)

This trail begins at Round Barn Field on the shore of Flagstaff Lake, crosses East Flagstaff Rd., and climbs to the Appalachian Trail at Safford Notch.

The trail can be approached by water or by road. Round Barn Field is located on the east side of a cove on the south shore of Flagstaff Lake, which can be identified from the lake by a large sawdust pile on the lake shore. To reach the trail by road, turn north off ME 16 on the blacktop Long Falls Dam Rd. in North New Portland. At 16.7 mi. turn left (northwest) on Bog Brook Rd. (gravel). At about 0.8 mi. East Flagstaff Rd. leads left (north and west); it crosses Safford Brook at 4 mi. and the trail at 4.5 mi.

From Round Barn Field the trail passes through the woods and crosses East Flagstaff Rd. at 0.3 mi. The trail follows a graded tote road, then climbs steeply, crosses Safford Brook, and enters Safford Notch. At 2.6 mi. reach a junction with the Appalachian Trail.

Fifty yd. east (left) on the Appalachian Trail is a blue-blazed trail south (right) 0.2 mi. to Safford Notch Campsite with two tent platforms and a privy. (The Appalachian Trail east reaches the highest peak of Little Bigelow at 3.7 mi.) The Appalachian Trail west rises steeply toward Avery Peak for a mile, with several excellent vistas. At 3.4 mi. it reaches the crest of the ridge. There, a side trail leads left 500 ft. to the top of Old Man's Head (a cliff on the side of the mountain). The trail continues to climb steeply, reaching the timberline and, shortly thereafter, the abandoned tower on Avery Peak.

Safford Brook Trail and Appalachian Trail
Distances from Round Barn Field

> *to* East Flagstaff Road: 0.3 mi.
> *to* Appalachian Trail junction (via Safford Brook Trail): 2.6 mi.
> *to* Little Bigelow summit (via Appalachian Trail east): 6.3 mi./10 km. (4 hr.)
> *to* Avery Peak (via Appalachian Trail west): 4.5 mi./7.2 km. (3 hr 45 min.)

LITTLE BIGELOW MOUNTAIN
(3040 ft./927 m.)

Little Bigelow lies to the east of the main Bigelow Range, separated from it by a deep notch, known as Safford Notch. It is a long, narrow ridge, with steep cliffs along the southern side. The northern slope descends steadily for some 2 mi. to Flagstaff Lake. The natural structure of the mountain makes extremely rough terrain. The trail is part of the Appalachian Trail and therefore marked with white paint blazes. Refer to the USGS Little Bigelow Mountain quadrangle, 15-minute series, or map 5 in the MATC *Guide to the Appalachian Trail in Maine*, if you want to supplement the map in this guide.

The approach is via the Appalachian Trail. See the Safford Brook description for Avery Peak for the approach from the west. To approach from the east, follow Long Falls Dam Rd. north from North New Portland. At 16.7 mi. the former route of ME 16, Bog Brook Rd. (flowed out by Flagstaff Lake), diverges left. Follow this well-graded road for 0.8 mi. Turn left on East Flagstaff Rd., which crosses the Appalachian Trail in 0.1 mi. The Appalachian Trail leads through hardwoods and follows a brook. At 1.2 mi. a blue-blazed side trail leads right 0.1 mi.across the brook to the Little Bigelow Lean-to. The trail continues through the woods, leaving the brook, and climbs on a series of open ledges which comprise the northeast buttress of the mountain. At 3 mi. it reaches the summit.

Little Bigelow Mountain
Distances from East Flagstaff Road (via Appalachian Trail)

to Little Bigelow Lean-to: 1.3 mi.
to Little Bigelow summit: 2.8 mi./4.5 km. (2 hr. 30 min.)
to Avery Peak: 7.5 mi./12.1 km. (6 hr.)

Kennebec Valley

This section includes several mountains on the lower and middle sections of the Kennebec River and other mountains that are accessible from US 201 and roads running off this highway. There are MFS fire towers on several of these summits. US 201 generally follows the Kennebec River as far as The Forks. It then runs through mountainous country past Parlin Pond to Jackman and on to the Quebec border. ME 15 diverges east from US 201 at Jackman and follows down the Moose River valley to reach Moosehead Lake at Rockwood.

The highest mountain in this section is Coburn Mountain (3718 ft.). Boundary Bald Mountain is 3640 ft., but the majority of the rest are much lower. Most of the mountains described in this section are in Somerset County; two are in Kennebec County.

MOUNT PISGAH (809 ft./246 m.)

On the summit of Mount Pisgah in Winthrop there are an MFS fire tower, a microwave relay tower, a log cabin equipment building, and a small enclosed shelter building (unlocked). Refer to the USGS Wayne quadrangle, 7.5-minute series.

From the intersection of US 202 and ME 41 in Winthrop, go 3 mi. west on US 202. Turn right (northwest) at St. Stanislas Catholic Church on the road to North Monmouth. Continue past the Globe Albany factory on the left. At 0.5 mi. the road reaches the crossroads in North Monmouth. (A dam and a bridge over a stream are on the left.) Turn right, go 0.2 mi. to Pisgah Rd., turn left (northwest), and drive for 2 mi. to the warden's cabin on the right. The trail follows the line of the driveway, crosses the yard to the rear of the cabin, and immediately crosses a brook (dry in dry weather). After a 0.3-mi. climb following telephone wires, the trail bears left and levels out at a stone wall. From the wall, the trail gently rises over a distance of about 0.7 mi., at times following the telephone wires or a jeep road, which also runs from the warden's cabin to the tower. The trail's last 100 ft. traverse open ledges to the summit, where views in all directions take in the entire sweep of western Maine's mountains, from Pleasant Mountain to Sugarloaf, as well as the Presidentials in New Hampshire. Views of surrounding lakes add sparkle to the scene.

Mount Pisgah
Distance from warden's cabin
>   *to* Mount Pisgah summit: 1 mi./1.6 km. (45 min.)

MONUMENT HILL (660 ft./201 m.)

Monument Hill, in Leeds, is just west of the Androscoggin Lake and offers good views to the south and southwest from its summit, though in other directions views are largely obscured by trees. On the summit is a granite monument to Leeds soldiers and sailors of the Civil War. Refer to the USGS Turner Center quadrangle, 7.5-minute series.

To reach the trail from US 202 between Lewiston and Augusta, take ME 106 north for 6.2 mi. to Leeds. Take Church Hill Rd. left for 0.9 mi. to North Rd. on the right. The trailhead is at 0.9 mi. (sign) and the well-worn trail is marked by faded and sporadic blue blazes. It leads east and southeast through varied forest and berry patches to the rocky summit.

Monument Hill
Distance from North Road
>   *to* summit: 1 mi./1.6 km. (40 min.)

COOK HILL (472 ft./143 m.)

Cook Hill, in Vassalboro, is topped by a 60-ft. MFS fire tower, with a 360-degree view, and a microwave facility, which is 120 ft. high. Refer to the USGS Vassalboro quadrangle, 15-minute series.

From US 201/ME 100 in Vassalboro, take the road northeast at Coburn-Oak Grove School and drive 2 mi. to an unsurfaced service road on the left (northwest) with a double overhead wire. From ME 32 in North Vassalboro, take the same road southwest at the Mid-State Machine Products brick factory building and drive 1.2 mi. to the same side road on the right (northwest). For a pleasant walk, or in wet weather, leave the car on the main road. Walk 1 mi. to the summit where, besides the towers, there is a picnic grove with a table and fireplace.

Cook Hill

Distance from main road
  to Cook summit: 1 mi./1.6 km. (30 min.)

CHASE HILL (774 ft./235 m.)

This summit in Canaan offers a 360° view from the firetower on its summit. Refer to the USGS Skowhegan quadrangle, 15-minute series.

From the junction of US 2 and ME 23 east of Canaan village drive 4 mi. northeast on ME 23 to a town road on the left (west). From the junction of ME 151 and ME 23 in Hartland drive 6 mi. southwest on ME 23 to the same road on the right. After turning onto the the town road drive 0.3 mi. to a fork in the gravel road. Follow the right fork (a small cemetery is just past the junction) for 0.3 mi. to a house on the right, ignoring a private driveway curving to the left. Park here, and on foot follow a recently bulldozed logging track

0.2 mi. to a jeep road on the left (west). On the jeep road walk past the warden's cabin and an excellent picnic area with a fireplace and a table (*spring* nearby). It is 0.2 mi. to the tower rising above the trees on the wooded summit. This tower is one of the few in Maine still manned during the forest fire season.

Chase Hill

Distance from parking lot
   to Chase summit: 0.4 mi./0.6 km. (20 min.)

KELLY MOUNTAIN (1675 ft./511 m.)

This mountain is in Brighton Plantation, east of Bingham. There is an abandoned MFS fire tower on its summit. The present approach is from the northeast. The route up the eastern side from Brighton Village (trail shown on 1948 edition of USGS Kingsbury quadrangle, 15-minute series) can no longer be followed.

Since use of the fire tower ceased, the trail has become overgrown, and hikers should check with the MFS fire warden supervisor in Caratunk before driving to the mountain. To reach the trail, take a woods road leading west from ME 151, 2.7 mi. north of Brighton and 1.6 mi. south of the ME 151/16 junction (Mayfield Corner). Park off the highway at the locked gate at the start of the road. Follow the road around the northern end of Smith Pond to the start of the trail. The warden's cabin is 0.1 mi. farther and straight ahead (*water*).

The trail goes right, following the telephone line. It climbs gradually through open woods for about 1 mi. and then more steeply for 0.5 mi. to the summit.

Kelly Mountain

Distances from ME 151

to start of trail (via woods road): 2 mi. (1 hr.)
to Kelly summit: *est.* 3.6 mi./5.8 km. (2 hr.)

MOXIE BALD MOUNTAIN (2630 ft./802 m.)

This mountain, located in Bald Mountain Township northeast of Bingham, is a long ridge running north to south for about 4 mi. Although the summit is not very high, it has many features of above-timberline summits because of the extended ledges and open crest. The trailless North Peak, easy to reach from the Appalachian Trail, is worth exploring. Refer to the USGS The Forks and Bingham quadrangles, 15-minute series, or map 4 in the MATC *Guide to the Appalachian Trail in Maine*.

The views from the summit are excellent. Katahdin is to the northeast, beyond many other peaks in Piscataquis County; Bigelow, Sugarloaf, and Abraham are to the west; and Coburn and Boundary Bald to the north.

The approach is via the Appalachian Trail, which leaves from a point on a Scott Paper Company road just south of Joe's Hole, the southernmost point on Moxie Pond. To reach the trailhead from the south turn off US 201 in Bingham onto ME 16 and follow it for 0.8 mi. Turn north onto a gravel paper company road. Two roads join the highway at this point; take the right, which follows Austin Stream for much of its length. At the stop sign, 1.7 mi. from the highway, proceed straight; at 9.9 mi. join the power line for a short distance, and at 10.3 mi., where the road forks, take the left fork. At 14.8 mi. the Appalachian Trail sign is seen on the right. There are few places to park here, but there are some places farther up the road. Be careful not to block camp driveways. (The Appalachian Trail approach to Pleasant Pond Mountain from the east begins a little over 100 yd.

north, just beyond a powerline crossing and across from a small boat landing.)

To reach the trailhead from the north leave US 201 at the Forks and take the road toward Indian Pond. At Lake Moxie Station, 5.3 mi. from the highway, turn south on the road that follows the old railroad bed along Moxie Pond. The road is rough and very narrow in places and there are many camps located on this shore of the lake, so drive carefully. At 8.1 mi. from Lake Moxie Station the sign for the Appalachian Trail and Moxie Bald is located on the left.

The Appalachian Trail up Moxie Bald leaves the east side of the road and crosses Baker Brook (in times of high water hikers may choose to use a tricky two cable footbridge located just downstream near Joe's Hole). At 0.3 mi. a power line is crossed and at 1.1 mi. a side trail leads south to Joe's Hole Brook Lean-to, with space for six. The trail ascends gradually, then more steeply over open ledges before breaking out above the treeline. At 3.8 mi. reach a junction with a 0.5 mi. blue-blazed side trail used to bypass the summit in bad weather. It rejoins the Appalachian Trail north of the summit along the crest of the mountain. At 4.2 mi. reach the open summit of Moxie Bald with the remains of an old MFS fire tower.

Moxie Bald Mountain
Distances from Scott Paper Company road via Appalachian Trail

    to lean-to: 1.1 mi.
    to Moxie Bald summit: 4.2 mi./6.8 km. (3 hr. 15 min.)

PLEASANT POND MOUNTAIN
(2480 ft./756 m.)

On the Appalachian Trail between Moxie Pond and the Kennebec River at Caratunk, Pleasant Pond Mountain has open ledges that offer fine views in all directions. Hikers can approach the mountain from either the east or the west, although the western approach is generally favored. Refer to the USGS The Forks quadrangle, 15-minute series.

From the east the approach by road is the same as for Moxie Bald Mountain. The Appalachian Trail, relocated in 1987 to avoid a 2-mile road walk along the Moxie Pond Rd., leads west up the mountain from a spot on the Scott Paper Company road near Joe's Hole, the southernmost tip of Moxie Pond. The trail crosses a power line after 0.1 mi. and ascends to a long ridge, which it follows to the summit 4.9 mi. from the gravel road. A small spring is 0.1 mi. east.

The road approach from the west starts by turning off US 201 to the east at the Maine Forest Service Station in Caratunk. At a spot 0.5 mi. from the highway reach a junction and turn left, following the signs to Pleasant Pond. At 3.7 mi. take the left fork, and in another 0.6 mi. the pavement ends. Continue on the noticeably rougher gravel road another 0.8 mi. to a spot where a narrower gravel road leaves right. Take the road to the right. At 0.5 mi. from the fork, or 5.6 mi. from US 2, the Pleasant Pond Mountain Lean-to is on the left. The Appalachian Trail leaves the gravel road about 100 yd. beyond it. Parking spots are scarce along this road, but there are a few more turnouts farther back toward the last intersection.

The trail leads steeply uphill. At about 1 mi., pass the remains of an old warden's cabin, and shortly thereafter break out onto open ledges, where all that remains of the old firetower are a couple of concrete and rock footings and some broken glass.

Pleasant Pond Mountain from the East
Distances from Scott Paper Company road via the Appalachian Trail

to powerline: 0.1 mi.

to Pleasant Pond Mountain summit: 4.9 mi./7.4 km. (3 hr. 10 min.)

Pleasant Pond Mountain from the West
Distances from Pleasant Pond Mountain Lean-to

to old cabin remains: 0.9 mi.

to Pleasant Pond Mountain summit: 1.2 mi./1.9 km. (1 hr. 15 min.)

COBURN MOUNTAIN (3718 ft./1130 m.)

This mountain, west of US 201 between The Forks and Jackman, is the highest in the region. It offers excellent views from its abandoned MFS firetower. The mountain formerly supported the Enchanted Mountain Ski Area, but it has been shut down for several years and the ski trails are rapidly growing in; all buildings have been removed.

For the easiest and shortest trail (as of 1986), turn west off US 201 on the ski area access road (no sign) about 11 mi. north of The Forks and about 16 mi. south of the US 201/ME 15 junction in Jackman. The access road is badly eroded, and only the first quarter mile or so is passable by two-wheel-drive autos, although four-wheel-drive vehicles with a high wheel base can make it another mile to the location of the former ski area buildings.

At the base of the mountain there is a three-way fork in the road. Take the hard right fork and follow a wide gravel road. A sign on the tree on the left side of the road says Road 9851. About 100 yd. beyond the sign turn left on a jeep road and begin climbing. About 0.7 mi. from the location of the former ski area buildings reach the top of the old ski slope, where a new solar-powered radio repeating station is located. Immediately behind the station is a narrow, but easily followed footpath marked with alternating orange and blue surveyor's tape that leads very steeply uphill about 0.4 mi. It exits the woods onto the summit at a second new repeating station and just south of the firetower. Past the firetower and the summit buildings is the old fire warden's trail, which leads off the northeast ridge and circles back down past the few remains of the old warden's cabin onto an old logging track that intersects the jeep road about halfway down the mountain. This trail is much more easily found at the top than at the bottom. For those with compass skills and some bushwacking experience it can make a nice loop trip when combined with the former trail.

Coburn Mountain
Distances from the US 201

to base of mountain via access road: *est.* 1.2 mi.
to top of ski area: *est.* 2 mi.
to summit via new trails: *est.* 2.4 mi./3.9 km. (2 hr.)

SALLY MOUNTAIN (2221 ft./675 m.)

Sally Mountain is southwest of Jackman, between Wood Pond and Attean Pond. It has a long summit ridge running northeast-southwest, with the highest point at the southwestern end. The northeastern and southeastern slopes rise fairly steeply above two ponds, and the climb to the summit ridge is very steep from these directions. The MFS firetower has been demolished, and although the trail is no longer regularly maintained it gets sufficient use to keep the route clear. Refer to the USGS Attean quadrangle, 15-minute series.

Leave US 201 on a dirt road to the west just south of Jackman Station and nearly opposite ME 15 east. Follow the dirt road for about 3 mi. until it approaches the stream connecting Wood and Attean ponds, where the Canadian Pacific Railroad crosses. Park here and follow the railroad line to the west for about 1.8 mi. The trail crosses the railroad tracks about 200 ft. beyond a west-facing trail signal post with the marking "770." As of July 1987 the start of the trail is marked by a piece of pipe wrapped in surveyor's tape on the south side of the tracks; there is no sign. The trail, marked by red surveyor's tape on trees, runs fairly level for a time before climbing steeply through a pleasant forest of mixed hardwoods to the summit ridge. Among the rocks and and scrub growth of the summit ridge the trail becomes fainter, but it generally runs along the east-facing edge of the ridge on a gradual ascent toward the summit, where four pieces of steel bolted to the rocks mark the former site of the firetower. The views from the top are excellent, taking in several large ponds and mountains from Katahdin to Bigelow to the border peaks.

A more pleasant alternative to hiking along the railroad tracks is making the approach to the trail by canoe. Follow the dirt road mentioned previously to its end at the public landing on Attean Pond. By boat follow the the north shore of Attean Pond west. The trail begins at the second established campsite in a small cove directly opposite Birch Island. The trail can be easily followed for about 0.1 mi. to a spot where it crosses the Canadian Pacific tracks.

Sally Mountain

Distances from road
  to start of trail (via railroad line): 1.8 mi.
  to Sally summit: 3 mi./4.8 km. (2 hr.)

BOUNDARY BALD MOUNTAIN
(3640 ft./1107 m.)

This rocky summit is north-northeast of Jackman and about 8 mi. southwest of the Canadian border. Its long, open summit ridge offers 360° views of the mountain and lake country of northern Somerset County. Over the past decade the former firewarden's trail has succumbed to logging operations, blowdown, and lack of maintenance. As of May 1987 it no longer exists. However, the mountain and the collapsed fire tower at its top can be reached by a 1.2-mi. bushwhack from the former warden's cabin, now rented to a snowmobile club. Refer to the USGS Penobscot Lake and Long Pond quadrangles, 15-minute series.

From the bridge on US 201 in Jackman, drive north 7.7 mi. to The Falls picnic area on the right. Take the second right after the picnic area (the first right leads back, parallel to the highway). This narrow, unmaintained gravel road leads 5.8 mi. to the former warden's cabin. It is generally suitable for pickup trucks and four-wheel-drive vehicles; some front-wheel-drive vehicles with high clearance might be able to make it most of the way. Drivers may want to carry a saw or shovel to deal with washouts and blowdowns.

Pass over a height-of-land, and at 2.5 mi. cross the Heald Stream gorge and immediately take a right at the fork. The road passes north of Mud Pond and crosses another small stream. At 1.8 mi. after the the gorge take a left at the junction, and in another 0.2 mi. take a right. Another 1.3 mi. of steady uphill driving brings you to the former warden's cabin on the left. Park here, taking care not to block the road. The trail formerly began behind the cabin. Scraps of telephone wire now lead into thick scrub and slash. Set a compass course here.

Boundary Bald Mountain
Distance from former warden's cabin
   to summit: 1.2 mi./1.9 km.

Piscataquis Mountains

This section includes the mountains of Piscataquis County west and southwest of the Katahdin area. Moosehead Lake, about 34 mi. long with an area of 117 square miles, is the state's largest lake. The approach to most of the mountains in this section is through Greenville, a convenient climbing center, at the southern end of the lake. Squaw Mountain (3196 ft.), west of Greenville, and Mount Kineo (1806 ft.), reached by water through Rockwood, are the most frequently climbed and best-known peaks in the area. The Appalachian Trail crosses White Cap Mountain (3644 ft.), the highest peak in the section. The Appalachian Trail, in its northeast-southwest course, also passes over the Barren-Chairback Range and close to the interesting and striking Boarstone Mountain (1947 ft.).

Lily Bay State Park is on the eastern shore of Moosehead Lake, 8 mi. north of Greenville on the Greenville-Ripogenus Rd. This area of 576 acres offers picnicking, camping, boat launching, and swimming. (In 1974, the Scott Paper Company donated the Squaw Mountain Ski area and considerable land on that mountain to the state for a park. In 1976, the state added to the area by exchanging land with another paper company.)

An expanding network of private roads, open to the public, serves the wilderness country north of Rockwood. (See the section in the introduction to this guide on the North Maine Woods Association.)

SQUAW MOUNTAIN (3196 ft./974 m.)

Squaw Mountain (or Big Squaw Mountain) dominates the country to the southwest of Moosehead Lake. It is located west of Greenville and is known for its exceptional views of the lake area. An abandoned fire tower (reconditioned in 1985) marks the site of the first fire lookout in the state, which was established in 1905. There is a major state-owned ski area on the mountain's eastern slope. This area is north of the hiking trail. Refer to the USGS Greenville quadrangle, 15-minute series.

From ME 15, turn left (west) on the Scott Paper Company road just north of the bridge over Middle Squaw Brook and 5.3 mi. north of Greenville. Drive up this road for about 1 mi. to where the fire warden's trail leaves the right side of the road (sign: Squaw Mountain Trail).

Though not regularly maintained, the trail is easy to follow and leads 2.5 mi. to the warden's cabin. There is water near the cabin and also a few hundred yards above. From the cabin the trail heads straight up the steep slope with many rocks placed as stepping-stones. Reaching the narrow crest of the ridge, it turns right (north) and climbs another 0.5 mi. to the summit tower.

From the tower, a short trail leads north to a ledge with a view down over Mirror Lake, an isolated pond on the northeastern spur of the mountain.

A trail has also been cut from the top of the ski lifts and trails to the summit.

Squaw Mountain Trail
Distances from Scott Paper Company road
to cabin: 2.5 mi.
to Squaw summit: 3.3 mi./5.3 km.) (2 hr. 45 min.)

MOUNT KINEO (1806 ft./550 m.)

Mount Kineo, with its sheer southeastern face, rises spectacularly 800 ft. above Moosehead Lake on a peninsula that juts from the eastern shore of the lake to within 1 mi. of the western shore at Rockwood. The view over the lake from the summit, where there is a vacant MFS fire tower, is quite remarkable. Refer to the USGS Moosehead Lake quadrangle, 15-minute series.

To reach the mountain, you have to take a boat from Rockwood. Since the Mount Kineo Hotel is no longer open, hikers must hire a boat locally or bring their own. There are two trails up the mountain. The Bridle Trail climbs the western slope. It has the easiest grades but is the longest. The Indian Trail climbs from the southwest along the top of the cliff. The Bridle Trail and the Indian Trail run northwest from the hotel for 0.8 mi. along the shore under spectacular cliffs of Kineo flint. At the northwestern end of these cliffs the trails divide (no sign). The Bridle Trail (no views) continues along the shore 0.3 mi. further before starting to climb; the Indian Trail diverges sharply right and rises along the top of the cliffs. The Indian Trail is the most interesting and affords the best views. There is *no water* on either trail.

Mount Kineo
Distances from dock at Kineo Cove

to Bridle Trail/Indian Trail junction: 0.8 mi.

to Kineo summit (via Bridle Trail): 2 mi./3.2 km. (1 hr. 20 min.)

to Kineo summit (via Indian Trail): 1 mi./1.6 km. (50 min.)

GREEN MOUNTAIN (2395 ft./730 m.)

This mountain is northwest of Pittston Farm and northeast of Boundary Bald Mountain. There is an MFS fire tower on the highest of its several summits. Refer to the USGS Penobscot Lake quadrangle, 15-minute series.

Take the Great Northern Paper Company gravel road for 20 mi. north from Rockwood to the toll gate ($4.00 per car). From the toll gate, continue left through Pittston Farm. Beyond Pittston Farm, Boundary Rd. to Green Mountain forks left from North Branch Rd. The trail leaves the right (north) side of the road about 7 mi. beyond this fork.

The trail starts as a steep driveway to the warden's cabin, which it passes in 0.3 mi. It then rises gradually, with several short dips, to the summit. The trail is well worn and easy to follow.

Green Mountain
Distances from North Branch Road
to cabin: 0.3 mi.

to Green Mountain summit: 1.5 mi./2.4 km. (1 hr. 15 min.)

LITTLE RUSSELL MOUNTAIN
(2400 ft./730 m.)

Little Russell Mountain is close to the Piscataquis County Line in T5 R16, Somerset County. (T and R stand for township and range and identify unincorporated areas in Maine.) There is an abandoned MFS fire tower on the summit. Refer to the USGS St. John Pond quadrangle, 15-minute series.

Take the Great Northern Paper Company road for 20 mi. north from Rockwood to the toll gate ($4.00 per car). Take the road right to Seboomook Dam, and then drive north on the road toward Caucomgomoc Lake. The trail (sign) leaves the right (east) side of the road about 19 mi. north of Seboomook Dam and about 1.3 mi. north of Lost Pond, which is in the saddle (about 1975 ft.) between Russell Mountain and Little Russell Mountain. (There is an MFS campsite at Lost Pond, 0.3 mi. from the road.)

The trail ascends gradually. In its upper half, it gets steeper, with expanding views to the north. The trail is wide, well-worn, and easy to follow.

Little Russell Mountain
Distance from road
   to Little Russell summit: 1.3 mi./2.1 km. (55 min.)

SOUBUNGE MOUNTAIN (2104 ft./641 m.)

This mountain is north of Ripogenus Dam and northwest of Doubletop Mountain. There is an abandoned MFS fire tower on the summit. Refer to the USGS Harrington Lake quadrangle, 15-minute series.

The trail leaves the north side of Telos Rd. about 8 mi. north of Ripogenus Dam. It runs generally northwest across level country for 1 mi. and then climbs north to the tower.

Soubunge Mountain
Distance from road
   to Soubunge summit: *est.* 2 mi./3.2 km. (1 hr. 30 min.)

BIG SPENCER MOUNTAIN (3240 ft./988 m.)

Rising sharply from the countryside to the north of Kokadjo, Big Spencer Mountain and its partner Little Spencer Mountain (2990 ft.) are prominent landmarks from many points in the Moosehead area. Big Spencer has an MFS fire tower on the northeastern end of its 2 mi. summit ridge (3230 ft.). The summit is about 0.3 mi. southwest of the tower. The unrestricted views in all directions are beautiful. Refer to the USGS Ragged Lake quadrangle, 15-minute series.

To reach the trail to the fire tower, turn northwest (left) from Greenville-Ripogenus Rd. on a side road about 8.3 mi. northeast of Kokadjo and 2 mi. southwest of Grant Farm. Drive 6 mi. on this road. The trail leaves on the left (south) side of the road (sign) and climbs to the right (north) of the mountain's nose. In its upper part, beyond the warden's cabin, the trail is quite steep and gains more than 1000 vertical feet in the last 0.7 mi. to the summit. The last *water* is at the warden's cabin.

Big Spencer Mountain
Distance from road

to Big Spencer summit: *est.* 2 mi./3.2 km. (2 hr. 15 min.)

NUMBER FOUR MOUNTAIN (2890 ft./881 m.)

This summit, with a vacant MFS fire tower, is at the northern end of the jumbled mountain mass lying between Kokadjo on the north, Lily Bay on the west, and Big Lyford and the West Branch Ponds on the east. Baker Mountain (3520 ft.) and Lily Bay Mountain (3228 ft.), other major peaks in this mass, are higher but have no trails. Refer to the USGS First Roach Pond quadrangle, 15-minute series.

Turn off Greenville-Ripogenus Rd. onto Frenchtown Rd., which is about 8.5 mi. northeast of Lily Bay and 1 mi. south of Kokadjo. The trail, not maintained but easy to follow, leaves the south side of Frenchtown Rd. 3.5 mi. from the intersection. The trail runs southwest, with little change in grade, for over 2 mi., passing through an out-of-use timber yarding area at 0.5 mi. Then, crossing Lagoon Brook (*last water*), it runs through the clearing where the fire warden's cabin used to be. From this point, surveyor's flags mark the trail, which climbs, first gradually and finally more steeply, through white birch and spruce to the summit ridge. The tower is locked.

Number Four Mountain
Distances from Frenchtown Road

to cabin site: 2.3 mi. (1 hr. 20 min.)
to fire tower: 3.8 mi./6.1 km. (2 hr. 30 min.)

WHITE CAP MOUNTAIN (3644 ft./1111 m.)

White Cap Mountain is the highest point on the Appalachian Trail between Katahdin and Bigelow and also the highest mountain in this section. There are outstanding views from its summit. Refer to the USGS First Roach Pond and Jo-Mary Mountain quadrangles, 15-minute series, or map 2 in the MATC *Guide to the Appalachian Trail in Maine*.

White Brook Trail

The Appalachian Trail in the Gulf Hagas-White Cap area has been relocated and now leads from Pleasant River past the Hermitage and then turns northeast to parallel Gulf Hagas Brook to Gulf Hagas Mountain, West Peak, and Hay Mountain. To reach the White Brook Trail—the former route of the Appalachian Trail, and still maintained by the MATC—turn left (northwest) off ME 11 5.5 mi. north of Brownville Junction. The sign ("Katahdin Iron Works") at the turn-off marks the start of a 6.8 mi. drive on a gravel road from ME 11 to a gate at the Iron Works, a very interesting State Historical Memorial with a blast furnace and a beehive charcoal burner. Register at the gate and pay a fee to the caretaker. Bear right after driving through the gate and cross the West Branch of Pleasant River. At about 3 mi. fork right. About 5.8 mi. from the Iron Works, the road crosses the high, narrow bridge over White Brook. At the next junction continue straight ahead. (The left fork leads to Hay Brook and Gulf Hagas.) Follow the major gravel road for nearly 4 mi., taking the main branch at each fork. The road parallels White Brook and ends in a large wood yard. The White Cap–Hay Mountain sag is clearly visible from this yard. Depending on logging operations, this road may be impassable.

A blue-blazed trail leaves the left side of the road and climbs the southern slope toward the sag through a heavily logged area. (Bad blowdown condition in 1986.)

At 0.5 mi. the trail crosses White Brook near the ruins of the warden's cabin. From there it climbs more steeply and reaches the junction with the Appalachian Trail at 1 mi. Turn right and climb the last steep stretch to the summit at 2.1 mi. There are panoramic views from the open ledge. They take in Saddlerock (2998 ft.), Little Spruce (3274 ft.), Baker (3520 ft.), Squaw (3196 ft.), Hay (3244 ft.), and Big Spencer (3240 ft.), along with the vast lake country to the north, rising to the Katahdin Range. The view is one of the finest in the state.

White Brook Trail
Distances from road at wood yard
to White Brook crossing: 0.5 mi.
to Appalachian Trail junction: 1 mi.
to White Cap summit (via the Appalachian Trail): 2.1 mi./3.4 km. (1 hr. 30 min.)

GULF HAGAS

Just off the Appalachian Trail between the Barren-Chairback Range and White Cap Mountain, Gulf Hagas is a unique scenic area consisting of a deep, narrow, slate canyon about 4 mi. long on the West Branch of the Pleasant River in northern Piscataquis County. The West Branch falls about 400 ft. in the 4 mi., and in many places the canyon's vertical slate walls force the river into very narrow channels that form a series of waterfalls, rapids, chutes, and pools. The falls are particularly spectacular in late spring during peak runoff. During winter, ice builds up on the walls and, because the sun rarely reaches certain faces, often lasts into late June.

The St. Regis and Great Northern paper companies own the property. In 1969 the canyon was designated a Registered Natural Landmark, and the owners agreed to set aside 500 acres, including all of the canyon, for the public's enjoyment. While retaining ownership, the paper companies have agreed not to harvest wood on the reserved land as long as the area is designated a landmark.

Loggers first harvested the area more than a century ago when Pleasant River Rd., the approach from both ends of the canyon, was built. Trails were cut to the rim of the canyon in the last century but fell into disuse. The last extensive logging took place during the 1930s, when new trails were cut. The trails are still well marked and well maintained. The trail system runs near the rim of the canyon, with frequent side trails to viewpoints and falls. By using the old Pleasant River Rd., hikers can make a circuit from the south. Refer to the USGS First Roach Pond, Sebec Lake, and Sebec quadrangles, 15-minute series, or map 2 in the MATC *Guide to the Appalachian Trail in Maine.*

See the preceding description of the approach to White Cap Mountain. After crossing the high bridge 5.8 mi. from the Katahdin Iron Works, go left off the major gravel road at the first junction. Follow this logging road for about 1.8 mi. to Hay Brook, which is about 7.5 mi. from the Iron Works. The approach road is rocky and rough but generally passable. There is a campground with tent sites along the West Branch of Pleasant River. You can make reservations (fee) at the control gate at Katahdin Iron Works.

From the parking area, cross Hay Brook and follow Pleasant River Rd., past Pugwash Pond, for 0.7 mi. There, the Appalachian Trail comes in from the left. Continue straight ahead. The trail shortly reaches the Hermitage, a beautiful stand of tall white pines now owned by The Nature Conservancy (a log cabin and other buildings have been removed). From the Hermitage area follow the white-blazed Appalachian Trail northwest along Pleasant River Rd. for 0.9 mi. to Gulf Hagas Brook, where the relocated

Appalachian Trail turns sharply right to follow Gulf Hagas Brook. Continue straight ahead and cross Gulf Hagas Brook (no bridge and dangerous in high water). Immediately after the crossing, the Screw Auger Falls Trail leaves left and descends steeply along the rim of the canyon to Gulf Hagas Brook, where it passes a series of spectacular waterfalls that are visible from viewpoints to the left of the falls trail.

The blue-blazed main trail on Pleasant River Rd. continues west for 0.4 mi. Turn left, and follow the trail that leads to the rim walk. In about 0.2 mi., after a sharp right turn, a spur trail leads left. (Blue and yellow blazes mark the trail, and the entrance is often swampy.) This trail leads to Hammond Street Pitch, a point high above the canyon that offers a fine view of the gorge. Return to the rim trail and turn left. At 0.9 mi. from Pleasant River Rd. there is a series of side paths that lead to views of the Jaws, where the river squeezes around a slate spur and narrows in many places. Back on the rim trail, at 1.3 mi. from Pleasant River Rd., a spur trail leads to a viewpoint below Buttermilk Falls. After that, the canyon gradually becomes more shallow and at times the trail approaches the banks of the West Branch. At 1.7 mi. from Pleasant River Rd., the trail passes Stair Falls, and at 2.3 mi. it reaches the ledge above Billings Falls, where the narrowed river drops into a large pool. In another 0.1 mi. the trail bears sharply away from the river. (At this point a short side trail leads left to the edge of the river near a rocky island called Head of the Gulf, where there are some interesting logging artifacts.) The trail rejoins Pleasant River Rd. in another 0.2 mi. Turn right (southeast) to follow Pleasant River Rd. along the side of the mountain high above Gulf Hagas back to Screw Auger Falls, the Hermitage, and Hay Brook. Although it is often very marshy and wet, the road offers a quicker return than the rim trail.

SECTION 12

Gulf Hagas Circuit

Distances from campground

> *to* Appalachian Trail junction: 0.7 mi.
> *to* Screw Auger Falls Trail junction: 1.7 mi.
> *to* rim trail junction: 2.1 mi.
> *to* spur trail to Hammond Street Pitch (via rim trail): *est.* 2.3 mi.
> *to* side paths to the Jaws outlook: 3 mi.
> *to* side trail to Buttermilk Falls: 3.4 mi.
> *to* Stair Falls: 3.8 mi.
> *to* ledge above Billings Falls: 4.4 mi.
> *to* side trail to Head of the Gulf: 4.5 mi.
> *to* Pleasant River Road: 4.7 mi.
> *to* rim trail junction (via Pleasant Valley Road): 6.7 mi.
> *to* Gulf Hagas Brook: 7.1 mi.
> *to* campground: 8.8 mi./14.2 km. (7 hr. 30 min.)

CHAIRBACK MOUNTAIN (2219 ft./676 m.)

This interesting, open peak is at the eastern end of the Barren-Chairback Range. It is a day hike from a logging road south of the West Branch of the Pleasant River. Refer to the USGS Sebec and Sebec Lake quadrangles, 15-minute series, or map 3 in the MATC *Guide to the Appalachian Trail in Maine*.

From Katahdin Iron Works follow the gravel St. Regis Paper Company road. At about 3 mi. take the left fork at the LLPC (Little Lyford Pond Camps) sign. The right fork leads to Gulf Hagas.

Park at 6 mi. from the Iron Works, where the Appalachian Trail crosses the road. Go left (south) on the Appalachian Trail, which climbs a short way on a hauling road then turns sharp left. At 1.3 mi. the Appalachian Trail reaches the top of a ridge, and a side trail right leads 0.2 mi. to East Chairback Pond. Continue over a series of ridges. The last half mile of the climb rises over very steep ledges to reach the summit, with its outstanding views.

Chairback Mountain
Distances from road (via the Appalachian Trail)

to side trail to East Chairback Pond: 1.3 mi. (1 hr.)

to Chairback summit (via the Appalachian Trail): 3.2 mi./5.2 km. (2 hr. 20 min.)

BARREN MOUNTAIN (2660 ft./811 m.)

Barren Mountain, at its western end, is the highest and most accessible mountain of the Barren-Chairback Range. It is in Elliotsville Plantation (USGS Sebec Lake quadrangle, 15-minute series). There are interesting outlooks from Barren Slide and Barren Ledges over Bodfish Intervale, Lake Onawa, and Boarstone Mountain. The panorama from the abandoned fire tower on the summit is excellent.

To climb Barren Mountain via the Appalachian Trail, drive from Monson on Elliotsville Rd. 11.8 mi. to Bodfish Farm. Then drive 1.6 mi. on the Long Pond tote road and park. The Appalachian Trail follows the road 150 ft. and leaves to the left (south).

Leave the road right (north) on the Appalachian Trail and descend 0.1 mi. Cross Long Pond Stream at the normally shallow ford. The trail turns east, passing Slugundy Gorge. At 0.8 mi. it reaches a blue-blazed side trail leading 0.5 mi. to Long Pond Stream Lean-to.

After the junction, the main trail climbs the northwestern slope of Barren Mountain. At 2.1 mi. another blue-blazed side trail (right) leads to the head of Barren Slide, an interesting mass of boulders with a view west. A little further, the main trail crosses the head of Barren Ledges, from which there is a striking view. The route then bears left and winds along the northern slope of the range over rough terrain to the base of the cone. From there, it climbs steeply through boulders for a short distance to the summit fire tower.

(The Appalachian Trail continues northeast over the remaining peaks of the range to the valley of the West Branch of the Pleasant River. This hike is a camping trip of several days over rough terrain. See the 1988 edition of the MATC *Guide to the Appalachian Trail in Maine* if you plan to take the trip across the range.)

Barren Mountain
Distances from Long Pond tote road (via Appalachian Trail)

> *to* side trail to Long Pond Stream Lean-to: 0.8 mi.
> *to* side trail to Barren Slide: 2.1 mi., 1 hr. 30 min.
> *to* Barren Mountain summit: 3.9 mi./6.3 km. (3 hr.)

LITTLE WILSON FALLS

A worthwhile side trip in this area is to Little Wilson Falls, a striking 57-ft. waterfall in the canyon gouged through slate by Little Wilson Stream. Driving from Monson on Elliotsville Rd., park just before crossing Big Wilson Bridge. Go left on a faint dirt road (formerly the Appalachian Trail). At 0.8 mi. pass MFS Little Wilson Campsite and cross Little Wilson Stream. At 2 mi. turn left on the relocated Appalachian Trail, and at 2.1 mi. cross Little Wilson Stream. At 2.4 mi. reach the rim of ledge to an outstanding view of the 57-ft. falls and a deep slate canyon.

Little Wilson Falls
Distances from Big Wilson Bridge

> *to* MFS campsite: 0.8 mi.
> *to* Little Wilson Falls: 2.4 mi./3.7 km. (1 hr. 25 min.)

BOARSTONE MOUNTAIN (1947 ft./593 m.)

This small but rugged mountain complete with its two peaks and its three small ponds well up on the southwestern slope, rises above Lake Onawa. The views from the bare summits are excellent. Subject to the usual standards of respect for private property, hikers have been welcome to climb Boarstone via the Moore's ponds route. Refer to the USGS Sebec Lake quadrangle, 15-minute series.

Moore's Ponds Route

From Monson follow Elliotsville Rd. After crossing the Big Wilson Bridge at 9 mi., bear left and cross the Canadian Pacific railroad tracks in another 0.7 mi. The route to Boarstone leads right 0.1 mi. beyond the railroad, following a private road through a gate. The road climbs steadily through switchbacks and then runs along a shelf to the lowest of the three Moore's ponds, where it ends. The ponds are known as Sunrise, Midday, and Sunset. Follow the trail around the southeastern end of the lowest pond and cross the outlet. After that, the trail, turning north and then east, steeply climbs up the main cone to the open western peak. It descends slightly into the saddle and then rises to the higher eastern peak.

Moore's Ponds Route
Distances from Elliotsville Road

to lower Moore's Pond: 1 mi. (40 min.)

to Boarstone, western peak: 1.8 mi./2.9 km. (1 hr. 20 min.)

to Boarstone, eastern peak: 2 mi./3.2 km. (1 hr. 30 min.)

HIGH CUT HILL (955 ft./291 m.)

High Cut Hill is in Garland, just south of the Penobscot-Piscataquis county line. There is a magnificent 360° view. Refer to the USGS Dover-Foxcroft quadrangle, 15-minute series.

Approach by turning west off ME 15 at West Charleston four corners. Drive 3.2 mi. to a dirt road on the right. The trail ascends north through open pasture to the summit.

High Cut Hill

Distance from road
  to High Cut summit: 1.3 mi./2.1 km. (55 min.)

Appendix

The Appalachian Mountain Club,
the New England Trail Conference,
and the Appalachian Trail

THE APPALACHIAN MOUNTAIN CLUB

The Appalachian Mountain Club (AMC) was organized in 1876 and was subsequently incorporated both in Massachusetts and in New Hampshire. It is the oldest and largest mountain club in the United States. It has made substantial contributions to various branches of geography, and it has taken a leading part in efforts to preserve the beauty and economic value of the mountains and forests, and to promote backcountry research and education. It has built and maintains about four hundred miles of foot trails and twenty shelters in New Hampshire and Maine.

The Club publishes a semiannual magazine, *Appalachia*, a monthly bulletin, and guidebooks and other books.

The AMC headquarters are at 5 Joy Street, Boston, Massachusetts. The information center and library are open to the public Monday through Friday, from 9:00 A.M. to 5:00 P.M. The information center is a resource for questions about trails and camping. It also sells guidebooks and books on outdoor recreation. Club-sponsored lectures, meetings, and social gatherings are held in Boston. The AMC also sponsors weekly outings and longer excursions, including some to foreign countries. Chapters in Maine, eastern New York, the Catskills, greater Philadelphia, New Hampshire, Connecticut, Rhode Island, Massachusetts, and Washington, D.C., also hold outings and meetings. There is opportunity to participate in trail clearing, skiing, canoeing, rock climbing, and other outdoor activities, in addition to hiking.

The Club now has more than 30,000 members. It invites

all who love the woods and mountains and wish to contribute to their protection to join. Information on membership, as well as the names and addresses of the secretaries of local chapters, may be obtained by writing to the Appalachian Mountain Club, 5 Joy St., Boston, MA 02108, or by telephoning (617-523-0636).

AMC Trails

Development, construction, and maintenance of backcountry trails and facilities have been a major focus of the AMC's public-service efforts since the Club's inception in 1876. Today, through twelve chapters, numerous camps, and its trails program, the AMC is responsible for maintaining and managing nearly a thousand miles of trails, including over two hundred fifty miles of the Appalachian Trail, many miles of ski trails, and more than twenty shelters and tent sites throughout the Northeast. The largest portion of these is in the White Mountain area of New Hampshire and Maine, where the AMC maintains over a hundred hiking trails with an aggregate length of some three hundred fifty miles.

In general, trails are maintained to provide a clear pathway while protecting and minimizing damage to the environment. Some may offer rough and difficult passage. The Club reserves the right to discontinue any without notice, and expressly disclaims any legal responsibility for the condition of its trails at any time.

As a well-known and respected authority on hiking trails, the AMC works cooperatively with many federal, state, and local agencies, corporate and private landowners, and numerous other trail clubs and outdoor organizations.

AMC trails are maintained through the coordinated efforts of many members who volunteer their labor and of trails program staff. Most of the difficult major construction projects are handled by the AMC trail crew, based in the White Mountains, which began operations in 1917 and is probably the oldest professional crew in the nation. Hikers can help maintain trails by donating their time for various projects and regularly scheduled volunteer trips with the AMC chapters and at AMC camps.

For more information on any aspect of the Club's trail and shelter efforts, contact AMC Trails Program, Pinkham Notch Camp, Box 298, Gorham, NH 03581.

Comments on the AMC's trail work and information on problems you encounter when hiking or camping are always welcome.

NEW ENGLAND TRAIL CONFERENCE

The New England Trail Conference was organized in 1917 to develop the hiking possibilities of New England and to correlate the work of local organizations. The Conference serves as a clearinghouse for information about trail maintenance and trail use both for organized groups and for individuals.

The annual meeting of this organization is held in the spring. Representatives of mountaineering and outing clubs from all over New England come together for a full day and evening program of reports, talks, and illustrated lectures on mountain climbing, hiking, and trails and shelters. All sessions are open to the public.

The work of the Conference is directed by the chairman, who is elected by the executive committee. For information, contact the chairman, Forrest House, 33 Knollwood Drive, E. Longmeadow, MA 01028 (203-342-1425 or 413-732-3719).

APPENDIX

THE APPALACHIAN TRAIL

The Appalachian National Scenic Trail (AT) is a continuous marked footpath that extends through the mountainous regions of the east for two thousand miles, from Katahdin in Maine to Springer Mountain in Georgia. Its maintenance is a volunteer project carried on by organizations and individuals, coordinated by the Appalachian Trail Conference. The trail west of Old Speck through the White Mountains in New Hampshire uses numerous AMC trails for its route, and AMC chapters maintain parts of the Appalachian Trail in Maine, Massachusetts, Connecticut, and New York. The AMC has been a member of the Conference from its inception.

In Maine, the Appalachian National Scenic Trail is maintained by the Maine Appalachian Trail Club, Inc. (MATC), also a member of the Appalachian Trail Conference (ATC). This club is comprised of individual members and organizations including such diverse groups as the AMC's Maine chapter, college outing clubs, fish and game clubs, and children's camps.

The Appalachian Trail starts in Maine at the summit of Katahdin; goes by Rainbow, Nahmakanta and Jo-Mary lakes and Crawford Pond; traverses White Cap, the Barren-Chairback Range, and Moxie Bald; crosses the Great Bend of the Dead River, in part following the Arnold Trail; goes over the Bigelow Range, the Crockers, Spaulding, Saddleback, Baldpate, Old Speck, and the Mahoosucs; and reaches the New Hampshire line at Carlo Col.

Due to the remote locations and changes brought on by storms, lumbering, beaver activity, etc., it is not advisable to attempt travel on the Appalachian Trail (other than by the routes described in this book) without explicit directions and maps. Both are incorporated in the *Guide to the Appalachian Trail in Maine* (eleventh edition, 1988) published by the Maine Appalachian Trail Club. It is available at many bookstores; from the Secretary, Maine Appalachian Trail Club, PO Box 283, Augusta, ME 04330 (also for memberships and trail information); or from the Appalachian Trail Conference, Box 236, Harpers Ferry, WV 25425. More detailed information on the sections of the Appalachian Trail described as approaches to some of the mountains discussed in this book will also be found in the MATC guide.

Glossary

blaze	a trail marking on a tree or rock, painted and/or cut
blazed	marked with paint (blazes) on trees or rocks
bluff	a high bank or hill with a cliff face overlooking a valley
boggy	muddy, swampy
boulder	large, detached, somewhat rounded rock
box canyon	rock formation with vertical walls and flat bottom
bushwack	to hike through woods or brush without a trail
buttress	a rock mass projecting outward from a mountain or hill
cairn	pile of rocks to mark trail
cataract	waterfall
cirque	upper end of valley with half-bowl shape (scoured by glacier)
cliff	high, steep rock face
col	low point on a ridge between two mountains; saddle
crag	rugged, often overhanging rock eminence
flume	a ravine or gorge with a stream running through it

grade	steepness of trail or road; ratio of vertical to horizontal distance
graded trail	well-constructed trail with smoothed footway
gulf	a cirque
gully	small, steep-sided valley
headwall	steep slope at the head of a valley, especially a cirque
height-of-land	highest point reached by a trail or road
knob	a rounded minor summit
lean-to	shelter
ledge	a large body of rock; or, but not usually in this book, a horizontal shelf across a cliff
ledgy	having exposed ledges, usually giving views
outcrops	large rocks projecting out of the soil
plateau	high, flat area
potable	drinkable
ravine	steep-sided valley
ridge	highest spine joining two or more mountains, or leading up to a mountain
runoff brook	a brook usually dry (intermittent), except shortly after rain or snow melt

saddle	lowest, flattish part of ridge connecting two mountains; col
scrub	low trees near treeline
shelter	building, usually of wood, with roof and 3 or 4 sides, for camping
shoulder	point where rising ridge levels off or descends slightly before rising higher to a summit
slab	(n.) a smooth, somewhat steeply sloping ledge
slab	(v.) to travel in a direction parallel to the contour of a slope
slide	steep slope where a landslide has carried away soil and vegetation
spur	a minor summit projecting from a larger one
spur trail	a side path to a point off a main trail
strata	layers of rock
summit	highest point on a mountain; or, a point higher than any other point in its neighborhood
switchback	zigzag traverse of a steep slope
tarn	a small pond, often at high elevation, or with no outlet
timberline	elevation that marks the upper limit of commercial timber
treeline	elevation above which trees do not grow

INDEX

281

NOTES

NOTES

NOTES